PERSONAL FINANCE

QuickStart Guide®

PERSONAL FINANCE

QuickStart Guide®

The Simplified Beginner's Guide to
Eliminating Financial Stress, Building Wealth,
and Achieving Financial Freedom

Morgen B. Rochard, CFA, CFP®, RLP®

Editors: Bryan Basamanowicz, Marilyn Burkley
Cover Illustration and Design: Katie Donnachie, Copyright © 2020 by ClydeBank Media LLC
Interior Design & Illustrations: Katie Donnachie, Copyright © 2020 by ClydeBank Media LLC

First Edition - Last Updated: July 4, 2023

ISBN-13: 9781945051012 (paperback) | 9781945051593 (hardcover) | 9781945051586 (eBook) | 9781945051654 (audiobook) | 9781636100227 (spiral bound)

Publisher's Cataloging-In-Publication Data
(Prepared by The Donohue Group, Inc.)

Names: Rochard, Morgen, author.
Title: Personal finance QuickStart Guide : the simplified beginner's guide to eliminating financial stress, building wealth, and achieving financial freedom / Morgen Rochard, CFP®, CFA.
Other Titles: Personal finance Quick Start Guide
Description: [Albany, New York] : ClydeBank Finance, [2020] | Series: QuickStart Guide | Includes bibliographical references and index.
Identifiers: ISBN 9781945051593 (hardcover) | ISBN 9781945051012 (paperback) | ISBN 9781945051586 (ebook)
Subjects: LCSH: Finance, Personal.
Classification: LCC HG179 .R63 2020 (print) | LCC HG179 (ebook) | DDC 332.024--dc23

Library of Congress Control Number: 2020944708

Author ISNI: 0000 0004 9220 0682

For bulk sales inquiries, please visit www.go.quickstartguides.com/wholesale, email us at orders@clydebankmedia.com, or call 800-340-3069. Special discounts are available on quantity purchases by corporations, associations, and others.

Copyright © 2022
www.quickstartguides.com
All Rights Reserved

ISBN-13: 978-1-945051-01-2 (paperback)
ISBN-13: 978-1-636100-22-7 (spiral bound)

OVER 850,000

READERS **LOVE** *QuickStart Guides.*

Really well written with lots of practical information. These books have a very concise way of presenting each topic and everything inside is very actionable!

— ALAN F.

The book was a great resource, every page is packed with information, but [the book] never felt overly-wordy or repetitive. Every chapter was filled with very useful information.

— CURTIS W.

I appreciated how accessible and how insightful the material was and look forward to sharing the knowledge that I've learned [from this book].

— SCOTT B.

After reading this book, I must say that it has been one of the best decisions of my life!

— ROHIT R.

This book is one-thousand percent worth every single dollar!

— HUGO C.

The read itself was worth the cost of the book, but the additional tools and materials make this purchase a better value than most books.

— JAMES D.

I finally understand this topic ... this book has really opened doors for me!

— MISTY A.

Contents

PART I – FINDING AND SECURING YOUR FREEDOM

PART II – SOLVING EVERYDAY CHALLENGES

BEFORE YOU START READING, DOWNLOAD YOUR FREE DIGITAL ASSETS!

 Net Worth Calculator

 Financial Goal Setting Workbook

 Goal Setting Questionnaire

Ideal Day Week Year Spreadsheet

TWO WAYS TO ACCESS YOUR FREE DIGITAL ASSETS

Use the camera app on your mobile phone to scan the QR code or visit the link below and instantly access your digital assets.

SCAN ME

or

go.quickstartguides.com/personalfinance

 VISIT URL

Introduction

"I don't know how we got here." A friend says this to you on a phone call. You can hear it in her voice; she's on the brink of tears and can barely get her words out. You tell her to take a breath and do her best to calmly explain what's going on.

"I have no income coming in from my business anymore. And Robert was laid off two weeks ago. We have maybe a month's worth of emergency savings. I keep looking around my home, thinking about what I could sell to make ends meet. I don't see how we are going to keep our home. The kids have no idea, how can I begin to explain this to them? I can't believe this is happening."

Your friend confides that she and her spouse, Robert, have been living on the financial brink for a long time, even before Robert's layoff. They never thought about it much, because they always found a way to pay for things, even though there was never much in the bank. You had no idea. To you, they seemed wealthy. "We need all the things we have; I don't know where or how I'm supposed to cut expenses. The kids need things. I have obligations. This is horrible."

As your friend pours her heart out to you, you can feel her fear and sadness. How do you respond? What do you say to her? Do you listen? Are you empathetic? Do you tell her that everything is going to be all right?

Most of us would respond with empathy. We would comfort and assure. We might even offer to pitch in and help our friend. We would be quick to offer advice and ideas, even if they were unwanted.

Every one of us has a story through which money weaves. You picked up this personal finance book because you want to change your financial situation. Changing your wealth picture takes more than reading a few tips. You'll need to see your finances through a completely different lens, one where you bury your old convictions that do not serve you, prioritize what is truly important, and make all your decisions based on the results you want to achieve. I invite you to offer yourself the same level of empathy you would give to any loved one. As we proceed through these pages, notice when you beat yourself up or find it too difficult to continue reading. Give yourself the grace you need to accept your situation and move forward. This simple act of self-empathy is the foundation for financial success.

Your Most Fulfilled Life

Think back to when you learned how to drive. It was exciting to move the mirrors and change the seat position. You put the car in drive and felt it roll. You didn't know how to press on the gas pedal efficiently or break without stopping short. When you turned, it was an awkward inching of your hands around the wheel until you got the car to point in the right direction. Slowly and steadily, you began to drive. You paid close attention, checked your mirrors obsessively, and used caution with the pedals. You gained confidence and speed. You practiced on different terrains.

Fast-forward to today. You probably have no trouble driving while eating a Big Mac with one hand and holding a drink in your lap, with your kids in the back shrieking about their iPads. It took you fifteen years to achieve this level of driving excellence! Those fifteen years encompassed an enormous amount of change. You likely embraced this change, because it offered new privileges and freedoms. Furthermore, for most people, learning to drive is a practical necessity. True and lasting change does not happen overnight, nor does it progress in a straight line. We must change what we *believe* to improve our daily habits and get us closer to our most coveted outcomes.

I know something about change. Usually, when a person or family seeks my help with their financial lives, change is at the top of their minds. Take, for instance, a couple that needed help with a pressing financial problem; we'll call them Gary and Christina.

For almost two decades Gary worked as a C-level executive for a large corporation. He and Christina, his stay-at-home wife, had two adolescent kids when they signed on as my clients. Gary had created wealth for himself— plenty of it—but he was unhappy. You could say he was burned out, tired.

Gary also regretted that he never saw his family, for whom he did everything. He gave his wife every convenience to make her life easier: a dog walker, house cleaners, extra childcare, spending money to see friends. But he was never around. His absence wore on their relationship. When they sat in my office together, you could feel the tension. He wanted to provide for her, and she wanted more of his time. But he didn't have any more time to give.

I asked them each to answer one question: Imagine you're already living your most fulfilled life; what does it look like?

> **Gary** (after pausing to think): In my most fulfilled life I work on something that gives my life meaning and purpose. I don't feel like an ant walking into a crowded elevator every day waiting to do my job. I get to see the daylight some afternoons because I can leave work early. I have more flexibility with my schedule. I can plan a vacation with my family, because I have more clarity about my long-term schedule.

Me: Anything else?

Gary: I'd like more time with my family. It would be nice to come home and help Christina cook or play with the kids a couple of nights a week. I'd love to help them with homework every now and then. I never get to do that. My kids are halfway to college now, and I don't spend much time with them at all. I want them to know me and I want to know them. I don't want them to look back and think that money was more important to me than they are. I work so that I can do things for them. But sometimes I wonder if they see that.

Me: Yes, I can see that's very important to you. Anything else?

Gary: I'd like time to play the guitar. It's been so many years since I've picked up my guitar and been able to play for more than ten minutes without interruption. I'd love to be able to play my guitar for a couple of hours. But I can't, because I barely see my family now, so imagine me telling Christina that I can't see them because I want to play guitar for two hours undisturbed in the garage.

Me: Yes, you seem passionate about music. Anything else?

Gary: I would have date nights with Christina. Back when we dated, before we were married, I made the time. I was less busy then. Spending more time with Christina would be nice. I know she wants more from me and I do want to give that to her. I just don't know how.

We continued to talk, and then I switched to Christina and asked the same question: Imagine you're already living your most fulfilled life. What does it look like?

Christina: In my most fulfilled life Gary is home more. I don't feel like I'm raising our family alone. With our current situation, I know I can pay for help whenever I need it. But sometimes I feel like a single mom. We never go anywhere as a family. I sometimes make up excuses as to why Gary isn't with us when I take the kids to a friend's birthday party or to soccer events. I see other dads there and I'm jealous.

Me: Oh yes, that sounds very hard.

Christina: Well, family is the most important thing to me. I just want to be a family. And part of being a family means spending time together. I don't need much; I just need something. I'm very involved in the kids' school. But I feel like if I went back to work in some capacity, I would have something that was just mine. I don't really do anything for *me* anymore. I'd love to start a small business. I used to be a yoga instructor, and I wanted to have my own studio one day. That would be a dream. I could run the studio and teach a class or two a week.

Me: That sounds very important to you; we should include that in your plan.

When Christina and Gary had the opportunity to communicate what they really wanted, the tension subsided. They noticed that they mostly wanted the same things! They both felt as if they were missing time together. They both wanted to do something different professionally.

Gary decided to start a consulting practice, and Christina began co-instructing yoga classes a couple of times a week as she prepared to open up her own studio. Once brought to light, Christina and Gary's shared objectives inspired teamwork. They became the dynamic duo.

Their financial life changed drastically. In a bid for true happiness, Gary walked away from a massive salary. Upon his leaving the company, they had only eighteen months of health insurance (a temporary plan called COBRA) before they would need to secure other health care. They moved into a less expensive neighborhood and a smaller home. They lived for a time off the savings and other assets they had accumulated, while Gary got his new consulting business off the ground. Their spending behaviors had to change during this sensitive transition time, with adjustments like less takeout food, less hired help around the house, and fewer expensive gifts.

Christina continued to learn all she could about running a yoga studio. Once Gary's business was humming, she would open her studio, as they didn't want to take the risk of two new ventures at once. They were worried about what the kids would think of the transition, particularly the change in residence and the tightening of material consumption. But after an adjustment period, it became clear that more time with Dad was a million times more meaningful to the kids than living in a bigger house or having the latest and greatest electronics and accessories. The family recently went to Hawaii for a two-week vacation. Before that, they had never had more than five days away together as a family.

Today, Gary not only spends more time with his family, but he also spends more time in the garage playing his guitar. Moreover, having settled comfortably into their new careers, the family's financial footing is once again strong, robust even.

Gary and Christina saw where they wanted to go and went there. They changed their entire outlook and prioritized what was truly important to them. No old habits or false needs dared stand in their way. Such a dramatic change was not easy. It was hard. It required a lot of effort and adjustments, none of which took place overnight. It took them years to arrive at their most fulfilled life.

You may be wondering how Gary and Christina were able to sustain such tenacity in pursuit of their goals. How did they weather the fear and doubt that nipped at their heels? *Are we crazy for walking away from an enormous, secure salary to pursue our most fulfilled life? Are we doing what's best for our children?* Perhaps an even more relevant question is how did they stay motivated. Starting two new businesses is no small feat, and when things get tough, as they inevitably will, a lot of new proprietors hit the panic button and scramble to find "stable" employment. Moreover, in Gary and Christina's case, they were pursuing these new business endeavors while concurrently rolling back a multitude of household expenditures. They were taking big risks, abandoning cozy and well-ingrained spending habits, and enduring the pains of change over a period of several years, without surrendering to fear or weariness. It was truly an accomplishment.

Think back to your most significant accomplishments in life. What are your most outstanding talents or attributes? Where are you the strongest? Maybe you are an outstanding parent and raised terrific kids. Perhaps you landed your dream job and were quickly promoted to the executive level. Maybe you achieved a hard-to-reach fitness or diet goal. Or maybe you are immensely skilled as a computer coder, plumber, or chef.

Behind each of your noteworthy accomplishments or attributes is a powerful motivator. Your love for your children gave you the focus and discipline you needed to become a great parent. Your intense desire for career success led you to chase down a big promotion at work. Your determination to look good and live well led you to succeed with your weight-loss goals. The common current underlying each of these scenarios is energy and enthusiasm fueled by a powerful personal motivator.

Like other major life accomplishments and milestones, big financial achievements are personal in nature. And like the others, when achieved, they can transform your life.

My goal in writing this book is to help you understand the human element involved in all facets of personal finance, to truly emphasize the "personal" in personal finance. Why is it, for instance, that we spend a lot of time and effort creating a budget one month, only to scrap it and go back to bad spending habits a few months later? Why do we pay high interest rates on credit cards when we know the rational thing to do is to pay down the balance? Why are some people comfortable taking risks, while others prefer to leave money in a checking or savings account offering no returns and withering under the steady tide of inflation?

The reason we often try and fail, give up, and quit is that our energy and enthusiasm for the endeavor wanes. Financial goals and resolutions have an unfortunate way of fading. We set out with a lot of ambition, but we fail to sustain the day-to-day actions that we need for real change. We quickly lose sight of our goals amid all the other things competing for our attention: our jobs, businesses, family obligations, and other distractions.

Let me share with you a secret, the first of many to be uncovered in this book: in order to make big changes that last, we must first establish—and clearly define—our goals and objectives, our personal motivators. This was the clear first step for Gary and Christina—*what does your most fulfilled life look like?* It was also the first step for many of my other clients, and, if you are serious about creating real change in your life, then it will be the first step for you too. You must find your financial raison d'etre.

> » What does your most fulfilled life look like?
> » What motivates you?
> » What will help you sustain that motivation and energy over time?
> » If you value spending more time with family, traveling the world, or pursuing your favorite hobby, what is stopping you from doing that now?
> » Why do you want more money, and what would you do with it if you had it?

NOTE

If you want to get ahead of the game, then take a few minutes to write down your answers to each of these questions. As we move forward, I'll present you with several specific "on your own" assignments that will prompt you to address these and other questions about your personal finance and greater life objectives.

Thoughts, Behaviors, Results, Repeat

The key to finding financial freedom and independence is identifying our personal motivators. The answers are always within us. Unlocking the secrets involves changing the way we think. I use a diagram to express the process. Now, keep in mind that I'm not talking about waking up one day and having a totally different outlook on life. Instead, the idea is to make incremental changes each day that become part of a feedback loop between our convictions (thoughts), our behavior, and the results (figure 1).

fig. 1

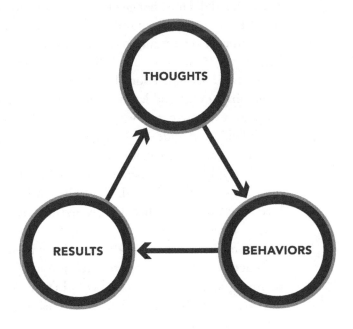

Source: Means in Progress

Changing the way you think requires some open-mindedness and flexibility. If you can change the way you think, then you can change the way you behave, which will, in turn, lead you to the results you seek. It sounds simple. It's not. I've made a career out of putting this process to work for the benefit of my clients, and I can tell you firsthand that the old adage "Nothing good comes easily" applies here.

My personal story is one that required a change in my convictions, as well as a leap of faith. In 2010, after working as an options trader for a couple of years, I noticed business was slowing. Roles like mine, involving a lot of math and quick decision making, were becoming increasingly automated. The future did not seem bright.

Looking for a new job in 2010 was not an ideal situation. The global financial crisis was top of mind for many financial firms. Furthermore, my skill set was not in demand. However, I knew I needed to change, and I noticed wealth management firms were hiring. Making a major switch from trading to wealth management was a very difficult decision for me. On the one hand, I wanted to be a trader for life! That's what I knew. It was sexy. I liked the status. On the other hand, it was obvious that the type of trader I had learned to be was not what the market wanted anymore, and I needed to do something different.

I accepted a position at Merrill Lynch in wealth management. I did not take to it well at first. The thoughts about my career and my role as a financial professional did not change overnight. For a long time, I continued to believe that wealth management was not for me. I felt adrift and disoriented, craving the action of the trading room, even though I knew that it was a relic of a bygone era. To move on and fully embrace my new career required enormous amounts of self-reflection. I had to invest immense time and energy into improving myself and learning new ideas. The deep convictions I had about the nature of my career were slowly replaced with new ones. Now, when I think back to the idea of "Morgen the trader," that perspective I had about myself seems foreign, comical even.

Today, I own and operate a successful wealth management firm. I make my own schedule. I have the best clients. I work with the best staff. And I love what I do. I wouldn't change anything about how I got here. It is exactly as it is supposed to be.

I am not part of Wall Street anymore, and that gives me great satisfaction. Wall Street, to me, ignores the human being. Financial planning and personal finance couldn't be more personal. It's what makes my career fulfilling. It gives my work meaning and purpose and it fills a void I didn't even know existed.

Agree to Succeed

The key to success is agreement. You must find the right information from a source you trust, internalize it, and apply the insights to your personal situation. The various facets of personal finance must be something that you want to do—you *agree* that the steps need to be taken.

For example, maybe dining out or ordering takeout is a significant part of your life. You do it all the time, even though, from a personal finance perspective, buying groceries and cooking would save you a lot of money each month. Yet, my simply telling you to start cooking at home is not likely to yield any results. You need buy-in. You must understand, accept, and be motivated to make the change. If you're not in agreement that this is the best path for you, then you will not take any steps toward cooking at home. Perhaps you can think of a different way to save money that you do agree with.

Finding ways to incorporate prudent personal financial decision making into everyday life is challenging but rewarding. Setting yourself on the path to financial freedom involves agreeing with practical advice, being open to new ways of thinking, and deciding between trade-offs.

If you are reading this, then it is fair to assume you want something in your financial life to change. In your choice to read this book and respond to the many challenges or "on your own" assignments I'm going to give you, you are already taking a significant first step. And in that first step, you agree that change is something you wish to do!

I am convinced that, once you begin to see measurable results, financial stresses will recede and give way to hope, optimism, enthusiasm, and energy. Here are some of the goals I have for you as a reader:

» You will learn how to find your "big ideas," goals, and objectives.
» You will model success, not failure, from the stories and examples you read.
» You will use inspirational exercises to steer you toward action-oriented solutions.
» You will know how to make adjustments if your plan is not working.

Ultimately, this book is designed for you to apply general financial planning principles and philosophies to your specific, non-general life. It is not meant to be like most other personal finance books, offering a generic presentation of financial advice, ideas, and strategies with no route to personal application. I want this book to be uncommon. Through an interactive, reflective reading experience, you will learn the necessary framework for applying big, powerful, general ideas to your unique circumstances.

Having these ideas readily available in writing gives me an unlimited opportunity to help people far and wide, beyond those whom I serve in my practice. Mine is a small practice, with thirty clients. My clients are like my family. In writing this book, I am expanding my message, support, and genuine empathy ever further, to a broader audience, an "extended family."

My radical idea is that personal finance should be personal. I know it can be difficult to find good advice that applies to you. I know it's not easy to convince you, wherever you are, that I really care about your life and your financial welfare. But believe it or not, I wrote this book for you. I'm interested in you.

I have a curiosity about human beings, what makes them unique and special, and what they want to do with their lives. Ultimately, the human element in each of us is what makes up personal finance. We are all human beings doing the best we can to make the right decisions about our personal lives with the information we have. In this book I will give you everything I have to make you successful. I want you to live your most fulfilled life, and I know you can.

Chapter by Chapter

In terms of the two parts of this book, part I explains the ways you can jump-start your personal finance improvement by changing how you think, by becoming more organized, and by developing an action plan. Part I also offers an in-depth look at how to navigate the financial world and the myriad of different investment options that exist today. In Part II, I will take you through a lot of common financial circumstances and problems, showing you how to use the tools you obtained in part 1 to overcome them.

» **PART I: Finding and Securing Your Freedom**

» Chapter 1, "Believe," is intended to help readers get into the right frame of mind before embarking on the road to financial wellness. The chapter explains some of the common obstacles that people face when dealing with decisions about money. We'll review several "money scripts," which are common but flawed ways of thinking about money, and we'll show you how, through awareness of your own money scripts, you can move forward in your endeavor to improve your financial predicament and pursue your long-term financial goals.

» In chapter 2, "Earning Money: Why and How," we'll compare your current income with your desired income and examine the gap between the two. Of course, most people want to earn more, and increasing one's income can be immensely helpful in meeting one's financial goals. But, as we will see, more income is not always the answer. Chapter 2 encourages readers to pursue an income worthy of their potential. We'll include some expert negotiating tips. We'll also examine how income relates, and doesn't relate, to other vital life desires, like the feeling of belonging, the need to express creativity, and a sense of community.

» Chapter 3, "Deliberate Saving and Spending," emphasizes the importance of focusing on your savings goals. If you can hit your savings targets, then you don't have to beat yourself up over your spending. The two, however, are inextricably related. I'll show you the right way to track personal income and expenses through budgeting. Where is money coming from and where does it go? Does your spending match your personal goals and values or is it driven primarily by habit? We'll go through several spending categories (house, car, food, insurance, etc.) and offer tips for lowering spending.

» Chapter 4, "The Basis of Wealth," provides actionable ideas for becoming more organized and diligent with saving and financial planning. Having savings (money in the bank) is one of the first steps in reducing stresses and finding financial freedom. However, increasing the rate of savings is easier said than done and often requires some sacrifice now in exchange for future security and flexibility.

» Chapter 5, "Net Worth: A Helpful Measure," begins with a walk-through examination of one's assets and liabilities. A clear-eyed assessment of one's current predicament is a necessary starting point on the road to progress. Whether we have negative net worth or are worth tens of millions of dollars, our goals are often remarkably similar. We want to improve our financial situation and develop greater life satisfaction along the way. Identifying where money is going and if our spending truly provides satisfaction are instrumental to the process. Tips for growing net worth are offered at the end of the chapter.

» Chapter 6, "Prepare to Invest," is a crash course in putting your savings to work for you. We will tackle the nature of fundamental economic factors, such as compounding and inflation, that create an undeniable need for investment at all stages of life. We will discuss how to attach specific financial objectives to your investments and how to tailor your investments to appropriate time horizons and risk tolerances. We'll also take a deep dive into the nature of risk itself.

» Chapter 7, "Asset Allocation," covers more specific investment strategies. If you do not know the difference between a stock and a bond, don't worry. Various instruments—and why I prefer mutual funds and ETFs—are covered in simple terms that readers of all levels will understand. Much of the focus of the chapter is on allocating assets (a fancy way of saying putting money to work in different investments), and the chapter ends with several sample portfolios for illustration.

» **PART II: Solving Everyday Challenges**

» Chapter 8, "Managing Debt," kicks off part II. We'll define different types of debt and common traps that people fall into. While taking on debt is not always bad, it must always be approached with caution. We'll review the key factors that must be considered when evaluating a loan. For those readers who are facing debt crises, we will include some actionable steps they can take to improve their situation and alleviate debt-related stress. For those already in debt-related financial crisis, chapter 8 concludes with actionable steps to improve the situation and alleviate stress right now. We'll also cover how credit scores work, the advantages of maintaining a good score, and steps you can take to improve your current score.

» Chapter 9, "Buying a Home," begins by refuting common myths related to homeownership: that buying is always better than renting, that homeownership is the only real way to build equity, or that buying a home is like leveraging other people's money. I explain my belief in a home as a "consumption item" as opposed to an investment and why the best reason to buy a home is not because you want to invest your money wisely, but because you love the home and want to live there a long time. Prospective homebuyers will also want to consider the implications associated with various types of home loans or mortgages, because they are not all created equal. The advantages and disadvantages of buying rental properties and vacation homes are also covered in this chapter.

» Chapter 10, "Insurance," presents ideas for protecting yourself, your property, and your loved ones in a cost-effective manner. Key differences between term and whole life policies are explained, and readers are encouraged to carefully consider the need for disability insurance. Various scenarios demonstrate how people of different ages and with different financial situations can maximize insurance coverage without breaking the bank.

» Chapter 11, "Taxes," offers specific strategies that are used to reduce income taxes. Current tax rates are explained in detail, such as how retirement withdrawals, dividends, and capital gains are taxed. Although few people relish sending money to the Internal Revenue Service, there are a few reasons why paying taxes is not such a bad thing. I explain these in chapter 11.

» Chapter 12, "Retirement and Saving for It," is a step-by-step guide to saving money, investing, and funding the retirement that you hope for. The discussion focuses on the different sources of retirement income and provides all the statistics you need to compute what your income needs will be after you decide to stop working. The amount you should save is a function of how much you have already saved and your age. If you are not on track, don't worry, because I provide some specific suggestions for bolstering your retirement savings and maximizing retirement plan contributions.

» Chapter 13, "Weddings and Family," will guide you through major life events such as getting married, having children, and sending them to college. I offer some general guidelines on how to finance your wedding day. Planning for a child's education can also be challenging, and I provide a few tips on tax-advantaged ways of setting money aside. Also, since few schools teach kids about personal finance, I include a checklist of important finance-related topics that parents may want to teach their kids at various ages.

» Chapter 14, "Making Your Own Living," is a chapter that aspiring entrepreneurs and business owners will want to pay special attention to. Topics include the advantages and disadvantages of working as a 1099 contractor rather than a W-2 employee, how to develop a business plan to determine cash flow needs, and unique retirement plan options for the self-employed or business owners. The chapter concludes with a discussion and example of how to handle highly irregular income, which arrives sporadically throughout the year. My main objective in this discussion, and in much of this chapter, is to keep you out of tax trouble.

» Finally, chapter 15, "Windfalls, Charities, and Estates," talks about the often unexpectedly challenging event of receiving a large lump sum of money. Although an inheritance, a lottery win, or even a large bonus from work can help resolve money challenges, emotional issues sometimes arise that can make it difficult for people to feel good about the one-time payment. I offer some tips on dealing with dilemmas associated with large windfalls. I also tackle the very important concept of giving. I offer tips about giving money away to charities and planning for gifting assets to heirs.

PART I

FINDING AND SECURING YOUR FREEDOM

| 1 |
Believe

Chapter Overview
- » Separating Thoughts from Facts
- » Money Scripts
- » Goals and Motivators

If a leader does not believe, he or she will not take the risks required to overcome the inevitable challenges necessary to win.

—JOCKO WILLINK

I believe in heaven and hell. I've seen it in my financial planning practice. Many who ask me for financial help are living in their own version of financial hell. As humans, we often create our own prisons and live within the walls.

Have you ever thought about what financial hell looks like for you? I once worked with a truly financially stressed couple, Molly and Richard. On the outside, they appeared to be a well-off family. Richard ran his own real estate business and Molly worked for a consulting firm. They had two absolutely darling children. Richard was bubbly and friendly, always ready with a lighthearted joke. Molly had a warm smile and was the kind of person who would bring you small gifts just to brighten your day.

At our first meeting, Molly brought me a hand-crocheted hat for my son. The magnanimous, jovial nature of this couple belied their very difficult financial predicament. Molly confessed to being anxious, scared, and angry about their finances. She told me through tears, "We have been living on the edge of our means for a long time. We'd occasionally take on some credit card debt but nothing we felt we couldn't repay. We both have student loans. We have a large mortgage. We like doing nice things for our children. Our daughter, Hannah, takes weekly ballet lessons. Our son, Henry, is obsessed with jiujitsu and competes in tournaments all over the East Coast. I tried to start my own consulting business a few years ago. We knew it would take a few years to get it running. At the time, Richard's business was booming.

It seemed like a great time for me to go out on my own. We started living on one income. Our expenses didn't change much. We essentially kept the same spending habits. We were kind of operating under the assumption that I'd eventually make enough money to stave off any budding financial issues. Richard handled all the finances, I'm not as good at it. We didn't communicate much about it. I really felt like everything was fine.

"And then, Richard's business had a hard year. It was the same year that my dad was diagnosed with Alzheimer's. My mother felt completely overwhelmed, and Richard and I wanted to help pay for my dad's home care. All throughout this time Richard continued to pay the bills and shelter me from the reality of our finances. I know he meant well. He knew I was already distressed about my dad, and he didn't want me to also have to worry about money. Had I known the details of our predicament, then I probably would have gone back to work."

Then it was time to hear from Richard: "The first thing we fell behind on was our taxes. As a business owner I would, under normal circumstances, pay my taxes in quarterly installments. But as our situation worsened I found myself using that money to pay the bills that were piling up. At the same time I began using our credit cards a lot more. Before long we'd burned through all of our liquid assets. We still had the equity in our home, but otherwise we were bust. When I finally told Molly, she was furious. She couldn't believe that I had shielded her from the reality of our financial situation for so long. She took the first available position at a consulting firm. However, I know she felt like it was too late. I just thought I could fix it all, but now we're paying 20 to 30 percent interest on our credit cards, and we owe the IRS a lot of money. We couldn't bring ourselves to share the financial news with our kids, so we've been hiding it. The kids are doing all their after-school activities as usual and asking for money. And it's flying out the door. We really don't know what to do."

There's a saying, "Rome wasn't built in a day." Rome didn't fall in a day, either. It took Molly and Richard a couple of years to end up living in financial hell. Each day, the decisions they made led them down a path they did not like, one that became increasingly difficult to reverse.

In his book *Atomic Habits*, James Clear explains his concept of "1 percent better every day." The idea is that small habits compound every day, and over time, this makes you better at whatever you're looking to accomplish. Conversely, small negative habits also compound and can leave you much worse off. It's like getting on an airplane in San Francisco and expecting to land in Washington, DC. If the pilot makes a very small change in his flight path and does not correct it, then you land in either New York City or Atlanta.

Mr. Clear's "1 percent better" approach seems easy enough. Replace little bad habits with little good habits, and you'll see positive results over time. In truth, it's not that easy. Little bad habits are harder to shake than you might expect. In fact, it is in the very quality of their "littleness" that they are the most dangerous and sneaky. In any given isolated moment, spending an extra twenty-five, fifty, or one hundred dollars here or there does not signal an oncoming financial hell. It's much easier, and comforting in the moment, to sustain the little bad habit rather than attempt to change it. Persistent, committed change, even on a seemingly small scale, requires real focus and willpower. And at the foundation of your efforts must be a vivid sense of belief. Believing in your mission is the most important part of financial success. Not only must you believe that you are capable of achieving your best financial life, but you must also believe that the little changes you are making will lead you to success. It is through this belief that you will find the tenacity to alter your habits and day-to-day decisions. Believing will change who you become.

Going back to our friends Molly and Richard—as I listened to their story of financial woe, I could see clearly from my end how the two of them could work together to change the household conversation, or lack thereof, about money. I could see them creating financial goals for their family and making the small, persistent changes necessary to set themselves on the right course. The trick would be getting them to see those possibilities. They would need to visualize and believe in their bright financial future.

It was clear from our conversation that Molly deeply wanted to run her own consulting firm. It was also clear how much they both loved their children and wanted to move heaven and earth for them. They also cared a lot about family and wanted to be financially supportive during this difficult time for Molly's mother and father. But given their current financial quagmire, were such lofty desires truly attainable? Of course they were. They could start by evaluating their expenses and eliminating nonessential spending. They could explore ways to increase income. They could sell items they no longer needed, or they could downsize their home or cars. Perhaps most importantly, they could begin taking the steps necessary to actualize their vision for their most fulfilled life.

When you understand your objective and believe in what you're doing, the path forward reveals itself. More appears possible.

Imagine Molly saying to Richard, "Honey, it's a dream of mine to start my own business one day. But we're already overspending, and we have student loan debt. Can we cut some expenses and see how we can increase income, so that I can start my business in the next few years?" Richard replies, "Well, we've never done that before, but that sounds good to me. I don't want to be in debt. I'd like our family to be financially successful." Molly says, "Me too.

I've already done the calculations. If we cut twenty thousand in expenses, then we can pay off our credit card debt over the next eighteen months. Then we can keep saving so I can start my business in three years, which will ultimately increase our income over the long term. What do you say?"

In this imagined dialog, Molly and Richard are having the conversation right now, amid their financial hell. What's changed is their belief that their most fulfilled life is out there, within their grasp. And they're surely going to get there by changing their habits, communicating openly, and committing to their vision. Sounds more like financial heaven to me! Most people think of financial heaven as winning the lottery and having everything and anything they could ever possibly want or need. I see financial heaven as being less about "having" and more about "choosing." You must choose what's incredibly important to you and rally and conform your financial efforts in support of those goals. This means abandoning habits that no longer serve you, to ensure that you have the time, money, and energy to pursue what you truly want.

Now that we've covered financial heaven, I want to touch on the often-discussed notion of "financial freedom." Financial freedom is having enough income, savings, and investments to support the lifestyle you want to have. Your version of financial freedom will look very different from that of others. You are unique. You have certain elements in your life that are incredibly important to you. I invite you to allow those elements to surface. Understand and believe in your mission to achieve financial freedom.

There will be challenges and obstacles to overcome. When you believe, you will find your way around them, and if you understand why they exist, then you can thwart them. Much of what we'll cover in this chapter centers around the "why" of our belief systems surrounding money.

Why Am I Not Wealthy?

If you ask, most people will say they want to be rich. They may even have a long list of things they'd want to buy or experiences they'd want to have if they were to become rich. There is an abundance of articles, podcasts, pundits, and workshops available to those seeking to improve their finances, though some offer zany or outright false information. Yet, out of the abundance of advice available, much of it ends up falling flat, failing to make an impact, and failing to truly transform people's lives.

I have some clients who, from our very first meeting, are focused and ready to make changes in order to attain their goals. I have other clients, many of whom take home enormous salaries and should be insanely wealthy, who suffer from ingrained habits and thinking patterns that make progress toward building wealth difficult.

The common feature in the first group is that they know what they want to accomplish and they have a fire burning to achieve it. This fire acts as motivation. They can overcome obstacles, poor habits, and deep-rooted convictions to get what they want.

The most common feature I find in the second group is that they have competing goals. There is a want for a wealthy future, but it competes emphatically with the comforts of *now*. The lack of clarity about what is most important makes it much more difficult to overcome obstacles, poor habits, and deep-rooted convictions.

Building wealth requires a certain mindset. Some can build and maintain wealth throughout their lives and even into subsequent generations. Others let every dollar they make slip through their fingers. A person capable of building wealth views the world differently than the average person. They evaluate trade-offs incredibly well. They often delay gratification in pursuit of long-term endeavors. They live below their means. Building wealth is part of who they are.

Let's look at some example topics in figure 2 and compare the mindset of the average person to that of the person who knows how to build wealth:

fig. 2

LIFE MILESTONE	AM Average Mindset	BWM Building Wealth Mindset
Earning an income	This is what my profession makes.	I'll negotiate, improve my skills, and demonstrate true value.
Buying a car	I'll research a few new, mid-priced cars to see which features I want, and then I'll lease or finance one.	I'll purchase a used vehicle that can get me from place to place. I'll only finance my purchase at a low interest rate.
Buying a home	I'll purchase the home I want at the maximum of what a bank will lend to me.	I'll purchase less than I can afford, so I have money for other endeavors.
Getting married	I guess this is what weddings cost.	I'll creatively celebrate this milestone on a budget.
Having kids	My kids need a lot. They need clothes. They need activities. They need camps. I need childcare. There's nothing I can do about it. Kids are expensive.	There are trade-offs between all the things I want for my children. I will evaluate what will best serve our family within the confines of our income.
Funding retirement	I'll save a bit and the state will take care of the rest.	I'll save what I need and not rely on others to provide for me.

In every financial decision, those looking to build wealth take responsibility for their finances. They don't blame the world or anyone else. They don't ceaselessly lament the high cost of this and that, but instead accept the realities of the world in which they live. They assess the choices available and make smart decisions. You can do all of this as well, if you learn to think like a person building wealth.

Since our convictions cause our behaviors and our behaviors cause our results, what convictions do you harbor that are not serving you? Something you believe is causing you to act in a way that results in poor financial outcomes. Without knowing you personally, I can't tell you what it is. However, I know how you can find out!

Thoughts versus Facts

We have thousands of thoughts on a daily basis, many of which are repetitive, the same thoughts we had the day before. Thoughts have tremendous power, and they are hyper-repetitive, fueling our emotions.

Our thoughts (convictions) cause our feelings. Our feelings cause our actions (behaviors). Our actions cause our results. All our results are due to our thoughts. Changing the mental script will lead to different results. It's not easy to do. You have to believe that you can, and you have to be focused on the goals you want to achieve.

In the accompanying infographic (figure 3), I show how a circumstance can create different thoughts that have their own associated feelings.

It is easy to see how different thoughts can lead to very different results. Let's take budgeting as an example. If you think of budgeting in terms like "it's restrictive and makes me suffocate," then I doubt you are going to start a budget anytime soon. On the other hand, if you and your husband have a clear goal—let's say you want to buy a house—and you know that budgeting will help you achieve this goal, then it's quite possible you can change the way you think about budgeting. "Results first" is my motto. First, think of the results you want. Then, work on generating the thoughts and the energy you need to get what you want.

fig. 3

CIRCUMSTANCE		THOUGHTS	FEELINGS
HAVING A BUDGET	☺	A budget will help me know where my money goes and, in turn, will help me be more deliberate with my finances.	capable, organized
	☹	A budget is restrictive and makes me feel suffocated.	uncomfortable, deprived
SAVINGS	☺	I know if I try, I can save more money.	determined, excited
	☹	No matter what I do, I can't seem to save. I shouldn't bother at all.	worthless, helpless
POTENTIAL EARLY DEMISE	☺	While it's unlikely that I will die young, it's important for me to think about how much my family would need if I did.	prepared
	☹	That won't happen to me (and therefore I won't take action).	overwhelmed, fearful
POTENTIAL DISABILITY	☺	Disability is scary, but as with life insurance, I want to make sure my family and I are protected in case something happens.	secure
	☹	It's too expensive! That won't happen to me (therefore I won't take action).	angry, fearful
INVESTING	☺	Investing over a long period of time will help my savings grow and help me reach my financial goals.	confident
	☹	Markets are unreliable and therefore I'm better off staying in cash or trying to time them.	worried, anxious
DEBT	☺	I've racked up debt, but I want to make changes in my life and pay it off.	decisive
	☹	I've racked up debt and it's so much that I can't even think about it or deal with it.	regretful, hopeless

CIRCUMSTANCE		THOUGHTS	FEELINGS
BUSINESS OWNERSHIP	🙂	I've always wanted to start my own business; I don't know how but I like a good challenge.	determined, powerful
	☹️	I don't know how to start a business.	insecure, frustrated
TAXES	🙂	Living in America is my choice, I like it here and therefore I pay my taxes (though I mitigate when possible).	content
	☹️	I hate taxes so much, I make all my financial decisions around them.	threatened
FUTURE RETIREMENT	🙂	Retirement seems far away, but planning for it now will give me flexibility and options later.	organized, resolute
	☹️	Retirement is so far away, I don't need to plan now.	overwhelmed, uneasy
ESTATE PLANNING	🙂	I want to protect my family. Working with a trusted attorney feels like the right thing to do.	able, supported
	☹️	My family can deal with papers after I die.	anxious, avoidant

Getting Out of Your Own Way

As soon as we become aware of money, we develop beliefs about it—beliefs we cling to, sometimes for the rest of our lives, often at the cost of our souls.
— GEORGE KINDER, *The Seven Stages of Money Maturity*

When you were a child, perhaps your mother said to you, "Turn off the light. You're burning your father's hard-earned money!" Or maybe it was your favorite uncle, after he bought an insanely expensive suit prior to an important sales meeting, who told you something like, "You gotta spend money to make money, kid!"

Maybe it wasn't something you heard, but rather something you experienced. Maybe you grew up on a financial roller-coaster ride. When Dad had good years, there were lots of vacations, new toys, and family dinners out. When Dad fell on hard times, you wore clothes that were too small for you and had turnips for dinner every night.

As children, we are incredibly impressionable. Our brains are like soft balls of Play-Doh, molded by our experiences. These experiences shape us into the adults we are today. In a lot of ways, this is a good thing, even a great thing. When we're young, our brain plasticity allows us to learn new ideas quickly. In other respects, such moldability is a hindrance. We learn bad lessons from our surroundings that warp our view of the world. Our past creates "truths" that we do not question.

Every day, we make choices. Sometimes we act intentionally, having considered the pros and cons of a choice, done some research, and consulted our friends and advisors. Most of the time we act using instincts learned long ago. When dealing with financial matters, the trick is knowing when these instincts are not helping.

In a way, instincts can seem like facts. They feel true, they are supposed to be true, but sometimes they are not. Our brains are filled with ideas that may or may not be true. These ideas jell into guiding principles in our minds, influencing so many of the decisions we make.

Some notions have been with us our whole lives. We have all kinds of untrue ideas in our minds that seem to help us. Every time we encounter a tough situation or a hard choice, our brain relies on our instincts. We listen to our instincts because they help to insulate us from the difficult realities of our lives. But they also inhibit us from progressing and achieving real and meaningful goals.

If you are struggling with money, the first step is to examine those instincts. When are you getting in your own way? Why? What is your brain telling you when you act instinctively?

We would like to believe that we at least understand our money problems, even as we struggle to manage them. However, we often carry inside our brains fully formed ideas about money that are questionable at best, and sometimes simply untrue. The financial psychologist Brad Klontz calls them "money scripts." Our financial behaviors, both good and bad, make more sense when we identify the money scripts that accompany them. We all have them, and our scripts have unique twists and peculiarities. But Dr. Klontz identifies a few core archetypes:

QUOTE

Money Avoidance

I don't like dealing with money, and that is never going to change.
— THE MONEY AVOIDER

This script is telling you that if you ignore your financial worries, they will go away. The result is that you habitually avoid dealing with money. When you get money, you spend it. Thinking about the future makes you anxious. You train yourself to avoid the subject that makes you feel bad.

Here are some other scripts regarding money avoidance:

»   **"Money is bad."** – It is not worth trying to accumulate any money when money is evil and the rich are shallow, greedy, and oppressive. The truth is that money is neither good nor bad, it just *is*. We attach thoughts to money, and it is our own relationship with money that determines how we feel about it.

»   **"I don't deserve money."** – You can't enjoy what you have when others are less fortunate. This often occurs to those in helping professions or who receive sudden money from a lottery, medical accident, life insurance settlement, inheritance, or sudden fame. This script keeps you emotionally poor.

»   **"There will always be enough money."** – In one sense this is a comforting script; money will be there when you need it. However, blind trust that the universe will provide causes you to take less responsibility for your finances.

»   **"Money is unimportant."** – While it is true that wealth doesn't bring love, happiness, or community, money still weaves its way through our lives. We can't ignore it. We must consider our finances seriously and exert financial maintenance, just as we would with any of our other personal resources, like time, energy, talent, health, and relationships.

»   **"People and institutions who work with money are evil."** – This avoidance script prevents people from getting help when they need it for fear of dealing with advisors, brokers, or other financial professionals whom they think are inherently untrustworthy. For some, this phobia can extend even to banks, investment firms, and other institutions that provide valuable services to those looking to accumulate wealth.

» **"Money is too complicated to deal with."** – This insidious script convinces fully capable individuals that they are not intelligent or patient enough to take control of their finances. If you shudder at the thought of all the paperwork that goes into purchasing a home or managing an investment portfolio, if you tremble at making a basic budget or tackling the stack of bills on your desk, then you may be oppressed by this script.

Money Worship

If I just had more money, my life would be better.
– THE MONEY WORSHIPPER

The money worshipper believes that money equates to the utmost in security and happiness. If you can't afford something, your first thought is, where can I get more money? Money worship is the perpetual hamster wheel: as you get more, you continually need more. Like the money avoidance script, this one leads nowhere. No matter how much money you get, you'll always want more.

Below are other scripts concerning money worship:

» **"There will never be enough money."** – If you believe there will never be enough money, you are destined to experience constant anxiety and insecurity about money, no matter how much you have. Workaholics tend to have this script. While it drives many positive outcomes, like ambition and a good work ethic, it can often lead to dissatisfaction if left unchecked.

» **"Money buys freedom."** – In some regards, this is true. Having money will allow you more flexibility and choice in your future. However, how you view freedom is entirely up to you. In the film *Braveheart*, when William Wallace said, "They may take away our lives, but they'll never take our freedom!" he wasn't talking about money.

Money Status

If I had more money, I would feel better about myself.
> – THE MONEY SHOWBOAT

Those who conform to the money status archetype believe that if you have more money, you have more self-worth. You have constant urges to buy the latest and greatest things and make sure that other people know you have them. When you see others with these expensive things, you think they must have everything they want in life.

Here are other scripts regarding money status:

» **"I will not buy something unless it's new."** – This goes hand in hand with net worth equaling self-worth. The person holding this script feels great when buying something new, but feels grungy when buying something used. This thought and the feelings that arise from it are not based in reality. There are many cases where buying something used is both financially prudent and wholly appropriate.

» **"Money is what gives life meaning."** – If you hold this script, then you believe that money will help you achieve what you want in life, like fulfillment, lasting relationships, or a place in the world. In reality, money does not make these things happen. Money is just a tool that, when well handled, can help you create the life you want. It does not give you that life; only you can do that.

Money Vigilance

Everything could go wrong tomorrow! I have to make sure everything is okay today.
> – THE FINANCIAL NEUROTIC

As a money-vigilant, you constantly think you need to do more to protect your finances. While being thoughtful and responsible is healthy, it can quickly turn unhealthy if it borders on obsessive. You may be very wary of your financial future, constantly checking your accounts or worrying about your investments. You may distrust financial professionals, feeling as if only you can manage everything. And you may be prone to workaholism, because you need to see your income rising and your accounts growing.

Below are some other scripts about money vigilance:

» **"It's not nice to talk about money."** – This is quite common in our society. We will talk about sex before we'll mention a salary figure. It is important to have open communication about your finances. I'm not saying to shout it from the rooftops, but it does help to trust those close to you and to talk openly about money.

» **"Money should be saved, not spent."** – While it is good to save, it is also important to recognize that money is a tool that helps us live our most fulfilled lives. Spending is a good thing when done mindfully and with purpose.

The four money archetypes have commonalities. First, none of the thoughts are based on fact. Avoiding your finances is not going to help your financial situation. More money is not going to make you happier. Having more status is also not going to make you happier. Obsessing over money is not going to make your life any better, either.

Second, each script pretends to offer you the solution to your problem but in truth further exacerbates it. If you're anxious about money, then avoiding it is ultimately going to make your anxiety worse, not better. If you think you need more money to be happier or to gain self-esteem, then you are using money to avoid the work that you really need to be doing within yourself. The money-vigilant person may scrimp and save his way to a higher bank account balance, but he will find himself perpetually dissatisfied, because he's allowed his obsession with money to unbalance his life.

And the final commonality between all the archetypes is that their scripts ultimately cause individuals and families to make the same decisions over and over again, expecting different results.

In order to change, you need to notice your scripts.

Which archetype do you most relate to? Think of a few times when the scripts associated with that archetype have run through your head. How did it make you feel? Now, try to think of the financial result you want to have. Does it challenge your usual script?

If you have a money script, or three, do not despair! Your script is only an issue if it prevents you from living your most fulfilled life. If you are floundering, then I highly recommend focusing on the results you want to have. Putting your results first will help you decide what behaviors and thoughts you need to change to arrive at your cherished future.

For example, a main money script for one of my clients was "there will never be enough money." He grew up in a household where they never had enough, and times were often hard. He recalled going to bed without dinner and not always having clothing for all seasons. Because of this, as an adult, he worked many extra hours to provide for his family, even at the expense of being able to spend time with them. Though he and his wife both desired more time together as a family, he had difficulty in cutting back on his work hours. Rationally, he knew they had enough, but his script held him back.

To help him free himself from the grip of his money script, I encouraged him to focus like a laser on his objective—to spend more time with his family. He and his wife evaluated their true needs and what they could live without. My client prioritized working fewer hours, knowing that he would still be able to provide for what was most important while also being able to spend more time with his family.

If I had to submit a moral of the story, it would be this: if you can remain focused on the results you want, then you will inevitably uncover more opportunities for flexible, creative adjustments to your ingrained habits, and the path forward will become clear.

Money Maturity Is a Process

Life planning is the process by which we prioritize what is important and move toward living the life we want to have. In imagining our most fulfilled lives, we can see the direction in which we need to go. George Kinder, widely recognized as the father of financial life planning, has trained thousands of advisors worldwide through the Kinder Institute of Life Planning. He wrote three books, *The Seven Stages of Money Maturity*, *Lighting the Torch*, and *Life Planning for You*, which describe the process through which a person can launch into their most fulfilled life.

The Seven Stages of Money Maturity outlines three phases that Kinder calls childhood, adulthood, and maturity. In childhood, we have innocence and pain. We receive messages from those around us and if we are not careful, they follow us into adulthood. Adulthood is reframing our experiences through knowledge, understanding, and vigor. Knowledge helps us rationalize and work through the messages we heard throughout childhood. It involves facts, figures, and financial concepts. It is what you typically think of when imagining financial planning. Understanding involves developing an ease concerning your finances, despite the difficult feelings that may arise. It is what allows you to move past the pain of childhood to become who you are meant to be. Vigor gives us the energy we need to move into action. When we reach maturity, we have vision into what can be, and we are able to pass a blessing on to those around us.

Our goal is to graduate from childhood to adulthood in a series of steps:

» Gaining knowledge
» Understanding new things about ourselves and how we process information
» Becoming at ease with our negative thoughts and emotions about money
» Generating the energy we need to do what we need to do

My hope is that through this process you will reach maturity regarding your money and can pass your most important virtues on to those around you.

Pain and Suffering

It's pain that changes our lives.

— STEVE MARTIN

When we think of financial planning, we typically think of knowledge: what to do with money and when to do it. We think of the rational process of personal finance. The problem is that the process is far from rational. Thus, it is important to be at ease with the negative feelings that arise as we walk a new path. These feelings are quite normal and perhaps ones we often push aside.

In addition, truly painful events in our lives cause much suffering and affect the way we deal with our finances. Even small purchases are sometimes a reaction to pain or suffering. For example, if you walk into a drugstore to buy gum, you might be reacting to uneasiness about having bad breath.

In the world of financial planning, most clients come to my office because they have some problem or issue that needs to be addressed. While the perception might be that only wealthy people with too much money hire financial planners to help allocate and invest their assets, that is not true based on my experience.

Instead, people ask about my services because they are having some hardships or problems; they are experiencing a sense of unease with their finances. Maybe that is why you are reading this book? Maybe there is something in your financial picture that is uncomfortable or unpleasant?

A common reaction to something that is difficult or unpleasant—whether with money or anything else—is to pretend it does not exist. We want to get rid of it and never see it again. Unfortunately, this tendency is at odds with resolving the pain and moving forward.

Consider the following story: One day, a man noticed a young butterfly struggling to make its way out of the cocoon. It struggled there for hours as the man watched. It appeared to be stuck and unable to make any progress. Finally, he couldn't take it anymore and decided to put a pin into the cocoon to help the young butterfly out. With ease, the butterfly emerged. But something was wrong. The butterfly had a swollen body and shriveled wings. It was unable to fly. Energy with finances is like that. Challenges help us grow stronger. Too much help and dependency, and we never learn anything.

Since you are reading this book, I don't need to emphasize the importance of being proactive and taking charge of your finances. The important point to take home, however, is that it is normal to feel some pain or discomfort when dealing with money and finances. The solution is not avoidance and pretending the problems don't exist. The solution is to build energy, overcome common obstacles, and accomplish your goals.

Enthusiasm and Energy

The Dutch athlete Wim Hof is known for his ability to withstand extremely cold water temperatures for long periods of time. I'm in awe, because even a two-minute cold shower makes me jump! He can teach you how to do it with the Wim Hof method, a combination of breathing tactics, frequent cold weather exposure, and meditation. Behind the ice marathons, the underdressed Everest climbs, and the prolonged exposure to cold weather and water is a man with intense energy. His discipline, focus, and concentration come from a fire burning within him, a calling.

Energy and enthusiasm are the most important tools you have. You will never accomplish anything without finding the energy to do it and the enthusiasm to want to do it well. The drive must come from within.

Enthusiasm and energy are all about motivation and discipline.

For example, I have a friend who really wanted to be in good physical shape for his kids' sake, but he wasn't finding the energy to do it. As a motivator, he put a picture of his kids on his exercise bike, a *trigger*. This trigger gave him the energy to start a regular fitness program.

I have a client—a husband and wife—and they really want to send their kids to private school and pay for their college educations. They are laser-focused on this goal. As a result, a lot of their personal spending and savings endeavors are pursued with these goals and values in mind. Their trigger? A dollar amount. If something they want costs one hundred dollars or more, they discuss it together with their kids' education in mind.

Finding the triggers and motivators that will energize you is usually a matter of asking the right questions:

- » What would give you the most fulfilled life?
- » Who do you need to be to have your most fulfilled life?
- » What is getting in the way?
- » Who can you be accountable to? (Someone other than yourself is always best!)
- » What can you do right now to get closer to your goal?

Think of key items that you have been thus far unable to deal with due to a lack of enthusiasm or energy. Can you think of a trigger you can rely on to inspire motivation every day? Will this or another trigger continue to inspire motivation, even when it wanes on day 8, 28, 58, or beyond?

Identifying your motivators is essential for long-term success, because maintaining energy over time is challenging. Many people are motivated about dieting or fitness at one point or another but then run out of enthusiasm after one or two months. If you hit a low, find something that can pick you up. Know what your triggers are and find a way to incorporate them into your daily life.

The most important thing to me is my family. I am incredibly close with my sister and parents and hope to foster similar relationships with my son and future child(ren). I also run a business that I absolutely love. Sometimes these are at odds with each other. For example, several clients may need attention at the same time, leaving me little time to spend with my son. Or my son can be needy (but lovable!) and leave me little time to work with clients. My trigger is the word *balance*. When I think of that word, I know what I need to do. I remind myself that my most fulfilled life is one where I spend part of my time working and the remainder with my family.

If you change the way you think and believe in your goals and objectives, you will know where you want to go and what you want to accomplish. Repeat these goals to yourself every day. Identify the trigger that will keep you on track. By knowing exactly where you want to be and what you need to do, you can break old habits and replace them with new ones that achieve your desired results.

Setting Yourself Up for Success

Personal finance is deeply personal. It is often why I answer "it depends" to many questions I get on the subject. It depends on who you are, what you value, and what you want to accomplish. Imagine that you are standing on a dock and you want to get to the other side of a lake. There are many ways you can get from point A to point B. Perhaps you will take a sailboat or a kayak, or maybe you'll windsurf. You might even swim if you have the stamina for it. You evaluate your options and choose what appeals most to your senses and objectives; then you journey from point A to point B. Personal finance is exactly like that.

Setting financial goals is the most important part of the process. A goal is like a beacon in the night—it keeps you moving forward and stepping in the right direction. It gives you the reason to make behavioral changes that will lead you where you want to go. It helps you believe.

How to Set Goals, Step by Step:

» **Step 1: Establish the big picture**. What would give you your most fulfilled life? These are your goals.

» **Step 2: Prioritize**. Rank your goals from most to least important; choose three to five on which to focus.

» **Step 3: Visualize**. What can you do right now? What can you do in the next ninety days? What can you do over the next year? Be specific.

» **Step 4: Create your system**. Make a road map that will take you from where you are today to where you want to be in the future.

» **Step 5: Evaluate your motivators**. Your energy will wane. That is a fact. Everyone's energy wanes at one time or another. What do you need to stay motivated when you have little energy to keep going?

For example, Peter is a painter whose dream is to be an entrepreneur and start his own painting company in a few years. Peter's goal is to save $75,000 to buy the needed equipment, supplies, and marketing materials. Eventually, he also wants to hire a junior painter.

In imagining his dream business, Peter is feeling determined and excited. He has a sense of how important his goal is and he is thrilled to work on it. This energy moves Peter into action. He creates the system he needs to reach the $75,000 goal.

Peter says he can do the following: first, he will start saving 10 percent of his paycheck specifically to be used to start his business. He changes the direct deposit instructions on his paycheck so that 10 percent immediately transfers into a new high-yield savings account, where interest can accrue. Next, Peter creates a catalog of items in his home that he is no longer using and puts them online for sale. Every weekend, he carves out a couple of hours to clean, organize, and list the items. Peter finds energy in an old photo of his parents standing in front of the grocery store they owned. When he loses energy, this photo reminds him of how hard his family worked to be entrepreneurs.

Ask yourself what it would be like to live your best, most fulfilled life. Write down anything that comes to mind. Keep asking yourself, Anything else? When you're out of answers, rank them from 1 to however many you came up with. This will help you prioritize what is important. Add a time frame for accomplishing your top three to five priorities. Rewrite your top goals clearly and make sure they are what you really want to accomplish. Draft a list of tasks you can do right now to move yourself closer to your goals. Schedule when you can do them. Write down any motivators that will help reignite your energy along the way.

Setting and prioritizing goals is the only way to live your best life. Doing this will help you tap into the energy you need to set up systems and make necessary sacrifices. If you just set a goal but do not believe in your ability to achieve it, then you will not act in a manner that will accomplish the goal; that is, you will not put any systems in place to get yourself from point A to point B.

Chapter Recap

» Our preconceived thoughts and convictions often determine our results. By focusing on facts, we allow new and greater possibilities for success and fulfillment.

» If we let them, our money scripts can obstruct positive change.

» Pain points often lead to avoidance behavior, but by tackling the issues with energy and enthusiasm, many problems can be readily resolved.

» Triggers can be used to help us routinely reconnect with our motivations and values.

| 2 |
Earning Money: Why and How

Chapter Overview
- » Money and Happiness
- » Increasing Income or Reducing Spending
- » Under-Earning
- » Getting the Job Done

It has been my observation that most people get ahead during the time that others waste.

– HENRY FORD

The formula for financial wealth is not complicated. You earn money. You spend less than you earn. You invest your savings. You repeat this process again and again. You attain wealth.

A lot of financial advice revolves around spending less. In some regards, I agree. Changing how much you spend will help you build wealth. Nevertheless, there are two parts to the wealth equation, with income being a huge part. You can only cut your expenses so much before you're couch surfing, hitchhiking, and stealing food from your family's pantry.

Therefore, more income typically means more savings. More savings means more optionality on what you can afford in the future. If you can keep your spending relatively the same as your income increases, you will be able to build wealth.

Time and again, as income increases, lifestyle costs increase as well. If that occurs, your financial picture will remain the same regardless of your income level. This explains those who seem to have it all but, in reality, have very little saved. They may have a lot of stuff and a big house, but the second their income decreases, it all comes tumbling down. Your spending is not a good indicator of your wealth. Your savings are.

Often, we want to make more money because we want to afford more stuff. More income seems like a good shortcut to solving problems. With more income we can balance the budget and reduce overall financial stress. While this practical incentive is a valid one, there are often other motivators that lurk beneath the surface. I want you to be honest with yourself right now: *why do you want more money?*

Why Do You Want More Money?

What is the truth? Do you want massive wealth? Is your goal to be richer than your neighbor, sister, or Uncle Donald in Tucson? Or is the real reason that you want to feel secure, empowered, and happy? Being a billionaire might help you feel secure, empowered, and happy, but I hope we have shown that happiness can be procured at a much smaller price tag. As the adage goes, money doesn't buy happiness.

We often blame our income or our jobs for financial problems. We don't make enough, we picked the wrong career, our boss is holding us back. Excuses, excuses, excuses.

There are certainly a lot of *if onlys* out there. If only I were a billionaire and did not have to worry about money or working. If only I could retire at the age of forty-five, I would be able to travel and spend more time with my kids. If only … all this struggle would go away.

The thing we often overlook is that everything we do in life, every problem we solve, generally comes with a new set of challenges. That *is* life.

If traveling and spending more time with your kids is what truly gives you energy, what is stopping you from prioritizing that right now? For example, a client recently told me that she wanted to get away from the city and own a cottage in the woods. This was her most precious dream. "If only I had more income, then I could afford my cottage," she said. But our discussion revealed that it was the *feeling* of being in the cottage that was appealing to her. She said she could rent a cottage all summer, but it was outside her price range. "What is within your price range?" I asked. "Well," she said, "I could rent a cottage for a few weekends per summer. That would feel really nice." We calculated that she could rent one five weekends per summer and not sacrifice saving for the future. She could have that right now! She does not need to wait ten years to accumulate the funds for a down payment.

I would like you to take a few moments and think about what you truly want. Is it possible that you can have a small part of your most fulfilled life right now? How?

More income is great, but what is it really doing for you? I'm not here to tell anyone that they shouldn't strive for more income; I think if that's what someone wants, they should go for it.

But evaluate why. What is the feeling you want from having more income? What is the result you wish to create? Is more income the answer, or is there something else you can do right now?

A common example is wanting an upgraded living situation. But how much space do we really need? Evaluate your current space. Is it possible you already have enough and just need to organize a bit? It is a lot cheaper to hire a professional organizer than it is to upgrade a home. When we're in my parents' house, my mom often says, "3,600 square feet and we're all sitting in three square feet!" What's life all about if you are not smushed together with the people you love? No matter what the world looks like, we all have a handful of vital needs in our lives:

- » **Family**: being with those we love and want to protect
- » **Spirituality**: seeking comfort in something bigger than ourselves
- » **Creativity**: using our mind to accomplish our personal and professional dreams
- » **Community**: being with those we trust to celebrate life's milestones and daily rituals
- » **Place**: wanting to fit in somewhere and be a part of something

Money weaves into these needs, but more money doesn't get you any of them. Sometimes more money is the result of seeking or achieving them, but you can't buy any of them.

The truth is that additional money makes us more of who we already are, not somebody new. If you are overspending today, you will overspend tomorrow, regardless of how much income you have. If overspending is a problem for you, it is *you* that needs to change, not your income.

You Do Have the Time

When assessing the "why" of their desire to make more money, many of my clients express a belief that more money will allow them to spend more time with their families. I am left thinking to myself, hmm, it doesn't sound like you need to make more money; just focus on spending more time with your family.

As I write this book, we are amid the COVID-19 pandemic. While many are busier than they've ever been, others have extra free time without their commutes and their nine-to-six jobs. There are folks who find the energy and enthusiasm to cook new things, work out at home, create artistic content, sew masks, and more. There are others who, despite this extra time, cannot get the fire burning to accomplish things they really want to do. It's not the time you are missing. It's the energy. Where there's a will, there's a way.

Here's another reason for making more money that I hear a lot: if I had more money, then I could work on passion projects. My response: what is stopping you? Just do it. If you focus on what you are passionate about, you will not miss the time you take from other things.

Many individuals feel that their time is excessively taxed. If this is you, I suggest you do one thing right away. Start a time journal. Take a week and write down everything you do. Where does your time go? Where would you prefer your time to go? I think you will find that you have many hours in the day to work on your passions. Maybe it's just the two hours you spend every week scrolling through Facebook or Twitter. Discover and own the facts of your time usage. Accept that having a lack of time is not a problem readily fixed by having more money. Think of the results you want to have, and generate the energy for your passion projects.

In the Digital Assets associated with this book, I have a nifty workbook that will help you track and visualize where your time is currently going by hour per week. It's called the IDEAL DAY WEEK YEAR workbook. This resource will allow you to create a plan to recalibrate your time usage to more closely align with what's most important to you. Download this and all your Digital Assets at go.quickstartguides.com/personalfinance.

#3

Why do I want to earn more? What do I need this income for? What is the feeling I want? What is the result I wish to create? These questions may lead to more questions, such as, How do I want to spend my time? or, With whom do I want to be spending my time? Go ahead and ask yourself those questions and give yourself the time to think about your answers.

I can think of perfectly sensible reasons for wanting to earn more money, such as paying off debt more quickly or paying for your wedding because you just cannot wait to be married! And there are great long-term reasons to earn more money, such as boosting your retirement savings or raising the capital to start (or buy) a business. When you truly value and prioritize goals, you can generate the energy you need to earn additional income.

Perhaps more money is a way to avoid a completely different problem. Say you want more money so that you can travel more. What is the feeling you get from traveling? Is this a quality you can have in your life now? Perhaps it's the feeling of freedom you experience when you're out of your routine and in a new place. Find a way to feel it right now within the parameters of your current financial position. Go to a local museum that you've never been to (or haven't been to in a while) or drive out to a neighboring town you have never explored. You'll find you can venture far from your routine while being only a few miles away from home.

Speaking of expensive habits, if you want to earn more money so you can upgrade _____ (fill in the blank with your desire, be it a bigger house, a vacation home, more guitars, a new car, or an antique car), ask yourself key questions:

> » Why do you want to upgrade?
> » What, exactly, is your upgrade going to change?
> » What value will it add to your life?
> » Is it worth the sacrifices you will make to afford it?
> » Have you calculated the salary you need to maintain it?
> » Are you going to appreciate every minute of time you spend with that upgraded thing after you get it, or will you soon become accustomed to it and begin pining for some other upgrade?

Be honest. And be mindful of the following well-known adage: what begins as a pleasure often ends as an expectation.

The bottom line is that there are great reasons to earn more money, but a zombie-like pursuit of "more, more, more" will not solve your financial or personal problems. What will help you evolve, and work toward having a secure financial plan, is figuring out what you *really* want, and why.

Under-Earning

"Under-earner" refers to someone who is earning less than what they are capable of and wants to earn more money. There is nothing fancy about it, except that the desire to earn more money typically means that you *can* earn more, and the only real problem is *you*. In other words, you are getting in your own way.

Under-earners think more about money than others do. Their money thoughts become a weight around their neck that holds them back.

Rather than thinking about ways to make more money, the under-earner is consumed with worry about affording everything. It causes problems between spouses as well: fights about money and endless conversations about how they will be able to pay for things. It can completely erode quality of life. Truly. Here are some of the warning signs that someone is an under-earner:

» Blatant self-sabotage, like sloppy or late work, not showing up, missing meetings, not caring about work as much as others, or binge-watching Netflix instead of working.

» Not asking for more money. As a W-2 employee, you must ask for raises and show your accomplishments to get them. As a business owner, you must evaluate pricing (and probably raise prices to be commensurate with the value you provide).

» Not looking for other ways to make money, like a new job, part-time work, or different ways to make money from an existing business.

» Focusing on short-term immediate pleasures rather than focusing on results wanted in the long term.

» Quitting a high-paying job because of lack of energy, motivation, or inspiration and becoming an under-earner only to regret it later.

For example, say you quit your job because you were unhappy, or you wanted a job with more "purpose." You thought a lower-paying position would make you happier. But it turns out you were simply unhappy; it was not the job's fault. Now you are unhappy while making less.

On the other hand, I have a client who is a highly paid attorney and always talks about a career change because being a lawyer is no longer satisfying. But she hasn't quit, because the high income provides enough motivation—fueling energy—to go to the office each day. The solution to this problem is to channel the energy into finding a career that pays similar wages but also provides meaning and personal satisfaction.

Your happiness and your job are not the same thing. They are separate things. The bottom line is the notion that under-earning is symptomatic of an underlying lack of energy and enthusiasm concerning personal finances, and this enthusiasm is critical for meaningful transformation.

Find Your Value

Have you ever opened a bag of candy and offered a piece to a three-year-old? After they take one, what do they usually say? They want more, right? And after the second piece, they start jumping up and down screaming *more, more, more!*

The three-year old does not understand why they cannot eat one piece after another until the candy is all gone. They do not understand that the first piece is usually the best and, after the tenth or eleventh, they might not feel so well. In economic terms, the process of eating an entire bag of candy has *diminishing returns*.

And the three-year-old has no idea that candy costs money. They only know that you control the dispensing of it. They also understand that they likely won't get any if they color on the living room wall with crayons, throw a fit at the grocery store, or try to kick the cat in the face again.

Grown-ups evaluate cause and effect as well and understand that rewards (like income) can increase if they display certain behaviors that get noticed and add value. The good news for those aspiring to make more money is that many things are within our control:

- » How do we show up for work—unmotivated or excited to get things done?
- » Are we on time for work?
- » Are we willing to stay late to get the job done?
- » Are we just trying to get by, or are we a force of nature at work?
- » Do we help the team or sabotage it?
- » Do we view the job as a paycheck or as something that adds meaning to our lives?

Value is more than the amount of money you earn. It is the person you are every day. Knowing that you add value will make you feel better about yourself and the money itself probably will not.

A salary is not fixed. There is no magic formula or market "out there" that dictates exactly how much we can earn. We think everybody who does our job gets roughly the same amount of money for doing it. This is not true. In every job, from minimum wage to multimillion-dollar salaries, the actual value that each employee brings to the table is different.

Employees think they show up to do the work, and in return they get their paychecks. But what employers really want is your value. When an employer is considering making you an offer, the only thing they want to know is whether you can help their business, organization, or group become more successful.

It does not matter what the profession is or what the job is. The employer is making you the offer because they think you can help them. Employers don't pay you for the job itself or for the time it takes you to do it, but for the value behind it. The position could be managing the drive-through at a fast-food chain or being the CEO of a major technology company. In both cases, you are going to make a million small decisions every day. You are going to be creative and communicative. You are going to add value.

Be the person that your manager knows they can depend on. This does not mean being the suck-up that the rest of the team resents. Be the person who is reliable, who does hard jobs, who shows leadership qualities, even in a role that seems like it doesn't need any. You will shine and show true value.

The same concept applies to business owners. Clients or customers pay owners because they offer a valuable good or service. The amount charged is based on value or the value-creation process. Whether you are owner, boss, or employee does not matter so much. What is important is the value that is being provided.

Your value may meet common expectations for your current position and salary, or it may exceed them. The interesting question is, how much value can you provide? Or, if you are a business owner, are you charging enough?

#4

What do you think you are worth? Sit down and think to yourself: How much money can I make? What is the limit for me? And why is that the limit for me?

A lot of people struggle with these questions because, while we all have certain ideas about what we are worth, many of the notions are inaccurate. They reflect more fear than fact. They don't take into account the confidence others have in us. Developing a sense of our own personal value takes awareness, practice, and repetition.

The key takeaway is that an objective, fact-based knowledge of your own value is essential for maximizing your income.

How to Get More

Many of us will, at some point, find ourselves in a position where we feel underpaid. Generally, employers want to pay you at the low end of what you are worth. I want to help you manage that complicated and often stressful negotiation.

Doing your best work will help your employer succeed and will help you build the skills you need to be successful. Doing your best work will boost your confidence and make you feel good about both the quality of your work and its value. It will also help you get noticed by your employer and make it much more likely that you will get a good recommendation from your boss.

In addition, teammates will know and like you. They will learn they can depend on you. In turn, you will build relationships, which will ultimately lead to success in your career.

If you're bad at something, practice! If you're great at spreadsheets and not great with clients, start talking to whomever you can. Become comfortable connecting with people. I know that whenever I get too comfortable, it means I'm not doing anything to grow. You must grow. It's good for your brain; it's good for your soul.

The simple truth is that people are hesitant to get out of their comfort zones. It is hard. You must generate energy and enthusiasm to do it. It requires work and discipline. It requires ownership of your path.

Maybe you do not have the skills you need for the job you want. If you want to be _____ (fill in the blank with your desired profession) you must work to build your skills in that profession. Stop waiting for someone to hand you the job you want.

While the need to build skills applies to everybody seeking a promotion, it is starkest among those seeking to change professions. For example, long ago my husband was an accountant but wanted to become a software engineer. He taught himself to code. He worked on side projects after work and on the weekends. Then he worked on "open source" projects, meaning he did not get paid. His investment paid off! Now he is a software engineer. As an upshot, he is also making more money and is more fulfilled in his work. It was a long road, over which he maintained a high level of energy to fuel his goal. He taught himself to be an engineer for three years before he was hired and paid as a developer. Changing careers requires grit, motivation, and resilience.

MY TAKE

Be a team player. Help your team no matter what, even if it means that you do not get credit. This is known as "playing the long game," and it is the right thing to do. Eventually you will get a raise or a promotion. It will not happen this week, but eventually your leadership and commitment to the team will be noticed and lead to more senior jobs. Good teamwork is valuable and is rewarded.

If you commit to steadily developing and expanding your value, then you will find the negotiation for a pay increase will be easier than expected. It will help if you remember the results you want. If you fancy a boost to your compensation but think your company can't afford it, then consider what else you value—perhaps more paid time off, or a more flexible schedule.

I have a client who wanted to spend more time with her kids and negotiated a three-day workweek at the same salary. She did not get a pay raise, but she did get what she really wanted!

Depending on the company or industry, maybe a pay bump is simply not possible. It is not in the budget. If you can't negotiate more money, consider asking for something else:

» Benefits (or a better benefits package)
» Bonus programs
» Longevity bonus
» Retention bonus
» More *paid time off (PTO)*
» Educational leave with paid conferences
» Remote workday options
» Additional hourly options outside of the workday
» Childcare subsidy
» Flextime (ability to alter start and end times)
» Cutting hours but not pay

And keep in mind that there is more than one type of pay raise:

» A *COLA* (cost-of-living allowance) is an upward adjustment of your pay to keep pace with increases in costs of living.

» A merit raise is an increase in salary for a job well done.

» Variable pay (or bonus) is payment determined by specific performance, where you can devise and propose a custom arrangement.

» In a competitive pay raise, your salary is adjusted to meet what you could get elsewhere (it helps to have an offer showing you could get this amount elsewhere, and you also have to be willing to leave).

» A salary adjustment is very similar to a competitive pay raise, but this is a correction to bring your pay in line with industry standards. You need to have data showing what the industry standard is; you can't just make it up.

Many people enter these negotiations with their employer armed with an offer letter from another company. The advantage of this tactic is that you are bringing a clear statement of your worth to another party. However, when you use this approach, you must be willing to walk away from your current job if they cannot or will not match your offer letter.

Finally, remember that you cannot control every outcome. Do not take the result of your negotiation personally, whether it goes well or badly. At end of the day, it is about two parties coming together, one with a problem and one with a solution. You are the party with the solution. It is your job to know and articulate the real value you are bringing to the table.

ON YOUR OWN

What specific things do you believe hold you back from making more money? What steps would you need to take in order to grow your income?

#5

The Employer's Perspective

We are fortunate to live in a world full of opportunities. Maybe you are an executive or a business owner and understand the challenges that hiring managers face when negotiating salaries, benefits, and bonuses. It is a balancing act to retain top talent, stay on budget, and meet company profit objectives.

My experience is that the best leaders put their people first. A potential employee is going to be a lot happier to work in a company where they are valued more than the numbers.

When interviewing an applicant, I encourage you to submit a number to the employee right out of the gate. This will anchor the conversation around your budget. The employee is likely to accept the proposal or possibly begin negotiations from there.

NOTE

On the employee side, I encourage them not to mention a number or a range, but to let the employer provide the initial number.

Good employers also take the time to empathize with applicants and attempt to understand why they want to get hired. Is it their first job? Offering them a market rate for their first job is pretty standard.

Or are they leaving a company to join your company? Why are they leaving? It may not be salary-related. That is, a person who really wants a particular job might jump on the right opportunity regardless of the salary offered.

The only way to know a person and to find out their true motivation is by taking the time to ask. *People first.*

Understanding Your Unique Assets

Underlying all discussions about income lies the concept of ***capital***. What is it?

Capital is typically associated with ***assets***, like deposits in a checking account or stock held with a brokerage firm. It can also include real estate, business interests, retirement plans, bonds, annuities, or any financial instrument that has tangible value. In the world of personal finance, however, capital can also come in the form of knowledge, expertise, and experience.

Even if you do not have a multitude of investments or assets, you have capital. Your brain, your knowledge, and your experience are all forms of human capital that can help to improve your personal finances.

Think of how much it costs to become a doctor. Many people graduate from medical schools with debt levels in excess of $100,000. These students have made a tremendous investment in their human capital! Once they are actively helping patients and saving lives (providing immense value), then their investments will generally achieve financially satisfying returns.

The degrees and skill sets acquired by medical professionals are very clear examples of human capital investment, but, in fact, everyone has human capital. It is the sum of an individual's skills, knowledge, experience, and way of being. By pursuing investments (time and money) in our own capital value, we position ourselves to provide more value to the world and to increase our income if we so desire.

Chapter Recap

» Find ways to add value, and increased income will likely follow.

» Sometimes we think we want more income, but what we really want is more meaning and responsibility in our career.

» Changing industries mid-career is difficult but often worth it for those who can learn new skills.

» The best employers empathize with their employees and put people before numbers.

» Human capital is your experience, education, and brainpower.

| 3 |
Deliberate Saving and Spending

Chapter Overview
» Budgeting with Purpose
» Saving by Way of Budgeting
» Spending Less

The advertising industry and Hollywood have done a wonderful job conditioning us to believe that wealth and hyperconsumption go hand in hand.

– THOMAS J. STANLEY

No one likes to **budget**. No one. Budgeting implies restriction. It suggests the party is over.

Income minus spending equals savings. It is just math. Your savings builds wealth. The rest of the thoughts you are having about spending and budgeting are just drama.

The other reason why no one likes to budget is because it's super-annoying. You have to track every little thing you purchase. It takes time and energy. It's tedious and frustrating.

But it doesn't have to be that way. There are ways for you to accomplish your savings goals without tracking every little penny. Don't mistake what I'm saying—if you track all your spending, you will be successful. In fact, budgeting works quite well, if you can stick with it. However, if you are a person who absolutely loathes tracking, then I have other solutions for you.

Have you ever read the kids' book *Go, Dog. Go!?* Spoiler alert: on the last page all the dogs go to a party on top of a tree. Big dogs, little dogs, black dogs, yellow dogs, green dogs, all the dogs are there with their party hats and their ping pong paddles and their streamers. They are having a grand ole time.

We are going to transform your budgeting process into a zany, lighthearted soirée. It may not feel like the *Go, Dog. Go!* party right now. But it will by the end of the chapter.

Where Does Your Money Go?

To make changes to your spending, you need to know where your money is going. This is not a budget. This is simply a record of what you are currently spending. All you want are the facts. There is no judgment, no prescriptions, no *shoulds*, just facts.

You can do this in two ways:

1. Download all your credit card and banking transactions over at least the past six months, up to a year. Categorize them. Subtract your expenses from your income earned over the same period. See what is left over.

    a. **Advantage:** This will give you a detailed picture of where you spend your money and how much you are saving.
    b. **Disadvantage:** It takes a lot of time and energy.

2. Take an average of all your credit card purchases on a monthly basis, plus an average of your monthly spending from your checking account. Subtract your averages from your income. See what is left over.

    a. **Advantage:** This will give you a quick idea of how much you spend and save on average.
    b. **Disadvantage:** You will not have a detailed picture of your expenses and therefore will not know where to make changes.

You can access my Simple Budgeting Spreadsheet in your free Digital Assets at go.quickstartguides.com/personalfinance. This will help you categorize your current spending, and, as we proceed through this chapter, you can return to this asset as you design a more mindful approach to your spending.

Having taken a look at where your money goes, are you at all surprised? Are there any particular numbers catching your attention? Do you notice any patterns? Is there anything you would like to change?

Now, refer to the "How to Set Goals, Step by Step" exercise you completed at the end of chapter 1. What are you looking to accomplish? Does your current spending support your most fulfilled life?

When I meet with new clients, we spend a few meetings discussing goals and creating a system to achieve them. Afterward, we evaluate where spending has been and where the client would like it to be. You must begin with your goals. If you begin elsewhere, it will be exceedingly difficult for you to see what changes need to be made.

For example, I had a client named Alton. He worked as an administrator for a university. He came to me because he was very worried that he was not saving enough. He thought he needed to cut expenses, and he wanted budgeting tips. After a long discussion about Alton's most fulfilled life, it became clear that he wanted a completely different job. With a little investment in new skills, Alton was able to transition into a new career doing project management for a technology company. His salary nearly doubled. He was immediately able to save more by creating a simple savings plan. As we mentioned in the last chapter, your income is a huge part of the equation. Never forget that.

I have another client, Michelle, who is retired. She lives off her Social Security checks and income from her investments. Her spending looks vastly different than Alton's, who is at the beginning of his career and has years to save and invest. Michelle's goals are to live comfortably in retirement, travel three times per year, and give gifts to her children and grandchildren. Because she is crystal clear on her goals, she knows how to spend her money. She resists spending when it does not align with her goals.

Planning Your Spending

There is an old joke told by comedian Myron Cohen. Two men, Irving and Morris, are sitting on a park bench.

Irving: Morris, have I got a deal for you! I've got an elephant you can buy for five hundred dollars. This is the best elephant out there. And five hundred dollars, what a deal!

Morris: Irving, what am I going to do with an elephant? Forget it.

Irving: Morris, this is quite an elephant. He's tamed. He'll be your butler. He'll sit down and pass you your pants. He could hang up your coat, high on the rack. He'll give you a shawl.

Morris: What do I need a shawl for?

Irving: He eats peanuts. And what a memory on this elephant. He'll remember anything you need.

Morris: I live in a walk-up apartment on the fourth floor. I haven't even got room for a tiny dog. What am I going to do with an elephant?

Irving: All right, all right. I'll give you three elephants for six hundred dollars.

Morris: Now you're talking!

We all have proverbial elephants lying around the house. I recently went to the grocery store for milk. All we needed was milk. Yet I arrived home with twelve other bags. My thought process was *Well, I'm going to need these things pretty soon anyway, might as well buy them now.* The problem is, this mentality leads to mindless spending. If you are thinking, *I may need this later* or *I may want this at another time*, it's a good sign that you don't need it now. This is the type of spending over which you have the most control.

Choice is one of the greatest indicators of satisfaction. We feel good about our money and our spending when we have a choice in the matter. It is the reason why everyone hates spending money on fixing a leaky pipe. There was no choice! The good news is, you can choose how to spend your money when you are deliberate about how you save.

Here is my simplest "un-budget" plan, the 80/20 rule:
1. Multiply your after-tax income by 20 percent
2. Put the 20 percent directly into a savings, investment, or retirement account. You can also use it to pay off debt.
3. Spend the rest however you choose.

EXAMPLE

You make $75,000 per year. After taxes and deductions you have $55,000, or $2,115 per pay period when paid biweekly. You calculate that you need to save $423 per paycheck, or $11,000 per year. You put $115 per paycheck into your 401(k) to get the company match. You directly deposit the remaining $308 into a savings or investment account, depending on your goals and financial position (we will discuss this more in chapter 6). You have $44,000 per year left over for spending. Spend your $44,000 guilt free. It is yours!

This is not a budget; it is a savings plan. A savings plan enables you to feel good about your purchases while growing wealth.

If you are living paycheck to paycheck and find you cannot stick with a savings plan, then there is more work to be done. You must understand why you cannot save. Most people know what they make and therefore have a good idea of what they can spend. They may even be good at planning for future expenses, like a wedding or a sweet sixteen party. However, they forget to account for the unexpected expenses (figure 4).

For example, say you make $75,000 per year. You set aside 10 percent, or $7,500 per year, in savings. Then your hot water heater goes out. Your kids severely damage the carpet and it needs replacing. Your laptop is on the fritz. You have an unexpected medical emergency and have not yet met your deductible. Just like that, your savings evaporates.

SIZING UP SURPRISES

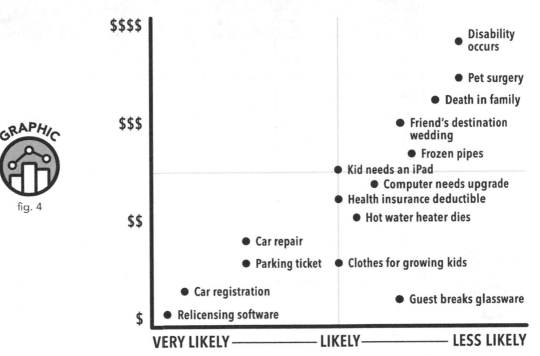

fig. 4

Completely out-of-the-blue expenses always seem like "one-time" items. Yet we all have one-time items every year. You must include them in your spending. The good news is that we can make an easy plan for the unexpected too. You can enhance the 80/20 rule by using the 80/20–90/10 rule. It is simpler than it seems. Here is what you do:

1. Calculate 20 percent of your after-tax income and directly deposit it into savings.
2. Of the 80 percent left over, calculate 90 percent; this is the amount you can spend on whatever you want, guilt free.
3. The remaining 10 percent is for any surprises.

Imagine you make $75,000 per year pretax, $55,000 after tax and health benefits. You set aside $11,000 for savings (20 percent). You have $44,000 left over ($55,000–$11,000). You can spend $39,600 per year ($44,000 x 0.9). You save an additional $4,400 per year for unexpected expenses ($44,000 x 0.1) and directly deposit it into a savings account. If you do not have any surprises, you save a little extra, or you can spend it on whatever you like.

Here's what spending might look like at $75,000 per year in income (figure 5):

fig. 5

SPENDING		SAVINGS/DEBT REPAYMENT		UNEXPECTED EVENTS	
Rent	$13,464.00	401(k) contribution	$3,000.00	Unforeseen car trouble	$580.00
Utilities	$812.00	Debt repayment	$8,000.00	Surprise medical bill	$705.00
Cell phone	$1,296.00			Wedding gift and travel	$435.00
Groceries	$8,215.00			Cat ate a marble	$365.00
Car	$3,180.00			Kids ruined the fence	$1,000
Insurance	$538.00			New air conditioner	$685.00
Dining out	$2,550.00			Last-minute concert tickets	$230.00
Clothing	$1,140.00			Leftover savings	$400.00
Vacation	$2,905.00				
Kids' activities	$1,200.00				
Personal care	$1,320.00				
Gym	$480.00				
Housecleaner	$1,400.00				
Gifts	$1,000.00				
TOTAL	**$39,500**	**TOTAL**	**$11,000**	**TOTAL**	**$4,400**

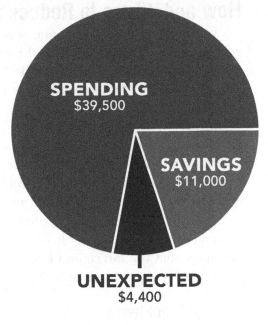

SPENDING
$39,500

SAVINGS
$11,000

UNEXPECTED
$4,400

Keep your goals in mind. Remember those motivators we discussed in chapter 1? Now is a great time to remind yourself of yours. Let's say family vacations are important to you, or eating out once per week is a joy; make sure to prioritize these when thinking through your spending. When you are ready to make a purchase that will compromise your savings targets, think of your motivators. Imagine that family vacation. Feel what it would be like. This will help you stay on course.

Kevin and Priscilla are clients of mine. When I met them, they lived in New York City close to Priscilla's workplace. She worked long hours and did not want to commute. They paid an inordinate amount of money for their tiny apartment. They had a high income and no savings. They both desperately wanted to change, so that Kevin could start his own business in the future. They also wanted more space to start a family. Priscilla admitted their rent was astronomical, and they didn't even like where they lived. So, she negotiated working from home three days per week. This allowed them to move out of the city and reduce their home expenses, while increasing their space. Other spending habits changed as well when they moved. They began cooking more. They spent less on expensive city activities. These reductions in spending created savings. And the knowledge that they were accumulating savings made them feel better about spending on items or experiences that truly brought them joy. Priscilla keeps a picture of their old apartment saved to "favorites" on her phone. When she longs for New York City, she looks at the picture and it reminds her of the stress of their old life.

How and Where to Reduce Spending

Generally, we like to spend money because it makes us feel good. Feeling good is more than emotions; it is the chemical messenger dopamine being released in our brain. Dopamine is the "happiness hormone." It plays a huge role in how we perceive rewards, how we are motivated, and what we are attentive to.

Dopamine is released in your brain not only when you are rewarded, but also when you anticipate being rewarded. Purchases are rewards for us. Perhaps you have seen experiments where mice are encouraged to press a button in anticipation of a reward to come. Think about that mouse the next time you click the "buy now" button and wait for your new stuff to arrive.

That dopamine high is what drives us to continue spending, even when it would be more prudent not to do so. You can't fight your brain's release of dopamine. But you can control how you spend, so you can continue to feel good about your purchases, at both a chemical and a rational level.

Big-Ticket Items

Generally, when we spend more money, we end up saving less or taking on debt. I advise against this. If you want to build wealth and have money for future goals, then you need to have savings and investments. Instead of spending away your savings, you need to adopt a "swapping" mentality. If you spend more in one place, you must spend less somewhere else. The easiest way to spend less is to evaluate your monthly fixed expenses, like your home or your car. Your monthly fixed expenses dominate your budget. Changing these will move the needle the most.

Housing

I recommend that your total spending on housing be 20 percent or less of your pretax salary. Housing spending includes your rent or *mortgage*, insurance, maintenance, and utilities. When you look at the numbers, you may think, "Whoa, 20 percent is not a lot—I spend way more on rent alone, or twice that if you include lawn and pool care." And, yes, a lot of us do spend more than 20 percent on housing, but a lot of us are in debt or live paycheck to paycheck, too. Keeping your housing expenses at or below 20 percent will make it much easier to save.

Here's an example: Krista and Martin make $85,000 per year. The bank is willing to lend them $400,000 to purchase the $500,000 home they want. If they purchase the home, they will end up spending 36 percent of their income on their mortgage, insurance, and taxes. Additionally, they will spend another $5,000 per year on home maintenance, which brings their total home-related expenses to nearly 42 percent of their pretax income! On an after-tax basis, the number is more like 50 percent. It is going to be incredibly difficult for Krista and Martin to save, when half of their money is spent before they wake up and put their feet on the carpet.

NOTE

Homeowners can expect to pay 1 to 3 percent of the total price of their home in annual maintenance expenses. For Krista and Martin's $500,000 home, this added expense is expected to be $5,000 to $15,000 per year. When deciding which home to purchase, you should include this estimate of maintenance expense in your total cost expectations.

Many people make the mistake of symbolically associating the size and grandeur of their homes with their self-worth. What this means is that they're not living in that home for themselves, but to impress or satisfy the expectations of others. If your home is costing you more than 20 percent of your pretax income and it is not an essential component of your most fulfilled life, then I highly recommend downsizing. This may seem like a dramatic step to take, but at the end of the day it will be a huge relief for you. You will finally have the cash flow to do what is important to you, rather than doing what you thought you were supposed to do.

We will continue to discuss all facets of housing in chapter 9.

ON YOUR OWN

#6

Look up the price of your dream home and estimate how much you would pay annually on your mortgage. Be sure to add in the costs of property taxes, homeowners insurance, maintenance, and home security. How much income would you need to spend only 20 percent on your dream home?

Car

I want to be straight with you. Buying a new car is one of the worst financial decisions you can make. Cars are rapidly depreciating assets. As soon as you drive one off the lot, the vehicle loses a substantial amount of value. Leasing is even worse: it is an infinite car loan. It ensures you will have car payments until your adult children take away your license—though I am hoping for driverless cars before that day comes for me!

Which would you prefer?

» **Option 1:** Pay $400 per month for seventy years (total: $336,000).

» **Option 2:** Pay $400 per month for five years, then pay off your vehicle and drive it for another five to ten years, spending about $1,000 per year in maintenance. Then, get a new vehicle, pay $400 per month for five years, pay off that vehicle, and drive it for another five to ten years, spending about $1,000 per year on maintenance, and so on and so forth for seventy years (total: $165,000).

Option 1 is leasing. Option 2 is buying. When you buy a car, there is a nice period between payments and the demise of your car when you have minimal car expenses. Thus, buying is much cheaper. Think of all the things you could do with an extra $171,000. Leasing is literally costing you your retirement.

Let's do another fun example. Which would you prefer:

» **Option 1**: Pay $579 per month for five years for a new 2020 Honda CRV (total: $34,740).

» **Option 2**: Pay $461 per month for five years for a used 2018 Honda CRV with 17,000 miles (total: $27,660).

Is there any difference between options 1 and 2 other than the fact that you save $7,000? You could take a nice family vacation to Disney World. You could eat seventy $100 meals at a restaurant. You could have a subscription to your favorite newspaper for thirty-five years. And if you were willing to buy a three-year-old car or one with a few more miles, then you could do even more!

I am not trying to scold you here; I am bringing you back to reality. We all think we are supposed to have everything: the nice car, the nice house, all the "things." But is your car a primary source of satisfaction? Do you enjoy every feature every time you enter the vehicle? If the answer is yes, great. Your car is worth it, and you may need to change your spending in other areas. But if that new car smell has figuratively faded, then you have a wonderful opportunity on your hands to cut large fixed expenses. Sell your car and downsize.

Whatever you decide, the rule of thumb is the same: add up all the vehicle's expenses (loan or lease payments, gas, maintenance, and possible repairs), and the number should stay under 5 percent of pretax income. No one likes being car-poor.

Clients often tell me that they want to spend a lot of money on a very fancy car. When it does not make financial sense, my answer is, what would give you the same feeling as owning the Ferrari or whatever car you want? Perhaps you can think of a way to have that feeling without sinking your financial freedom with massive car payments.

Insurance Premiums

We will discuss insurance at length in chapter 10. In the meantime, here are a few ways to reduce your insurance expenses:

1. **Increase your deductible**. Your deductible is the amount you must pay before the insurance company will contribute to your expenses. If you have a low deductible, it means the insurance company will pay sooner than if you have a high deductible. Because of this, the insurance company likes to cover itself by charging you more in premiums for a low deductible. I suggest increasing deductibles to create savings. You can use this savings to "self-insure" if something comes up. If nothing comes up, then you keep your savings. I generally recommend starting property deductibles for your home or car at $1,000.

2. **Don't buy insurance you don't need**. My husband and I are anti-warranty people. We do not buy warranties. We self-insure. This saves a lot of money. When we need to replace a laptop, couch, or other typically warrantied item, we use savings. You will also want to evaluate other insurance you may have. For example, your dental plan offered through work likely covers little and may not be worth the money. If no one is dependent on you, then you do not need life insurance. Insurance is there to cover catastrophic losses, not everyday expenses. Pick and choose what you insure, or else you are spending money that you could otherwise save.

Subscriptions and Recurring Costs

Anything you pay for on a recurring basis is a subscription, like your cell phone, cable and internet, or streaming services. Companies love this.

You are spending money without any friction. It is sticky revenue for them and a bonus if you are not even using the service that much.

Let's use an example. You have a $75,000 salary, and you have the following subscriptions (figure 6):

GRAPHIC

fig. 6

Cell phone	$89/month
Internet	$49/month
Spotify	$15/month
Netflix	$9/month
Hulu	$6/month
PBS Kids	$5/month
ESPN	$5/month
Dollar Shave Club	$3/month
Makeup subscription	$12/month
Gym	$42/month
Wall Street Journal	$43/month
Wine club	$35/month
TOTAL	**$313/mo or $3,756/yr** (nearly 7% of your after-tax income)

No wonder it's hard to save money! You spend money in your sleep! I highly recommend reviewing your monthly statements to see what subscriptions you have. Be honest with yourself. Do you use them? Do you get value out of them? Can you cut a few?

I once had a client who was subscribed to so many individual streaming services that it was cheaper for him to go back to cable. Everyone thinks unbundling is cheaper. Sometimes it is not. However, if you value television and enjoy it, you should include it in your plan in the most cost-effective way. If you spend little time watching television, then it is a great place to make cuts.

Food and Drink

Every financial planner likes to rip on this one. I think you only need to make changes here when your food spending is beyond what one person or family should spend *and* it is preventing you from saving.

How much you spend on food is going to vary wildly based on where you live and your daily habits. On average, grocery bills will cost approximately three hundred dollars per month per person in your household. If you live in a big city, this expense will be higher. If you shop at organic stores or have dietary restrictions, the costs will be higher still. Buying premade foods will also increase the cost. If you dine out frequently, your grocery bill will be lower but your overall food expenses will be higher. If you shop at wholesale stores, your bill may be lower.

In general, cooking at home is cheaper. However, most people enjoy a meal out. Here is my best advice for dining out while continuing to save: avoid ordering beverages, especially alcohol, and keep appetizers and desserts to a minimum. You and your spouse can dine out reasonably if you are willing to order two entrees and then share some wine at home after dinner.

Clothing and Personal Care

Unless you are a toddler going through a naked phase, you will probably need to wear some clothes! You may also appreciate the occasional or frequent haircut, and you may want to continue to purchase your preferred selection of makeup products. While some of these expenses are unavoidable, most of them are choices we make. Here are my tips for saving on personal care and clothing:

» Minimize shoe, handbag, and jewelry purchases or buy them secondhand.

» Abstain from clothing that needs dry cleaning.

» Buy more basic or classic clothing so it does not go out of fashion quickly.

» Space out haircuts more reasonably and opt for a less trendy stylist.

» Consider manicures, pedicures, facials, massages, makeup, and hair removal to be a pleasure rather than a necessity.

» Make sure you use your gym or any other health subscription you have.

» Eliminate expensive purchases for young kids; they grow out of their clothing so quickly.

The number one thing I have seen with my clients is that they like knowing how much they can spend. If they have a number in mind before they go to the store, they have the freedom to choose whatever they want, guilt free. I have one client who knows she can spend $1,000 on clothing three times a year. What does she do? She enjoys the heck out of buying and wearing the things she really wants!

Unhealthy Purchases or Purchases You Would Not Miss

We often spend out of habit. Those habits may or may not be serving us. A great way to cut expenses is to remove poor habits from your life. For example, if you smoke a pack a day, you are spending at least $2,000 per year on cigarettes. Or perhaps you drink often. If you and your spouse split a bottle of wine every night, you are spending over $4,000 per year on wine alone. Kicking these habits is good for both your physical and financial health.

Another way to consciously cut spending is to evaluate places where you simply would not miss those items. Even financial planners are not immune to spending money randomly! I used to buy and drink a kombucha every single day. I loved every minute of that drink. And I paid four dollars a day for it! That is $1,460 a year! And then I noticed myself sucking them down and not even enjoying them. After a few weeks, I clued in and cut the habit. I don't miss it. Now, when I occasionally have a kombucha, I really enjoy it.

You may have a coffee out every day, and you would be just as happy with a go-cup from home. Maybe you pay for *The Washington Post*, but you only read it once per month. Or maybe there are a bunch of Amazon purchases you made that you haven't used and should return. Whatever it is, it's always better to be conscious of your choices.

I don't like the "drink coffee at home to save money" mentality that pundits often tout. I don't think saving a thousand dollars a year on coffee is going to create huge amounts of wealth. Cutting down your big expenses, like your home or car, will. If your big expenses are incredibly important to you, then you must look at other aspects of your spending to see where you can make changes. You can have anything you want but not everything.

#7

On what do you most enjoy spending money? Make a list of those items or experiences. Keep it handy. Refer to your list when making purchases. Are other purchases holding you back from having more of what you really love? Are there expenses that brought you joy in the past but, under your honest scrutiny, do not give you satisfaction now?

Chapter Recap

» Even if you loathe the idea of being constrained by a budget, there are many creative ways to plan and monitor your spending.

» Before you begin budgeting, you need to take a cold hard look at the facts. Where is your money going?

» The 80/20 rule offers an astonishingly simple approach to spending and saving.

» A variety of unique approaches can be used to reduce both fixed expenses, such as housing and car payments, and variable expenses, such as food, clothing, and miscellaneous purchases.

| 4 |
The Basis of Wealth

By sowing frugality we reap liberty, a golden harvest.

– AGESILAUS

Savings is the basis of wealth. In the last two chapters, we discussed the inputs that create savings: your income and your spending. If you make more money and spend less money, you will have more savings.

Why bother saving? Why not spend it all? You have important elements in your life that you want to accomplish. Many of those elements require money. Your savings will foster your ability to have what you want. It will give you the flexibility to do things when you want to do them. Saving is the most effective way to insulate yourself from uncertainty. And saving liberates you when the future arrives, because you will find more choices available to you.

In this chapter I will show how to wisely manage that 20 percent of after-tax income which, in accordance with the 80/20 rule, you will devote to savings. I will also show you how to think about your savings as your income, life, and goals change.

Creating an Emergency Fund

The order in which you financially plan matters. For instance, it would be crazy to consider early retirement when you do not even have an emergency savings fund.

To have an emergency fund, you need to create savings, which is why we've spent a lot of time talking about income and spending. Once you've created savings, you can start on your journey to building wealth.

Creating an emergency fund is the next step in your planning process. Remember how we set aside 10 percent of your spending money to account for anything that may come up? Your emergency fund is a little like that, only it will take care of you when times are hard.

Recently, we experienced a crisis. COVID-19 hit our country and many people were out of work in what seemed like an instant. Your emergency fund protects you in times like these. Your emergency fund is there when income is not. Your emergency fund is the reason you can sleep well at night.

If you currently have no savings, you will want to build a small emergency fund that accounts for two months' worth of your essential expenses. These are your rent or mortgage (and associated homeowner expenses), groceries, utilities, health care, etc. Eventually, you will want your emergency fund to have six to nine months' worth of necessities. This is in case you lose your job, become disabled, or have any other catastrophic loss of income that would require you to dip into savings.

However, before you start stashing away additional emergency cash, you must take stock of your overall financial picture. Do you work for a company with a retirement plan? Does that retirement plan match a portion of your contributions? If so, after you build your small emergency fund, you will want to take advantage of your company's plan. This is so you can build wealth quickly. If you have acute emergencies covered, you can feel confident in saving for retirement. Many companies will match the first 4 percent of contributions. I highly recommend taking advantage of this, as it is equivalent to your contributing 8 percent. You'll want to read your plan rules to learn the particulars.

Next, you must look at the debt you have. Do you have high-interest debt, such as credit card debt? Do you have moderate-interest debt, such as student loans? If so, after your retirement contribution, you will want to start paying down high-interest debt first. Next, you'll want to pay off moderate-interest debts (not including your mortgage). We will discuss debt and repayment at length in chapter 8.

After debts are repaid, you can continue to add to your emergency savings fund, aiming to accumulate enough funds for six to nine months' worth of necessities.

MY TAKE

In terms of where to store emergency funds, I recommend to clients that they keep roughly one to two months' worth of expenses in their standard checking or savings account. The rest of their emergency funds should be put into a high-yield savings account. Doing so will allow the money to earn something while it waits for an emergency. Hopefully, they (and you) will never have one.

Here are the steps to build your emergency fund:

1. Spend less than you earn and generate savings.

2. Build a small emergency fund to account for two months' worth of essential expenses.

3. Begin taking advantage of your employer's retirement plan if it offers contribution matching.

4. Pay down high-interest debt.

5. Build on your small emergency fund until it accounts for six to nine months' worth of expenses.

Planning for Additional Savings

Once you have an emergency fund under control, you are well on your way to meeting your goals. Now, any money you save can go toward accomplishing everything you want to do or have in your life. Without seeing your particular list, it would be difficult for me to tell you exactly what to do. That said, there are some good basic guidelines for you to follow.

Retirement Savings

Retirement may not be on your list of exceedingly important goals; however, at some point you will retire. I promise when you get there, you will want to have money available. Typically, I recommend that at least 10 percent of your pretax income go toward retirement. If you're using the 80/20 rule we discussed in chapter 3, then you should be setting aside at least 50 percent of your savings for retirement. This ensures that you will be able to retire at a reasonable age. You may always want to work, but your body may feel otherwise. Therefore, it is important to plan for retirement.

The best way to save for retirement is in tax-advantaged accounts. We will discuss your retirement planning options in chapter 12.

Saving for Non-Retirement Goals

Often, due to spending habits, people tend to save all their money in retirement accounts and have few funds in other types of accounts to accomplish other goals. It is important to balance the tax advantages of retirement accounts with what your other goals are. For example, if you and your wife want to buy a house, it won't help much if you have $10,000 in a checking account and $100,000 in company 401(k) plans. You can take a 401(k) loan, but I don't recommend it. What I do recommend is evaluating what you want to do and saving accordingly, using both retirement and non-retirement accounts.

Commit to Automated Savings

My motto is "automation equals realization." The more you automate, the more likely you will be able to save successfully.

If you work for a company, you have many options available to save automatically. To start, you can take advantage of your retirement plan. You can also contact human resources (HR) to have portions of your paycheck directly deposited into different accounts. For example, if you make $3,000 per paycheck and want to contribute $600 to savings, you can put $200 into your retirement account every pay period and then have HR directly deposit $400 to savings and $2,400 to your checking account. If you then want to invest half your savings, you can automatically transfer $200 to an investment account after every pay period. You can then further set up automatic investment of that $200. See where I am going here? You are saving and doing nothing. Put your feet up and let the money do its thing!

It gets more complicated if you get paid irregularly from running your own business, working on commission, or if much of your income is earned through bonuses. If this is the case, then you need to be more deliberate about how you save. You may not be able to save every pay period. You may only be able to save in "good" months. The trick is knowing when you have a good month and saving as much as you can during that time. For example, let's say you run your own business and get paid quarterly. The amounts you are paid are contingent on sales. Based on your marketing plan and the seasonality of your business, you expect to net $25,000 in the first quarter, $25,000 in the second quarter, $8,000 in the third quarter, and $30,000 in the last quarter. You will make $88,000 overall and $73,000 after taxes. You will want to set aside $14,600 in savings. Based on the fact that you will make very little in the third quarter and you'll need reserves from the second quarter, you will want to make the majority of your savings happen in the first and fourth quarters. You could save $6,570 in quarter 1 and quarter 4 and save the remaining $1,460 in quarter 2. Likewise, if you are paid a bonus in February of every year, you can either save your entire bonus or calculate what 20 percent of your after-tax income would be and save it accordingly. Unfortunately, this is not something you can automate, unless you can expect more regular income.

Saving More than 20 Percent

Given what comprises your most fulfilled life, you may want to consider saving more than 20 percent of your after-tax income to get there more quickly. In my planning practice, we strive for clients to save 20 to 25 percent of their pretax rather than their after-tax income. For example, if you make $75,000, we advise at least $15,000 in savings, rather than the $11,000 that we discussed earlier.

Knowing whether to save more depends on what you want to do. For example, if you have credit card debt, you may want to save 30 percent or more because it will help you pay off the debt more quickly and move on. Maybe you want to buy a house in a year or two, but you do not have enough saved. Or maybe you want to start a business and you do not want to wait five years until you have the money. Saving more corresponds with your urgent goal.

You need to balance your future goals with your quality of life right now. That means there will be some sacrifices for future endeavors, and there will also be moments of distinct satisfaction that arise from spending decisions made in the present. This balance is financial freedom.

Think About the Future

People who spend time carefully thinking about who they are, where they have come from, and who they want to be are more satisfied in life. They are generally less anxious and depressed and are also physically healthier. I want you to deeply recognize where you want to go, so that all the decisions you make are a compilation of that understanding. The goal is to realize a meaningful, healthy, and productive life supported by good financial habits.

We do not know what the future holds for us. This uncertainty causes anxiety. Giving yourself purpose and direction will relieve it. Proving to yourself over and over that you can do it will reinforce good behaviors. Repetition will lead to success.

I know—asking what you want in life is a lot like asking what you want to be when you grow up. Even though we struggle to find clear and simple answers to the question, we do have a sense of where we're headed and where we want to be. It is normal to have second thoughts as we progress. We may even have full-blown changes of heart. It is also okay to choose not to decide everything today.

I've asked you to think a lot about your most fulfilled life. I imagine themes arose for you as you came up with answers. Those themes likely had some overlap. The Venn diagram in figure 7 demonstrates how the major thematic elements of our life interrelate with one another. Take a moment to consider your themes. Can you list some of the experiences you would like to have? Do you know what kinds of things you want? Do you know how comfortable you are with risk?

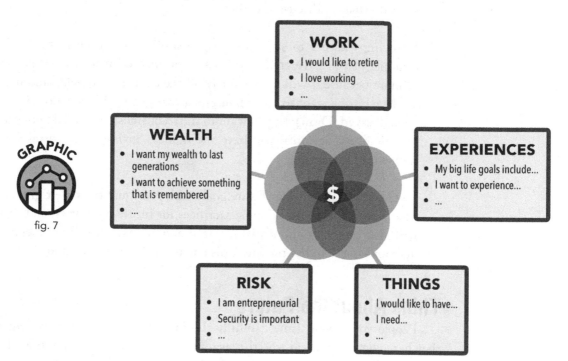

GRAPHIC

fig. 7

There are certainly other important categories not included in figure 7. Furthermore, many of the answers to the questions posed will surely lead to even more questions. Start by choosing one category that's important to you, review the prompts or the examples, and then have an honest discussion with yourself about the topic. See what else comes to mind, both in the way of answers *and* additional questions.

For example, if you want to have children, where would you want to raise them? In a town, in a city, in a rural community like the one in which you were raised, or perhaps somewhere quite different? What kind of school would you want your children to attend? Are you going to begin saving for college early? Or would you be content sending them to a good state school? Or perhaps in your family it's Ivy League or bust? How do you plan on spacing your children? Is it important to you that your children be close in age or do you mind if they are five or more years apart?

The answer to each question is brimming with major financial implications and, as you can see, tends to spur additional questions. I could go on forever with the having-children thread alone. The bottom line is that you need to think about what you want in your life, and you need to address the smaller questions that arise in the wake of your answers to the bigger ones. You may not have all the answers right now, but that does not mean you should avoid asking the questions. In fact, the sooner you start asking, the more time you'll have to plan and prepare. Start today!

Our Story: Making a Decision to Move

As I write this book, my husband and I are living in Brooklyn. But we will be moving to Austin, Texas (and will be there by the time you read this!). Making the decision to move was not easy; we had to ask, and answer, a lot of hard questions.

My husband and I have a young child at home, and we know we want to have at least one more child. So the first question we asked ourselves was, What kind of parents do we want to be? That question was not too hard. We knew we wanted to be the kind of parents that raise healthy, active, independent children, who learn to make their own decisions and who are confident being who they want to be.

How the heck do we do that, though? Well, we talked about it, and we agreed that physical space matters to us; we believe independent children should have room to do things on their own, and active kids should have large spaces in which to play. We also agreed that mentally healthy children don't have "helicopter parents." Kids need to be able to engage in activities on their own. So it became quite clear to us that we could not stay in New York City. We would not feel comfortable allowing our kids to roam around the city alone, and we do not have enough money to buy a giant home with a yard in the city. New York is expensive! And it is quite a dirty place to play if you don't have your own yard. We asked the questions, answered the questions, and figured out that we needed to move.

From there, a new question arose: Where else can we live? We knew we wanted convenience (you can take the girl out of New York ...). We also knew we wanted to live somewhere with a reasonable cost of living, so we would not be "house poor" and could hit our savings goals. Finally, we wanted to be near family.

In addition to New York, we have family in Austin and Seattle. Luckily for us, neither place has state taxes! Seattle is out of our price range. The suburbs of Austin are cheaper, and we have family there. We asked ourselves: are we good with the suburbs? Yes, so long as we can get to where we want to go in ten minutes or less (for the most part).

We also knew that we wanted an active community, with parks and sports for the kids—a vibrancy we were used to in Brooklyn. Check. Okay, so the next question was how much house could we afford (keeping in mind all associated home expenses including taxes, insurance, and maintenance)?

Save 1 to 3 percent of your home's value every year for maintenance expenses.

Do we need a house with every bell and whistle? Or if we need every bell and whistle, then can we commit to a house with a little less space? With a bit more research, the answer was clear: we would choose some bells and whistles and adequate space, and that would suffice to leave us on firm financial footing.

And on and on the questions went, until we worked through them all. We picked our house, committed to it, and began planning the logistics of the move itself.

It was a big financial decision for us, but by asking ourselves all these questions and taking each question to the next logical step, we were able to find the answers we needed, act, and feel really good about it. Hello, Austin!

Financial planning is all about looking carefully at your wants and needs, finding your values, and putting a price tag on them. Imagine you are debating the importance of life insurance and you have this thought: I want to protect my family if I die. It's a pretty simple thought, right? But notice the first part of the statement is even simpler: "I want to protect." You want to protect something. Every financial decision can be traced back to a value, something that is important to you, something worth protecting, improving, or acquiring. You should spend your money on what you value.

#8

What do you want? Look back to our Venn diagram in figure 7 and consider what you value. Try to be as broad as possible at first. You want to identify your core values now and build from there as you work your way through this book.

I trust you have given your questions some time, and I really hope they prompted additional questions for you to consider. You can achieve whatever you want, but only if you have the courage and focus to decide on what it is. While your tangible goals ("I want a sports car") are important to recognize, the more you can articulate a forward-looking vision for practical matters as well, the smoother your planning (and your life!) will go.

Chapter Recap

» Saving is essential for building wealth.

» Automating your saving habits and directing your savings efforts toward goals will help you succeed.

» Your current quality of life should be balanced alongside your dedication to achieving future goals.

| 5 |
Net Worth: A Helpful Measure

Chapter Overview
- » Assets and Liabilities
- » Household Operating Cash Flow
- » Grow Your Net Worth

America is built around this premise that you can do it, and there are an awful lot of people who are unlikely to have done it who did.

– MICHAEL BLOOMBERG

A healthy person tends to have good blood pressure and a normal blood sugar level. Perhaps this person also exercises three to five days per week and eats a balanced diet. Your financial health can similarly be measured through metrics. You can track your savings and you can work toward establishing healthy spending habits. These steps will move you toward being financially fit.

Net worth is the most widely used measure of financial health. It considers all aspects of your financial behavior and boils it down into one number. This chapter will help you understand your net worth, how to calculate it and what to do to increase it.

The first step is to face and assess your financial situation today. This will help you see if you are on track or if you need to make changes. Get ready to look at some hard numbers and ask yourself some tough questions!

Find Your Net Worth
Your net worth is the measure of how many dollars you have when you add up your assets and subtract your *liabilities* (assets – liabilities = net worth). This formula can feel a bit reductionistic: my worth is how many dollars I have? No, you're worthy no matter what! However, computing and tracking your net worth will tell you the most about your *financial* health over time.

So, what are financial assets and liabilities? Assets are bank accounts, investments, real estate, personal property, any businesses you own, and all your retirement accounts such as pension plans, individual retirement accounts (IRAs), 401(k)s, and so on.

Liabilities are debts. Any loans, like your car loan, mortgage, student loans, and credit card debts, are liabilities.

There are also *contingent assets* and *contingent liabilities*. These assets or liabilities are part of your net worth only if certain circumstances occur. An example of a contingent asset is part of your 401(k) balance. Your employer's contributions to your plan are contingent on you remaining an employee until these contributions become vested. An example of a contingent liability is paying taxes quarterly in your business. You make estimated quarterly payments throughout the year, but your final tax owed or refunded is contingent on how much total income you make.

In your Digital Assets, there is a downloadable, fillable Net Worth Calculator that can be used to calculate and visualize your net worth (figure 8). Find it at go.quickstartguides.com/personalfinance.

fig. 8

STATEMENT OF NET WORTH
WILLIAM AND ELIZABETH DARCY – JANUARY 1, 2020

ASSETS

NON-QUALIFIED ASSETS:	William	Elizabeth	Joint	Total
Cash & Equivalents				
William's Checking	$3,334	--	--	$3,334
William's Savings	$17,435	--	--	$17,435
Joint Checking Account	--	--	$8,675	$8,675
Elizabeth's Checking	--	$1,708	--	$1,708
Elizabeth's Savings	--	$2,430	--	$2,430
William's Business Account	$18,483	--	--	$18,483
Taxable Investments				
William's Trading Account	$3,477	--	--	$3,477
Joint Investment Account	--	--	$175,678	$175,678
Bitcoin			$8,153	$8,153
TOTAL NON-QUALIFIED ASSETS	**$42,729**	**$4,138**	**$192,506**	**$239,373**

ASSETS (continued)				
RETIREMENT ASSETS:	William	Elizabeth	Joint	Total
Qualified Retirement				
William's 403b	$252,988	--	--	$252,988
William's 457 Plan	$76,981	--	--	$76,981
William's Solo 401(k)	$38,752	--	--	$38,752
Elizabeth's 401(k)	--	$80,153	--	$80,153
TOTAL RETIREMENT ASSETS	**$368,721**	**$80,153**	**$0**	**$488,874**
TOTAL LIQUID ASSETS	**$411,450**	**$84,291**	**$192,506**	**$728,247**
PERSONAL ASSETS:				
House			$585,000	$585,000
Honda		$18,500		$18,500
Audi	$38,000			$38,000
Elizabeth's Engagement Ring	--	--	$15,000	$15,000
TOTAL PERSONAL ASSETS	**$38,000**	**$18,500**	**$600,000**	**$656,500**
TOTAL ASSETS	**$449,450**	**$102,791**	**$792,506**	**$1,384,747**

LIABILITIES				
SHORT-TERM LIABILITIES:	William	Elizabeth	Joint	Total
William's AMEX	($3,867)	--	--	($3,867)
Elizabeth's Visa	--	($2,765)	--	($2,765)
TOTAL SHORT-TERM LIABILITIES	**($3,867)**	**($2,765)**	**$0**	**($6,632)**
LONG-TERM LIABILITIES:				
William's Student Loans	($124,784)	--	--	($124,784)
Elizabeth's Student Loans	--	($38,765)	--	($38,765)
Honda Loan	--	($16,453)	--	($16,453)
Audi Loan	($36,759)	--	--	($36,759)
Home Mortgage	--	--	($465,000)	($465,000)
TOTAL LONG-TERM LIABILITIES	**($161,543)**	**($55,218)**	**($465,000)**	**($681,761)**
TOTAL LIABILITIES	**($165,410)**	**($57,983)**	**($465,000)**	**($688,393)**
NET WORTH	**$284,040**	**$44,808**	**$327,506**	**$696,354**

ON YOUR OWN

#9

Calculate your net worth. Using our Net Worth Calculator, found in your Digital Assets (go.quickstartguides.com/personalfinance), add up all your assets and liabilities. I understand it may take a little time to track down all the details, and even longer to remember every asset and every liability you have. But it doesn't have to be perfect your first time through. Just by getting started you will begin to think about your net worth, and in time more items will pop into your head. For example, if you rent an apartment, maybe you provided a rental deposit? It may help to scroll through some of the reports that your personal finance application or software can produce, as it may help you remember money you put aside (assets) or money you need to pay (liabilities).

When you are finished, put a reminder in your calendar app to update your net worth once a year, perhaps around the time you do your taxes. That way you can get everything updated when you are thinking about your big-picture financial situation.

What Should Your Net Worth Look Like?

If you finished the last on your own assignment, then you know what your net worth looks like. Hopefully, it is positive! If you're young, it might be negative. Remember that your net worth is just a number, like your salary. Just as your income is not a representation of who you are or what you are worth, neither is your net worth.

GRAPHIC

fig. 9

NET WORTH IN AMERICA	
HOUSEHOLD AGE RANGE	MEDIAN NET WORTH
Under 35 years	$11,000
35 – 44 years	$60,000
45 – 54 years	$124,000
55 – 64 years	$187,000
Retirement years	$224,000

Source: Yochim 2020

Median net worth figures are for American households (not individuals). They do not include home equity—the amount their home is worth after subtracting their mortgage.

For your financial security and peace of mind, you want to be above the national medians shown in figure 9. Consider the difference between the median and the average net worth across the nation: for families between the ages of 45 and 54, the median net worth was $124,000 and the mean was $727,500 (note that, in statistical terms, the median is the middle number, while the mean is the average). Wealthy families bring up the average; perhaps you will help them continue to do so!

Target Net Worth by Decade

In your twenties, you may have a negative net worth. It is quite common to graduate college with debt and no savings. Your goal in your twenties is to pay down debt and start accumulating savings.

In your thirties, your net worth should be at least equal to your current annual salary. You should have made some progress in eradicating the debt you accumulated in your twenties, and likewise made some progress in saving and investing money. Your goal in your thirties is to accumulate more savings in your bank, investment, and retirement accounts, as well as acquiring home equity (if you want to own a home).

In your forties, your net worth should be at least three times your annual income. Your only debt should be your mortgage. Your savings and investments will have had a good amount of time to grow from both your regular contributions and the power of compounding investment returns.

In your fifties, your net worth should have at least doubled, to seven and a half times your annual income. And by sixty, that figure should be closer to fourteen times your income, with a goal that as you approach the earliest date you can retire and receive Social Security (at age sixty-five), your net worth will be around twenty to twenty-five times your annual income (figure 10).

Targets for net worth are, of course, ballpark figures. A lot can change between age fifty-one and fifty-nine, for example. You might inherit money, which will change your net worth. Or you may have many kids, keeping expenses higher for longer. College and weddings seem to double in expense every decade, but we'll talk more about planning for these kinds of larger expenses in part II.

SAVINGS FACTORS TO HELP ON YOUR JOURNEY TO RETIREMENT

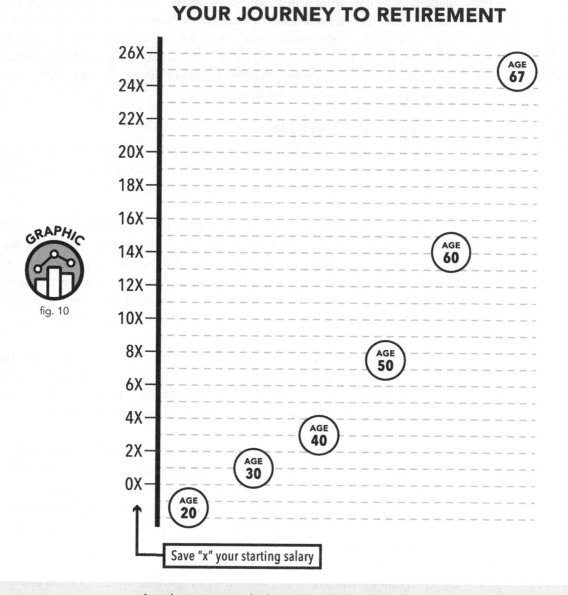

GRAPHIC

fig. 10

Save "x" your starting salary

AGE 67, AGE 60, AGE 50, AGE 40, AGE 30, AGE 20

MY TAKE

Another way to calculate income needs at retirement is to look at spending rather than income. For example, multiply your spending number. You need 25x your annual spending to retire before age sixty-five, you need 22.5x to retire between sixty-five and seventy, and you need 20x to retire at seventy. So, if you spend $60,000 per year and want to retire at sixty-five, you should have roughly $60,000 x 25, or $1.5 million in savings.

Household Operating Cash Flow

If you are spending less than you earn, your net worth grows. You gain security and freedom along the way. You maintain it by keeping enough cash on hand, known as liquidity. Living paycheck to paycheck is stressful! Having cash to pay for the unexpected ensures financial peace.

Imagine you are a business with operating cash flow (OCF) needs. OCF is the revenue a company generates through normal business activities. The amount of cash flow determines if the company can pay all its expenses and, more importantly, grow its business over time. Similarly, you want your household cash flow to cover your expenses with money left over for strategic investments.

Household Cash on Hand

The amount of money you need to feel comfortable and secure depends a lot on who you are, how you earn money, and how disciplined and organized you are. A full-time employee drawing the same salary every month will require less of a cash buffer than a freelancer going from gig to gig.

Some people like to focus on a dollar amount to determine how much cash they need on hand. If, for example, you have $5,000 in expenses per month and you have $15,000 in net income every three months, you will want to have at least $15,000 in *liquid assets* available to navigate any potential downturns, because the $15,000 represents one revenue cycle.

Thinking in terms of months is a great way to decide how much cash you need to have on hand. As with many aspects of personal finance, this is a *personal* question. At any given moment, would you prefer to have the next month's expenses covered by your bank balance, or three months' worth, or six months? Keep this in mind until chapters 6 and 7, when we review how much to put toward investing.

Responsible Household Borrowing

Receiving a no-interest loan from a family member would be ideal, but more often the lender is a bank or credit union. You can also borrow money from your brokerage using assets like stocks or bonds as collateral. In addition, the equity in your home can be a source of borrowing liquidity.

When is the right time to tap into available credit? Perhaps you are pursuing an advanced degree, or starting a worthwhile business, or making some other strategic investment that requires capital, such as purchasing a rental property.

Problems arise when borrowing is used for the wrong reason. If you're borrowing to cover consumption, for example, that is not good. Similarly, if you are borrowing money for a lavish vacation or an associate degree in dog walking, a $50,000 loan might be a little irresponsible. On the other hand, if you're borrowing so that you can start a business, that may be a worthy endeavor, so long as you are creating a thoughtful plan that demonstrates a high probability of success (more on this in chapter 14).

The bottom line is that it makes sense to approach borrowing liquidity as if you are the CEO of your life. A CEO considers how a loan will benefit the company over the long term. They understand the true benefit of the loan, explore their options among a variety of lenders, carefully consider the terms of the repayment plan, and calculate the true cost of the loan by factoring in the interest rate.

Growing Your Net Worth

> *Prosperity is only an instrument to be used, not a deity to be worshiped.*
> — CALVIN COOLIDGE

So, how are you doing? You have now measured your net worth. You have compared it to target net worth ranges for people in your age bracket. Now, unless you're ready to retire early, you are likely wondering how you can *grow* your net worth.

1. **Track:** In my practice, I measure our clients' net worth annually. Some years it will grow due to increased savings and growth from investments. Other years it will decline, due to money spent on a goal, market decreases, or simply a lower income year. The objective is to have your net worth trend up over time, even if there are bumps along the way.

2. **Budget:** I know, no one likes this step except crazy finance geeks like me. If you can change how you think about budgeting by making it fun, exciting, and rewarding, then you will be successful. At the very least, budget by creating a savings plan, as discussed in chapter 2. The key to growing net worth is living within your means, paying off debt, and saving money. You will accomplish all three through budgeting.

3. **Kill debt:** The sooner you can reduce or eliminate high-interest debt, the quicker your net worth will grow. Paying down **debt** not only saves you interest but also frees up additional funds for savings once the debt is paid.

4. **Save:** Your savings should be at least 10 percent of pretax income; ideally you are saving at least 20 percent. Higher savings levels increase assets, which increase net worth. Remember that another way to save is to increase your income without increasing your lifestyle.

5. **Invest:** Invest your savings according to your risk tolerance and time horizon. Investing helps your assets grow. We will discuss this at length in chapters 6 and 7.

6. **Embrace grace:** Life will give you hiccups. There will be pain and suffering. It won't always go your way. Things will come up. Accept this right now, so you will be psychologically (and financially) prepared when the wrench is thrown. You won't be surprised by it. You didn't keep your head in the sand, thinking it would never happen to you. You knew it would happen to you. And you will allow yourself the grace to understand that you are not a victim, only a human.

Given the six-step process above, what do you need to do to raise your net worth? Where could you make some changes?

#10

Many personal finance enthusiasts pursue very specific net worth goals. They want their net worth to be $300,000 by the time they turn thirty-five, or they want their newly established business to make them millionaires within five years' time. On a related note, the popular FIRE movement (Financial Independence, Retire Early) has captivated the imagination and financial ambitions of those willing to make bold sacrifices in the present in order to retire in their fifties, forties, or even thirties. While such goals can supply motivation, you also have to figure out the logistics. How are you going to grow and thrive financially? What specific steps will you take?

I'll have more to say on the FIRE movement in chapter 12 (see *A Most Fulfilled Retirement*). There are actually a lot of other factors in play, beyond finances, and it's very important that these factors be considered before you embark down the FIRE path. I don't want you to get burned (pun intended).

Chapter Recap

» Computing your net worth is a simple matter of subtracting liabilities from assets.

» Though many people begin with zero or negative net worth early in their careers, a person's net worth can grow exponentially over time.

» A household, like a business, has revenues, expenses, and an operational cash flow.

| 6 |
Prepare to Invest

A good plan must enable the highest chance of mission success while mitigating as much risk as possible.

— LEIF BABIN

There is an overwhelming amount of information available about investing—everything from how to conservatively invest to how to triple your tax refund in three days. Everyone has an opinion about what you should do with your money, yet when it comes down to it, the choice is yours. When someone recommends an investment to you, they do not know your total financial picture, your risk tolerance, or your intentions. Because of this, they cannot possibly know what is best for you. My recommendation is to take every piece of investment advice with a grain of salt.

These next two chapters will educate you about investing and how to think about it in terms of your most fulfilled life. Your objective is to combine these ideas to create your own investment plan.

Before we get to the investments themselves, we must lay some groundwork. There are factors that influence how you will approach investing, such as how compounding works, how inflation works against you, the difference between risk and uncertainty, and your individual appetite for risk.

The Power of Compounding

Compounding is like building a snowman. You start by creating a small ball of snow in your hand. Then you add snow to it. Then you roll the ball around the lawn while it grows and grows, and finally it stands as the giant base of your snowman. It works the same way with the money you save. You may only be able to save a small amount, paycheck by paycheck, but if you invest what you save, and regularly reinvest your interest and dividends, then over time you will observe dynamic growth in your investments. Your initial investment returns begin to earn returns of their own, and so on down the line—like a snowball growing in size.

Time is your biggest advantage here. If your investments compound at a steady rate over a long enough period, then your snowball will eventually become an avalanche. Let's look at an example (figure 11):

Milton is twenty-two, Adam is thirty-two, and Joseph is forty-two. They each commit to saving and investing $1,000 per month over fifteen years, and each earns an average of 6 percent per year in investment returns. They contribute the same total amount of money, but Milton will spend the longest time invested and Joseph, the shortest. How much money will they each have after they turn sixty-five and are looking to retire?

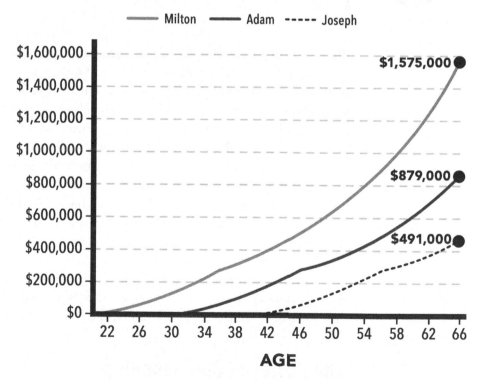

fig. 11

*Final totals assume investments are held throughout the 65th year of life, to the 66th birthday, technically.

Milton's modest ten-year head start resulted in a nearly $700,000 advantage over Adam and a $1.1 million advantage over Joseph. Milton's contributions during his twenties compounded throughout his career, resulting in the exponential pull-away from his peers who invested later.

The power of compounding was recognized by Einstein as being "the most powerful force in the universe." Your money can perpetually make money for you, if invested.

The Rule of 72

The formula for compounding returns is not something you can easily calculate in your head, or even on scratch paper. A simpler formula to keep in mind is called the Rule of 72 and is just this: the number of years it will take for your money to double is 72 divided by the rate of return. Say your interest rate on a bond is 10 percent; 72 divided by 10 is 7.2. Your money will double in a little over seven years. If your interest rate is 8 percent, your money will double in nine years (72 ÷ 8 = 9).

I use the Rule of 72 quite a bit in my practice because it is simple, yet so powerful when evaluating trade-offs. For example, if I invest $10,000 today, assuming I make 7.2 percent, I know my money will double every ten years, thanks to the Rule of 72. In ten years I'll have $20,000, in twenty years $40,000, in thirty years $80,000, and so on. So, let's say my hubby and I want to landscape our backyard and we get a quote for $50,000. I know that $50,000 today represents $400,000 thirty years from now, which could affect my retirement. So maybe landscaping is not something we want to spend money on right now! Maybe we'll just buy some mulch instead.

Furthermore, you do not need a large lump sum to begin investing. It's okay, even good, to invest smaller amounts on a monthly or quarterly basis. This is known as ***dollar cost averaging***. The combination of compound interest and monthly or quarterly investing is powerful and can build considerable wealth over time.

MY TAKE

The best time to invest is when you have the money to invest, and the best time to sell is when you need the money. Invest as money comes in, rather than waiting to accumulate a large lump sum before investing. This does two things. One, since you've started investing earlier, you'll experience compounding earlier. Two, you won't be waiting around with your cash depreciating due to inflation while you decide on the right entry point.

Inflation Hurts

There's an old joke about inflation. After years of scrimping and saving, a husband told his wife the good news:

"Honey, we've finally got enough money to buy what we started saving for in 1979."

"You mean a brand-new BMW?" she asked eagerly.

"No," said the husband, "a 1979 BMW."

If only this couple had invested their savings! The term *inflation* refers to a decline in purchasing power that results from the prices of goods and services increasing, or "inflating." It is widely known and accepted that your dollar will be worth less in the future due to inflation. From groceries to gasoline to wages paid to employees, every expense is subject to inflation. However, not every good or service inflates at an equal rate. While the average inflation rate in the United States over the last decade has been 1.8 percent, college tuition has increased 3 to 5 percent per year, and prescription drugs have inflated by as much as 10 percent per year!

If you have all your money in a checking account, inflation will devalue your dollars. Thus, there is real risk associated with not investing. Your money will lose its ability to purchase goods and services in the future (figure 12).

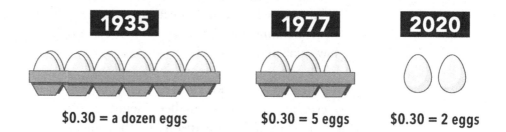

1935	1977	2020
$0.30 = a dozen eggs	$0.30 = 5 eggs	$0.30 = 2 eggs

fig. 12

Source: Bureau of Labor Statistics, CPI US City Average Price Data.

It's important to note that inflation is a real risk. Though America did not experience the 2007–2009 hyperinflation that occurred in Zimbabwe, our money still loses value every day. The only way to keep up with inflation is to invest and grow your money.

MY TAKE

Inflation necessitates investment; even if you feel more secure keeping several years' worth of cash on hand, the dollar is not a store of value. You must invest to keep up with inflation.

Your Time Horizon

Are you tired of me asking what your goals are? I hope it is helping to reignite your energy along the way. I invite you to recall your list of what would bring you your most fulfilled life. As we move into discussions about risk and uncertainty, it will be important for you to note *when* you want to fund a goal of yours.

The question of *when* is not always easy to answer. Sometimes goals have deadlines. For instance, your child may go to college one day. That tuition bill arrives no matter how much or how little you have accumulated. Other goals are more fluid. You may love your work and only want to retire when you feel ready. Retiring will be a moving goalpost, depending on how you feel. The more precise you can be, the easier it will be to plan. However, our lives are not on an ironclad timeline. Plans change, schedules change, people change. If you need flexibility regarding timing, then you'll want to be flexible with your investment approach, as well.

Imagine a couple, Ginny and Matthew. They have two teenage daughters. In exploring their most fulfilled life, Matthew wants to spend more time outdoors hiking, biking, and sailing. Ginny likes shopping with her daughters and swimming on a masters team. Together, they want to take family vacations until their girls are out of the house. They will pay for college, up to public university tuition. Once they are empty nesters, Ginny wants to downsize their home and move where she and Matthew can enjoy warmer weather and easier access to outdoor activity. They will move their business with them and retire when it feels right. Ginny and Matthew also want to take care of their parents if they need help with medical bills in the future.

Some of Matthew and Ginny's goals have specific timing, like planning annual family vacations for the next five years, paying for college, and downsizing their home. Other goals, like winding down their business and caring for their parents, have more fluid timelines, though we can assume these are longer-term.

You will want to make timing assumptions about your goals. If you cannot pinpoint a specific date, ask yourself how likely it is to occur in the short, medium, or long term. Then you'll be able to plan around it.

#11

Revisit your most fulfilled life assignment from chapter 1. Evaluate the time horizons of your top three to five goals. Note whether they are short (one to five years), medium (five to fifteen years), or long term (fifteen or more years).

In chapter 7 we talk a lot about investing, building a portfolio, and allocating assets. Outlining clear goals is an important part of the process.

Once you establish goals, you'll need a system to get you there. A savings plan is likely a part of this system. Automatic transfers to an earmarked account may prove to be a valuable system component. And while some of the money saved may end up in a standard savings account, most of it may be allocated toward various investment options. When investing, separating short-term and long-term goals is a good practice, because some investment types are better suited for longer time horizons. Stocks are generally used to fund long-term goals like retirement planning and funding of a college education in ten or fifteen years. This is because the path of returns from stocks is not a straight line. We will discuss this in more depth in chapter 7.

Risk and Uncertainty

> *There is a fundamental distinction between the reward for taking a known risk and that for assuming a risk whose value itself is not known.*
> – FRANK KNIGHT

Risk and uncertainty comprise investing. Investing is the potential to make money. This potential causes unpredictability, which most denote as risk. However, the terms *risk* and *uncertainty* are often mistakenly used interchangeably.

When you take risks, you know what the possible outcomes are. Sometimes you can even measure the probability of those outcomes. For example, when you flip a coin, there is a 50 percent chance it will land on heads and a 50 percent chance it will land on tails. You do not know which will occur, only that you have a one out of two chance of guessing correctly. Risk is something you can measure. You can prepare for it.

Let's contrast this with uncertainty. With uncertainty, you do not know the possible outcomes in advance. Therefore, you cannot assign probabilities to their occurrence. Uncertainty is the reality in which we live. The world is always changing. Transition brings new opportunities for business, careers, relationships, and more. With the opportunities come an imperfect knowledge of future outcomes. We typically devote much effort to reducing uncertainty because it is anxiety-provoking. We want to feel prepared. However, since we cannot have all the information in advance, much of this preparation is futile.

Investing involves both risk and uncertainty. Investment risk is based on whether the price increases or decreases. We can apply some probabilities to the outcomes, depending on what we know. Uncertainty, however, will be the main driver of our investments. An investor's willingness to withstand uncertainty is what prompts returns.

It is important to note that uncertainty is not always bad. A company can deliver profits due to something unknown in the marketplace. For example, when Apple released the first iPod, there was no way for them to know it would evolve into the iPhone you have today. Yet this has created billions in returns for Apple and improved quality of life for many.

In our lives, we evaluate risk and manage uncertainty. We accomplish this every day! We pack up and change locations for a new job, assuming it will work out. We borrow money to get a degree, trusting it will pay off. We buy a house, presuming we picked one in suitable condition. We know there is a risk that our home's value will fluctuate or even decrease. However, we derive a benefit from owning our home, and it may appreciate over time, compensating us for the inherent risk.

Before the global financial crisis of 2007–2008, the average house price in America had not declined since the Great Depression (1930s). Because of this, it was often assumed that one could not lose money on their home, or on any real estate purchase.

When most think of risk, they often perceive it as an investment's *volatility*, which refers to how much an asset moves around in price. An asset subject to declines in value can be scary. No one likes to log in to their investment account and see their money evaporating before their eyes.

Uncertainty is why there is risk. We don't know what the future holds. No one does. You don't know if your investments will recover after they've declined. It provokes fear and the thought, *sell everything!* And while your feelings are perfectly valid, true risk is not synonymous with volatility.

True risk is permanent loss of capital. It is commonly noted by savvy investors that if your stock went down and you didn't sell it, then you didn't take a loss. An asset's price moves up and down over time; it never increases in a straight line. Temporary declines do not mean loss of capital. Experiencing a decline and then selling the asset is what constitutes permanent loss of capital. This is an important distinction to remember as you set off on your journey to grow and build wealth.

There is a relationship between risk and reward. As we can see in figure 13, the greater the risk, the greater the expected reward.

The market compensates you for the use of your capital and for the risk you assume. You have probably heard people say "no risk, no reward." If you never take a risk, you may never see a worthwhile payoff. Conversely, if you're constantly taking *uncalculated* risks, you may also never see a worthwhile payoff.

RISK/RETURN TRADE-OFF

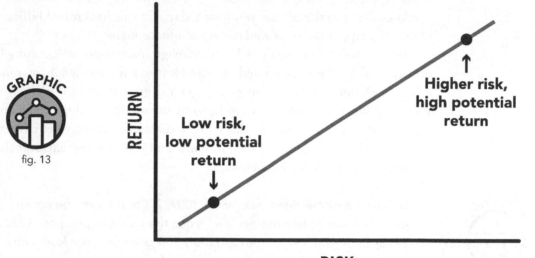

fig. 13

The most important thing is to take calculated risks rather than swinging for the fences. Understand the risks associated with any financial decision, from buying a car to investing in the stock market. A clear understanding of both risk and uncertainty will empower you.

Trees often take twenty to thirty years to grow to full size. Investments are like trees; just as you won't have a giant redwood in your yard in a year, your assets take a long time to grow. You wouldn't chop down a tree simply because it didn't grow quickly enough. Once you understand how long it takes to achieve returns, it will be easier to stick to the game plan during periods when investments perform poorly.

Know Your Risk Tolerance

What gets us into trouble is not what we don't know. It's what we know for sure that just ain't so.

-MARK TWAIN

A family friend of ours once dated a horse trainer, let's call him Paul. Paul called my dad and told him that his racehorse, Sundance, was a sure thing. At the time, my father worked across the street from an off-track betting place. He walked in and put two dollars on Sundance. Sundance lost. At the next family barbeque, my dad told the horse trainer, "We bet everything on Sundance, we'll probably lose our house!" Paul's face whitened!

How does losing money make you feel? Perhaps you also bet two dollars on Sundance, or bought a lottery ticket, or played blackjack at a casino. Chances are you lost money. Did that bother you, or did you take your loss in stride and move on?

Risk tolerance is a funny thing. We tend to feel overconfident when things go our way. We're popping champagne and feeling like the party can go on forever. We also tend to feel the pain of losses more than the pleasure of wins. People in general tend to have a higher risk tolerance as asset prices rise and a lower risk tolerance when they decline.

MY TAKE

Risk is the permanent loss of capital. Although that is risk most simply defined, your risk tolerance may also be skewed by the *amount* your capital changes in value. When investing, I want you to keep the former, simpler definition in mind. This will help put you at ease during volatile times. You'll be able to ask yourself, is my capital at permanent risk of loss? If the answer is no, then you can be calm in your heart amid all the financial chaos.

What is your financial risk tolerance? What would it feel like to have $10,000 invested in an asset of your choice that was worth $7,500 one day, $11,000 another day, $13,000 the next day, and then $7,500 again? Are you panicking? Are you uncomfortable? Do you avoid looking, holding fast to your hope and belief that it will work out over the long term? Are you totally fine, indifferent even? Conjure up the feelings you would have during intense market sell-offs and rises. Really imagine what it would be like. Then, take a risk tolerance questionnaire. The questionnaire will give you some insight into your potential behavior.

DIGITAL ASSETS

I recommend the free risk tolerance questionnaire offered by Vanguard. For your convenience, a direct link to the resource is provided in your Digital Assets at go.quickstartguides.com/personalfinance.

Willingness Versus Ability

Risk tolerance has two components: your willingness to take risk and your ability to take risk.

Your willingness is how inclined you are to invest in a risky asset and how well you tolerate portfolio losses. Willingness is comprised of your mental fortitude and readiness to invest and is generally a combination of both knowledge of the investment and emotional capacity to tolerate market movements. For example, someone with an exceedingly high willingness to take risk is prepared to lose 100 percent of their investment. Someone with a lower willingness to take risk may be prepared to lose only 15 percent of their investment. Willingness can be applied to more than someone's finances. A great example is willingness to try new things. Yuri Gagarin was the first man in space, in 1961. If that isn't willingness to take risk, I'm not sure what is!

Your *ability* to take risk is a combination of your level of wealth, how regularly you receive income, your stage in life, and the time horizon over which you plan to use your money. If you have more income and assets, you have more ability to take risk. If you don't plan to use your money for a long time, you have more ability to take risk. For example, a sixty-year-old person with minimal savings who wants to retire in the next five years has a lower ability to take risk than a thirty-five-year-old who recently inherited a significant sum of money and plans to work for the next thirty years.

Your ability to take risk is measured by the extent to which a loss from investing would affect your life. The often cruel irony at play here is this: as ability to take risk increases, you have less need to take risk and vice versa. Consider a billionaire who has everything she could want or need in terms of assets. She has a high ability to take risk, but she really does not need to; if she simply left her money alone to deflate, she'd be fine. Conversely, consider a young person in her twenties who has credit card debt. She has no ability to take risk but would certainly love to see her debt wiped away by a successful venture in the stock market.

For better or worse, it is a person's willingness, not their ability, that dominates investment decision making. In some ways this is a good thing. A person with a low willingness to invest in a risky asset should generally not invest in that asset. It would result in poor sleep, constant worry, and selling at a loss the second the asset declined in value. On the other hand, a person with high ability and low willingness can stifle her growth prospects by being too financially conservative.

It helps to evaluate exactly where you are in terms of both willingness and ability. If you have a high risk tolerance when it comes to ability but a low one in terms of willingness, then it is important to understand how you ended up that way. Perhaps it stems from something someone told you when you were young. Perhaps it is a thought you can change, so that your willingness matches your ability. Or maybe you need additional education to feel more comfortable with investing. Conversely, if you have a high risk willingness but don't have the proportionate risk ability, then you need to reflect on why that is. Did your excessive willingness play a role in your lessened ability? In other words, did you end up taking reckless risks that diminished your overall financial health?

Nobody can tell you what your tolerance for risk should be. It is up to you to take the time to consider how you might react in different scenarios. What emotions would you experience? What knee-jerk reactions can you see yourself having? It is also up to you to assess whether your ability to take risks aligns with the investment decisions you are making.

If you are unsure or would appreciate some informed feedback, then working with a financial professional can help. If you decide to hire a financial advisor, they will talk with you about your tolerance for risk and what is suitable given your point of view. If the advisor does not address the issue of risk at all, then you might want to reconsider hiring that person!

MY TAKE

If you have a low risk tolerance but most of your financial goals are seven years or more in the future, you will need to save significantly more to get to the same place. For example, say you need $100,000 for a goal in fifteen years. If you are willing to invest in moderate- to higher-risk assets and potentially obtain an average 7 percent return, then you will need to save $316 per month. If you are only willing to invest in less risky assets and potentially obtain only 4 percent per year, then you will need to save $406 per month. That is an additional $1,080 per year, $16,200 over fifteen years. Ask yourself if the discomfort you would feel from investing more aggressively today outweighs the discomfort you would feel from penny-pinching now so you can save enough to achieve your goals? Furthermore, what will your over-saving cost you in opportunity costs? If you have to save more to achieve your $100,000 goal but it comes at the expense of adequately funding your retirement account, then you have introduced a whole new dimension of potential discomfort that must be considered and weighed alongside your other competing financial interests.

Chapter Recap

» The phenomenon of compounding dramatically spotlights how important it is to invest early.

» The phenomenon of inflation shows how failing to invest can be risky.

» Investing strategies should be tailored to the goals you are pursuing.

» Risks can be calculated, whereas uncertainty refers to what is wholly unpredictable.

» A person's risk tolerance is defined by their ability and willingness to take risk. However, it is a person's willingness that usually drives their decision making.

| 7 |
Asset Allocation

Chapter Overview
- » Diversification
- » Asset Allocation
- » Investment Strategies
- » Financial Planners

October: This is one of the peculiarly dangerous months to speculate in stocks. The others are July, January, September, April, November, May, March, June, December, August and February.

— MARK TWAIN

In the last chapter, we introduced you to initial investing concepts. As you move through this chapter, there will be several questions for you to answer to discover your investment philosophy and design an *asset allocation* that best fits your needs and risk tolerance.

- » How should I allocate my money among stocks, bonds, cash, and nontraditional assets like gold or bitcoin?
- » How diversified do I want to be once I've decided which assets I will buy?
- » Do I want active or passive fund managers?
- » When should I rebalance my portfolio?
- » Given everything I know, do I want to seek professional advice?

Those are the questions that we seek to answer in this chapter. I want you to understand what investment options are out there and the risks involved with each one. The goal is to find the best strategy for success within your comfort range, something suited to your risk preferences that won't disturb a good night's sleep.

In the "Be Diversified" section of this chapter, we'll go through a virtual smorgasbord of investment assets available to the public. I'm going to explain each of these assets in some detail, but I don't want you to feel as if you have to understand each one backward and forward. What I recommend is that you skim through the "Be Diversified" section first and then read more closely through those passages as you approach designing your portfolio and investing your savings.

Some of these assets you may already own, and, hopefully, you already have some understanding of them. Others you may be interested in acquiring as you learn more about investing and diversifying your total holdings, and as you decide what you want to accomplish with your portfolio.

There is no single investment strategy that works for everyone. This is because everyone's goals, time horizons, risk tolerances, and experiences with investing are all different. A person in her thirties with few financial obligations may seek to generate growth over the long term, while another thirty-year-old may seek to purchase a home and pay for her children's college. Fortunately, we live in a world with tools available to accomplish almost any financial objective.

Before we get too deep into this exciting topic, I would like to advise you that the content provided in this chapter and throughout the book should *not* be construed as investment advice. To reiterate the preceding paragraph, there is no strategy that works for everyone, and any direct investment advice you take should be laser-focused on your particular situation and objectives.

Understanding the myriad of investment options takes time and effort. Keep your on your own assignment from chapter 6—your list of short-term and long-term goals—handy as you read through this chapter. By the end, you should have an idea of what types of investment strategies are best suited for each goal.

Be Diversified

By mid-March of 2020, amid coronavirus fears, 130 companies in the S&P 500 had declined 40 percent or more over the course of two and a half months. Sixty-three declined 50 percent or more. Sixteen companies dropped 70 percent or more. Imagine what it would be like to have 25 percent of your net worth invested in one of those sixteen companies. Your net worth would decrease by 18 percent or more from just one investment. This is the number one reason why you should never have all your money, retirement or otherwise, in one company's stock. It can significantly affect your financial health in times of crisis.

The old adage "don't put all your eggs in one basket" truly applies to personal finance. You can mitigate risk by diversifying your assets across many different categories including type, size, location, and economic sector exposure. For example, holding all your assets in a checking account will avoid investment risk but will subject you to *inflation risk*; that is, your money will lose purchasing power. Likewise, holding all your assets in one bond exposes you to default risk if the company or government is unable to repay its bondholders. The solution is to hold some cash in a savings account, invest some in a wide array of bonds, and invest the rest in a variety of stocks and perhaps bitcoin or gold.

Diversification is the most conservative way to be aggressive. It allows you to invest in assets at the highest edge of your risk tolerance without worrying about permanent loss of capital. For example, let's say you have a moderately aggressive risk tolerance. It is suggested that you invest in a portfolio that is 70 percent stocks and 30 percent bonds, based on your appetite for risk and your goals. If you invested 70 percent of your money in one stock, that would be a much more aggressive portfolio than if you invested 70 percent of your money in 13,000 companies around the world. Why? Because one company can go bankrupt, but the odds of 13,000 companies going bankrupt at the same time is very low. While the price of the 13,000 companies will fluctuate, idiosyncrasies from individual companies will not affect the total value of your portfolio.

The first step in building your diversified portfolio is understanding the investment options available to you. It does not make sense to time the market or make short-term trades. It is incredibly hard to achieve investment returns by timing the market. Even if you get it right one time, there is no guarantee you will get it right the next time, and in order to derive returns from your timing efforts you must be right twice, once on your way in and then again on your way out (or vice versa). If I knew when the best time to buy and sell was, I would tell you! I really would! Unfortunately, no one can tell you. No one knows! Creating a long-term asset allocation based on your life's goals and risk tolerance is the best way to get where you want to go. It won't be a straight path. It will twist and turn. The best way to create an asset allocation that fits who you are is to understand the investments you can buy that will help you reach your goals.

Bonds and CDs

Certificates of deposit (CDs) and bonds are fixed-income instruments that require a lump sum investment and pay periodic interest payments based on a predetermined rate. A bond or CD eventually reaches a *maturity* date, at which time the investor's lump sum is returned.

For example, an investor buys a five-year bond with a $1,000 face value and a 2.5 percent interest rate. The investor gives $1,000 to the company or government that issued the bond. In turn, the company or government pays 2.5 percent per year, known as the coupon, to the investor. It is generally paid semiannually, so the investor would receive $12.50 two times per year. After five years the bond reaches maturity, and $1,000 is returned to the investor.

A CD is similar to a bond, except it is solely offered by banks or other financial institutions, and the funds are tied up for a given period of time. In exchange for a higher interest rate, you give your funds to the bank with a lock-up period, which means that if you retrieve the funds before the CD matures, you will pay a penalty.

The thing to note about bonds and CDs is that, generally, the longer the time to maturity (when you are paid back your lump sum), the higher the interest rate the issuing institution must pay you for investing. A thirty-year bond should pay out a higher coupon payment than a five-year bond issued from the same authority. There are exceptions to this rule that are beyond the scope of this book.

Government Bonds

As of the year 2020, US government debt is $22 trillion. In order to fund its programs, our government issues three- to six-month bills, five- to ten-year notes, and thirty-year (long) bonds from the Treasury Department. These bonds are called Treasuries and are considered the safest types of bonds. As long as people around the globe are willing to hold US dollars, our government can always print more money to pay for its debts. Longer-term bonds are subject to *inflationary risk* and, as with any bond, there is also *principal risk*, which is best explained with an example:

Say an investor has a five-year $1,000 bond paying 2.5 percent, and suppose that six months after the bond is issued, interest rates have moved higher. The same issuing company needs more capital and decides to sell new five-year bonds, this time with a 3 percent interest rate. The old 2.5 percent bond is now less valuable because an investor can get 3 percent. Therefore, if an investor in the 2.5 percent bond wished to sell it prior to maturity, he would be unable to recover the $1,000 face value. He would receive "less than par" (figure 14).

INTEREST RATE / BOND PRICE

fig. 14

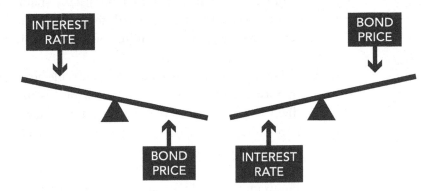

Corporate Bonds

Companies often issue bonds to raise capital. Just as you have a credit score that lenders use to assess your reliability, companies have something similar known as a credit quality rating. Credit quality ratings are determined by rating agencies like Standard & Poor's or Moody's. A company like Apple with a very high credit quality rating will be able to borrow at a lower interest rate than will Joe Schmoe around the corner. Bonds with a BBB rating or greater are considered investment grade and the company is more likely to pay back its bondholders. On the other hand, if the bond is rated CCC, the company may be deep in financial distress and unable to fulfill its obligations. (figure 15).

fig. 15

S&P	MOODY'S	GRADE	MEANING
AAA	Aaa	Investment	Risk is almost zero
AA	Aa	Investment	Low risk
A	A	Investment	Risk if economy declines
BBB	Baa	Investment	Some risk; more if economy declines
BB	Ba	Speculative	Risky
B	B	Speculative	Risky; expected to get worse
CCC	Caa	Speculative	Probable bankruptcy
CC	Ca	Speculative	Probable bankruptcy
C	C	Speculative	In bankruptcy or default

Municipal Bonds

Sometimes cities and counties issue bonds to meet certain needs like paying for new schools, office buildings, or law enforcement. The advantage of these municipal bonds, or "munis," is that the interest paid is often exempt from federal (and usually state) taxes. Like government and corporate bonds, the length to maturity, credit ratings, and interest rates can vary greatly depending on who is issuing the bond.

When looking at municipal bonds, taxable equivalent yield (TEY) is an important metric to consider. The formula is the muni bond interest rate divided by (one minus your tax rate). Its result tells you whether it's worth purchasing municipal bonds given your tax rate, or if you would earn more from taxable bonds.

For example, Molly has an effective federal tax rate of 23 percent and an effective state tax rate of 3 percent. Total tax rate: 26 percent. Municipal bonds in her state are yielding 1.8 percent.

Molly's taxable equivalent yield is as follows: $1.8\% \div (1 - 0.26) = 2.4\%$

If taxable bonds of similar credit quality and term yield more than 2.4 percent, she should own taxable bonds. If they yield less than 2.4 percent, then she should own municipal bonds.

NOTE

When calculating your TEY, you need to use your effective tax rate (total income divided by total taxes paid), not your marginal tax bracket, because you would be overestimating your tax liability and therefore overestimating the amount of yield you would need to receive from a taxable bond to be equivalent.

Generally, municipal bonds are priced such that it only makes sense to invest in them if you have a high tax rate.

Entire books could be written about the different types of bonds, and many already have been. From a personal finance perspective, it is not necessary to become a subject matter expert. The key takeaway is that highly rated bonds with shorter maturities are a great way to invest for short-term goals. As credit quality decreases and time to maturity increases, your initial investment is more at risk.

Stocks

A stock represents an ownership interest in an individual company. When a private company needs money to grow, it can choose to issue either stock or bonds. This allows the company to raise money through the public marketplace. Before a stock is listed on an exchange, the company issues stock through an initial public offering (IPO). Once the company has "gone public," you can buy or sell the shares through a brokerage firm.

Investors earn money on their purchase through *dividends* and *capital gains*. A dividend occurs when a company distributes a portion of its earnings to investors, typically on a quarterly basis. In general, larger, more established companies tend to pay dividends. Capital gains occur when the investor experiences price appreciation from holding the asset over time. Capital losses occur when a stock's value declines. We will have a fun tax-related discussion about capital losses in chapter 11!

To illustrate the distinction between stocks and bonds, consider the following scenario. You are entering the fashion design business and are making T-shirts in your garage. You're able to make and sell 100 T-shirts a month (or 1,200 per year). The cost to make each shirt is $5, and you can sell them for $15 each, making a $10 profit, or $12,000 per year!

You crunch some numbers and decide you need to hire more T-shirt makers and rent a warehouse to grow your company. Your expansion will cost $100,000. You have some options:

1. You borrow and assume debt. You find friends and family who are willing to lend to you at 5 percent per year for five years. You pay a total of $5,000 in interest and then repay $100,000 at the end of five years (this is the equivalent of issuing a five-year bond).

2. You find friends and family who are willing to accept a total of 10 percent ownership in your company in exchange for $100,000. In return, you pay a dividend equal to 10 percent of your profits forever. This is $1,200 per year with your current profits and will hopefully increase with your new expansion plans (this is the equivalent of issuing stock).

So which type of investment is correct? There is no right answer. Each investor must consider his or her own risk tolerance and investment objectives. The investor who lends you money at 5 percent (the bond investor) generally has less faith in your business than the investor willing to give you money in exchange for a 10 percent ownership stake (the stock investor). The investor who chooses to buy bonds rather than stocks says, "I believe you can pay me back over the next five years, but I am uncertain about becoming an equity holder (stockholder) in this business." The investor choosing stocks over bonds says, "I believe your T-shirts will earn me great profits in the future, much more than 5 percent per year for five years as with a bond investment." The stock investor must wait much longer to see a payoff than the bond investor, and therefore the stock investor is taking a lot more risk than the bond investor, though he stands to gain larger returns over time if the business performs exceptionally well.

Company Size / Market Capitalization

The global marketplace encompasses companies of many sizes, everything from the T-shirt business we just discussed to giants like Amazon and Apple. The size of a business is defined in terms of its market capitalization. A company's *market capitalization* is its current share price times the number of shares the company has outstanding. Imagine that you had the choice to make a loan to either Amazon or the T-shirt business discussed in the previous example. To which company would you charge a higher interest rate? The T-shirt business, right? It's much riskier!

Risk sets apart small companies from large ones. This does not mean that large companies never decline or go out of business. However, smaller companies are much more likely to declare bankruptcy or default on a loan. So why would you ever invest in these riskier endeavors? Well, let's say the T-shirt business only made $12,000 last year and has the potential to double, triple, or even quadruple its profits. Larger companies making billions of dollars need to do a lot more to record that kind of growth.

The outperformance of small companies over larger ones is known as the *size effect*. Smaller companies generally outperform larger ones over long periods of time (figure 16). This is because investors require a higher rate of return for their riskier investments. The T-shirt business may never get off the ground. But what if you diversified and invested in five thousand small companies? You'd worry a lot less about potential bankruptcies and over time earn a nice rate of return for the risk taken!

GROWTH OF A DOLLAR, 1926 – 2018
(COMPOUNDED MONTHLY)

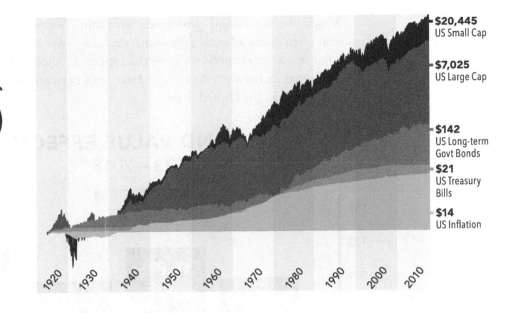

Source: US Small Cap Index is the CRSP 6–10 Index; US Large Cap Index is the S&P 500 Index; Long-Term Government Bonds Index is 20-year US government bonds; Treasury Bills are One-Month US Treasury bills; Inflation is the Consumer Price Index; 1-Month Treasury Bills Index is the IA SBBI US 30 Day TBill TR USD. Treasury Index data sourced from Ibbotson Associates, via Morningstar Direct. CRSP data provided by the Center for Research in Security Prices, S&P data copyright 2018 S&P Dow Jones Indices LLC, a division of S&P Global, all rights reserved. Past performance is no guarantee of future results.

Value vs. Growth

Just as we begin life as babies, grow through adolescence, pave our way in adulthood, and mature into the wise and elderly, companies also go through a series of phases over time. And just like us, companies have different attributes and traits. Instead of long hair, short hair, tall or small, we categorize stocks into sectors, such as financials, technology, energy, industrials, consumer discretionary, etc. We can also designate them as "growth" or "value" companies; this is known as "style." A growth company has revenue that increases rapidly over time. Shareholders pay a premium to be invested and are rewarded when shares appreciate, as most growth companies do not pay dividends.

A value stock is one perceived to be a bargain when considering fundamental factors. There are many financial indicators that investors use; some examples are price to earnings (the price relative to the amount of earnings a company can produce), price to book (the price compared to a company's net asset value) or return on equity or assets (how much income a company can earn per shareholder's capital or company assets).

Much like how small companies have outperformed over time, there also often exists a "value premium," meaning, over long periods of time, value tends to outperform growth. Figure 17 shows the difference in performance between small and large and between growth and value companies in the United States.

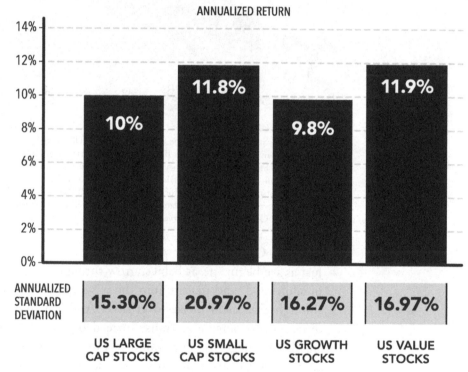

SIZE AND VALUE EFFECTS
1973 – 2018

ANNUALIZED RETURN

	US LARGE CAP STOCKS	US SMALL CAP STOCKS	US GROWTH STOCKS	US VALUE STOCKS
Annualized Return	10%	11.8%	9.8%	11.9%
ANNUALIZED STANDARD DEVIATION	15.30%	20.97%	16.27%	16.97%

fig. 17

For illustrative purposes only. Past performance is not indicative of future results. Indices are unmanaged baskets of securities in which investors cannot directly invest. Assumes reinvestment of income and no transaction costs or taxes. Standard deviation is a statistical measurement of how far the return of a security or index moves above or below its average value.

Over a forty-five-year period, small and value stocks outperformed large and growth stocks, respectively. However, over the past decade, value has significantly underperformed growth. Therefore, just because small and value have tended to outperform over long periods of time does not mean that you should exclude mid-size and large companies and growth-style companies. The key to a diversified portfolio is investing in all styles and sectors of companies, as some may outperform one year and underperform the next. We don't know when the outperformance or underperformance will be; therefore, it is important to hold some of everything.

Domestic vs. International

Since nearly half of all stocks trade outside of the United States, a truly diversified portfolio means exposure to international equity markets, of both developed nations (like much of Europe) and emerging economies (like China, Brazil, or Africa).

Your diversified portfolio should include companies all over the world, of every size and style and sector. Fortunately, you do not need to be a financial analyst to build the portfolio. Mutual funds and exchange-traded funds (both covered in detail later in this chapter) do the work for you.

Figures 18 and 19 show that nearly half of all stocks and two-thirds of all bonds trade outside the United States.

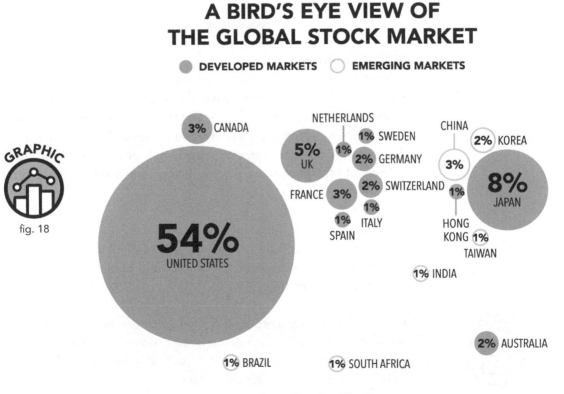

A BIRD'S EYE VIEW OF THE GLOBAL STOCK MARKET

● DEVELOPED MARKETS ○ EMERGING MARKETS

GRAPHIC

fig. 18

3% CANADA

NETHERLANDS
1% SWEDEN

5% UK 1% 2% GERMANY

CHINA
2% KOREA
3%

FRANCE 3% 2% SWITZERLAND 1%

8% JAPAN

1% ITALY
1% SPAIN

HONG KONG 1% TAIWAN

54% UNITED STATES

1% INDIA

2% AUSTRALIA

1% BRAZIL   1% SOUTH AFRICA

Source: Data from Bloomberg

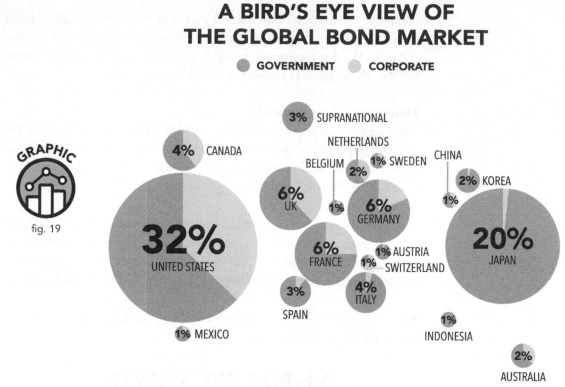

A BIRD'S EYE VIEW OF
THE GLOBAL BOND MARKET

● GOVERNMENT ● CORPORATE

GRAPHIC

fig. 19

3% SUPRANATIONAL

4% CANADA

NETHERLANDS

BELGIUM

6% UK

2%

1% SWEDEN

CHINA

1%

2% KOREA

6% GERMANY

32%
UNITED STATES

6% FRANCE

1%

1% AUSTRIA

1% SWITZERLAND

20%
JAPAN

3% SPAIN

4% ITALY

1% MEXICO

1% INDONESIA

2%
AUSTRALIA

Source: Data from Bloomberg

Mutual Funds

A *mutual fund* is a pool of money that is used to buy and sell assets with a certain investment objective. Fund managers make the day-to-day investment decisions. Each fund—and there are thousands of them—has its objectives, performance history, and portfolio holdings outlined in a document called the *prospectus*. This handy piece of literature must be delivered to the prospective investor before or at the time of investment.

Stock Funds

A stock or equity fund invests in shares of individual companies. Portfolios can be concentrated, holding only a small number of companies within the fund, or diversified, with the fund holding hundreds or even thousands of companies.

NOTE

A minimum deposit is required to invest in most mutual funds. For some, it can be as little as one hundred dollars, while others might require three thousand dollars or more. Make sure to check the fund's website and prospectus for the details.

Stock funds typically have a clear investment objective that the managers must adhere to. For example, the fund may focus on mid-cap stocks that include a blend of growth and value, or it may only invest in emerging market stocks of all styles. The fund's website and prospectus should give you a clear idea of the types of investments being pursued. If the investment targets and approach are not made clear in the prospectus, then be wary of the fund!

At this point, you may be asking yourself, with all the thousands of funds, where do I even begin to know how to put together a mutual fund portfolio? Great question! An easy way to distinguish the differences between stock mutual funds is by looking at a stock style box (figure 20). These boxes can be found on most mutual fund companies' websites and will give you a high-level overview of what the fund holds in terms of company size and style.

STOCK STYLE BOX

fig. 20

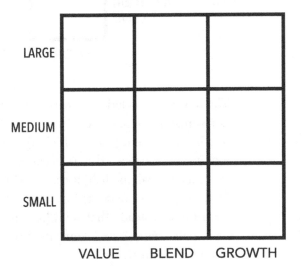

Bond Funds

Bond mutual funds typically focus on one type of bond category, such as government bonds, corporates, or municipal bonds. In addition, some funds focus on longer-term bonds that mature in twenty years or more, while others focus on short-term bonds.

To determine which bond funds to include in your portfolio, it is important to look at the relevant section of the mutual fund's website.

There you can find the yield of the fund, the duration of bonds it holds, the number of holdings, and any other pertinent information about the fund. You can also use a bond style box to give you an overview of what the fund holds (figure 21):

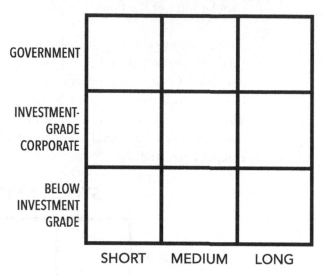

BOND STYLE BOX

fig. 21

You'll want to include maturities in your portfolio that match your time horizon and risk tolerance. In general, I like to include only high-quality bonds (investment grade or higher) in my portfolios, as well as short and medium maturities. This is because we generally use bonds to pay for short-term goals or liabilities. In which case, it doesn't make sense to hold long, risky bonds, as I can hold stocks over the same time period to fund those instead. That said, holding long-term bonds of high quality may make sense given your situation, so don't discount them without evaluating your needs!

Other Fund Types

You can find funds from stocks to bonds to commodities to currencies and every style and sector in between. While the sky is the limit when it comes to fund options, it's important to keep your goals in mind when choosing some of the sexier investments. For most of us, we want our money to be there when we need it or want to spend it on something important. For others, the investments themselves are part of the goal; that is, the goal is to be a savvy investor because that provides emotional value and fulfillment. If you fall in the former group, you'll want to keep your investments simple and easy to manage, so you can hold them through good and bad times. Because, baby, you'd better believe you will see both in your lifetime!

Active vs. Passive Investing

Finding the right mutual fund can seem daunting, since there are hundreds of categories and thousands of products to choose from. Let's make this process simpler by deciding now whether you want to take an active or passive approach to your portfolio.

An active approach means that either you or a fund manager will look at a wide array of investments and choose the ones you think will perform better than the overall market. This is typically done through rigorous research, although I have seen folks buy into a company simply because the price dropped or a neighbor told them to. You will want to take an active approach only if being a savvy investor is one of your lifetime dreams.

A passive approach means you accept the return the market is willing to give you. This is an easier way of going about investing. All you need to decide is what proportions you will hold in all the different markets, styles, and sectors, rather than choosing all the individual companies or managers within these categories as well.

You may now be asking, What if I want better returns than what the market can provide me with? Great question! I will answer your question with another question: How do you know you can consistently achieve better returns than what the market can provide? Unfortunately, you don't know you can do that. Even professionals have trouble doing it! Most fund managers fail to keep pace with the market over the years, and they're doing this full time as their job, not their side project after work, like you are!

Figure 22 shows the small proportion of fund managers that were able to outperform over a twenty-year period in both stocks and bonds. Bleak, isn't it?

Trying to outperform the market can be an exercise in self-sabotage. My experience is it is extremely difficult to do better than the market while keeping expenses and taxes at a minimum. Your investments should feel boring. The more boring, the better. I want you to feel as if you are watching paint dry. The idea is to build wealth over time and accomplish important goals and objectives, not provide some entertainment at the risk of your financial health.

BEATING THE MARKET IS CHALLENGING

fig. 22

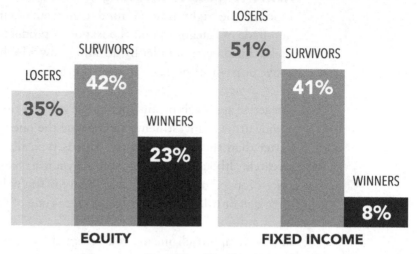

Source: Data from Bloomberg

The sample includes funds at the beginning of the 20-year period ending December 31, 2018. Each fund is evaluated relative to its respective primary prospectus benchmark as of the end of the evaluation period. Surviving funds are those with return observations for every month of the sample period. Winner funds are those that survived and whose cumulative net return over the period exceeded that of their respective primary prospectus benchmark. Loser funds are those that did not survive the period or whose cumulative net return did not exceed that of their respective primary prospectus benchmark.

Index Funds

John Bogle created the first index mutual fund, called the First Index Investment Trust, which later became the Vanguard 500 Index Fund.

The idea behind an index fund is that since most investors cannot beat the market (in terms of performance), a better idea is to replicate the performance of the market and minimize costs, or expenses.

Bogle outlined ten other investing rules:

1. Ignore the market on a day-to-day basis.
2. Be bored by the process but elated by the outcome.
3. Invest, don't trade.
4. Select low-cost funds.

5. Consider carefully the added costs of advice.
6. Do not overrate past fund performance.
7. Use past performance to determine consistency and risk.
8. Beware of stars (as in star mutual fund managers).
9. Do not invest in too many funds.
10. Stay the course: buy your fund portfolio … and hold it forever.

When we talk about "outperformance," in general we are looking at how we can outperform the S&P 500 Index. The S&P 500 Index is a market-value-weighted index that holds five hundred companies with shares listed on the US stock exchanges. *Market-value-weighted* means that the biggest companies are held in the largest proportion and therefore have a greater influence on the performance of the overall index. The methodology contrasts with a simple market average, where each component has an equal influence. Figure 23 shows the ten largest companies in the United States and their rank by weight.

GRAPHIC

fig. 23

#	COMPANY	SYMBOL	WEIGHT
\multicolumn{4}{c|}{**TOP 10 S&P 500 STOCKS**}			
1	Apple Inc.	AAPL	6.4%
2	Microsoft Corp.	MSFT	5.4%
3	Amazon.com Inc.	AMZN	4.5%
4	Facebook Inc. Class A	FB	2.2%
5	Alphabet Inc. Class A	GOOGL	1.8%
6	Alphabet Inc. Class C	GOOG	1.7%
7	Berkshire Hathaway Inc. Class B	BRK.B	1.5%
8	Johnson & Johnson	JNJ	1.3%
9	JPMorgan Chase & Co.	JPM	1.2%
10	Visa Inc. Class A	V	1.2%

Source: data from slickcharts.com, 11/19/2020

FUN FACT

The five hundred companies in the S&P 500 Index account for roughly 80 percent of the total market value, or market capitalization, of the US stock market. The top ten companies dominate the index and account for over 25 percent.

When people talk about the market, as in "the market was up 300 points today," they are talking about the Dow Jones Industrial Average, which is an index of thirty different companies. For professional investors, however, the S&P 500 Index is the more relevant barometer for performance of the stock market. But for you, neither one is all that important. Stop checking stock market updates and live your life!

While I strongly encourage you to take advantage of the wide array of index funds available, if you're set on active management I highly recommend evaluating the following questions before choosing a mutual fund manager:

» What is the process that the fund managers use to choose investments?
» Do the fund's goals and objectives match my goals and objectives?
» What are the fees and expenses?
» How many companies does the fund hold?
» Is the fund well-diversified or concentrated in specific groups or sectors?
» Are there penalties for early redemptions?
» Are there additional tax implications (see chapter 11)?

If you're planning to create your own portfolio of individual companies, ask yourself these questions: What is the process I will use to choose investments? How will I ensure consistency? Am I choosing assets that match the results I want to have? What expenses and taxes am I incurring with my strategy? How diversified do I want to be?

I have a client who wanted to trade actively with a small percentage of his portfolio. He opened an account with a discount broker and started trading individual stocks and exchange-traded funds. At the end of year one, the S&P 500 had risen 30 percent, and his account value had dropped 50 percent! In spite of that, it was a good time for him! He enjoyed the process and got a kick out of investing, especially because he didn't lose a large portion of his net worth doing it.

MY TAKE

There is nothing wrong with taking a small percentage of your portfolio and speculating with the money, just as there is nothing wrong with going to a casino from time to time and playing the tables. If you're trading for short-term profits because you think it is fun, call it what it is: entertainment. Never risk money that you really need for your longer-term goals and objectives.

Exchange-Traded Funds

The exchange-traded fund (ETF) is like a mutual fund: both are pools of money from which investments are made into stocks, bonds, or other assets. The main difference is that ETFs trade throughout the day and can be bought and sold like shares of stock. A mutual fund is bought and sold only once per day at a price called the *net asset value (NAV)*. As with mutual funds, there is a long list of ETFs available for purchase.

Compared to mutual funds, ETFs are typically more tax-efficient. Mutual fund managers buy and sell investments in their portfolio throughout the year. If there are gains on anything they sell, it is passed through to the investor at the end of the year in the form of capital gains. ETFs, on the other hand, are not subject to the same taxable events, due to the way they are structured. Therefore, mutual funds are often better in tax-advantaged accounts like IRAs or 401(k)s.

Real Estate Investment Trusts

Real estate investment trusts (REITs) allow investors to buy shares in commercial real estate portfolios and receive income from properties. As with stocks, you can buy REITs on the public market either individually or via an ETF or mutual fund. Each REIT has a unique portfolio. Some REITs contain apartment complexes or office buildings, and others might have data centers, health care facilities, storage buildings, or warehouses. While publicly traded REITs look and act like stocks, they are considered a different asset class, because they invest in real estate. Income from the properties is passed through to shareholders, and therefore most of the return is typically realized through dividend payments rather than capital gains.

Unless you want to be a landlord, holding REITs is the best way to add real estate investments to your asset allocation. As with stocks and bonds, I recommend diversifying your REITs rather than holding just one or two.

Hedge Funds

High-net-worth investors often turn to hedge funds in search of returns that are higher than those offered by traditional funds. Created as partnerships, these investment vehicles are handled by managers that are often paid 2 percent of the underlying assets plus 20 percent of the fund's profits. The popularity of hedge funds has declined over the years, because most have failed to achieve returns that justify the hefty fees charged. Nevertheless, some hedge funds are quite large and extremely popular with high-net-worth and institutional investors.

You have to be a qualified investor to participate. Don't worry, you're not missing out! Simpler portfolios are not only easier to build but also are more likely something you can stick with during hard times. This is because you'll always understand what you're holding, rather than being beholden to the black box of a hedge fund, not knowing what is inside.

Options, Commodities, and Currencies

The markets for options, commodities, and currencies ostensibly exists to provide solutions for those with true financial needs, such as the airline CEO who purchases petroleum futures contracts to insulate the business from volatile oil prices (commodities), or the investor who needs a guarantee of liquidity to meet an upcoming liability (options), or any executive or manager who needs to conduct business overseas (currencies). Though these markets do serve practical functions, they are perhaps best known for providing fodder for short-term speculators who seek profits from market movements. From reading this book, you now know that responsible personal finance management is not accomplished through speculation (aka recreation). You value your time, energy, money, and talent and therefore will spend more of it making smart decisions, like how to grow and build wealth in a diversified manner rather than speculating about what the Indian rupee will do versus the Swedish krona. Not only will you sleep better, but you will also become wealthy!

While I do not suggest that investors trade commodities as part of an investment plan, gold is something to consider because it has historically been a good hedge of inflationary risk. If you do not want to buy gold coins or bars, there are a handful of ETFs that represent ownership in the metal. It is important to note that when buying gold, you can anticipate receiving returns that are similar to the rate of inflation. Therefore, gold is not a good vehicle for growing wealth, since the inflation rate is historically 3 percent. I generally do not purchase gold positions in client portfolios in excess of 5 percent of the client's net worth.

Bitcoin

Most of the assets I talk about have a centralized third party controlling and influencing them. These assets require other people to perform specific tasks on your behalf as the shareholder, thereby generating cash flows for you. The CEO and board members are responsible for directing a company toward profitability, thereby increasing the value of your stock. Mutual funds and ETFs have portfolio managers and administrators. These assets also necessitate a custodian to hold assets on your behalf. Real estate investments often require a property manager and depend on tenants paying their rents.

Over the past decade a new kind of asset has appeared. This asset has a lot less utility. You can't live in it. You can't eat it. But it also has a lot less trust involved. You don't have to rely on others. You can use the magic of the internet to receive, hold, and send out this asset, all in a trust-minimized system. This kind of decentralized asset was only made possible by Satoshi Nakamoto's solution to the "double spend" problem. Without getting too technical, this means you can have a digital asset that, unlike most others, cannot be duplicated via a simple copy and paste. It is constructed to be scarce. Bitcoin's decentralized nature has invited a lot of skeptics as well as some almost religious believers.

My view is that bitcoin should be part of a balanced investment allocation. This is because it is so disconnected from the other investment solutions we use, like stocks and bonds. Though it is higher risk than most traditional investments we include in a portfolio, its fundamental properties allow it to be noncorrelated with the rest of our portfolio, which reduces overall portfolio volatility and may improve outcomes.

There are several reasons to believe this new currency is here to stay:

» Bitcoin is decentralized: the supply is not controlled by a government. It cannot be printed when politicians are trying to get reelected or when there is a crisis at hand. You also do not need permission from anyone to create a "bitcoin wallet," which enables you to send and receive payments through the Bitcoin network.

» Bitcoin's purchasing power is historically the most deflationary. Holding an asset that increases in value (deflationary) is better than holding an asset that decreases in value (inflationary) over time.

Bitcoin, over the long run, is deflationary, whereas fiat currencies (dollars and other government-backed currencies) are inflationary by design.

» The Lindy effect: the longer a money or currency exists, the longer we can expect it to continue to exist.

I view bitcoin as a savings technology. Though it is prone to volatile price swings, its proponents believe it will prove to be a more stable asset as its novelty wears off and its staying power is made manifest. Like gold, I consider bitcoin to be a non-core holding. I recommend holding 1 to 10 percent of your assets in bitcoin, commensurate with your time horizon, risk tolerance, and understanding of the technology. Additionally, you should consider this a long-term asset, much like how we view stocks, and it should not be used to fund any short-term goals.

Insurance Products

Some insurance products have an investment component to the policy. For example, with a variable whole life policy, subaccounts can be created with the cash value you accumulate, and the cash is invested into mutual funds. The policy will have a death benefit, and you can borrow against the cash value without tax consequences.

In nearly all cases, it is preferable to address insurance and investment needs separately. We'll talk a lot more about insurance in chapter 10.

Checking, Savings, and Money Markets

You probably have checking and savings accounts at a bank. While it may be practical to simply open your account with the big bank down the street, try shopping around for the best option. Some banks offer perks on checking accounts like free checks, waived account minimums with direct deposit of paychecks, Social Security benefits, or even airline miles. Additionally, the interest paid on savings accounts can vary widely from one financial institution to the next. It is also prudent to check online savings options, as the interest rate is often significantly higher than what a traditional brick-and-mortar branch can offer you.

Money markets are practical for cash savings, as well. This is a type of mutual fund that invests in high-quality short-term debt or cash. Most mutual fund families have some type of interest-bearing money market, which can be used to deposit periodic payments before allocating that money to other types of mutual funds, stocks, or other investments. The money market account can act as a placeholder investment that will garner a modest return for you while you decide how to deploy your capital more specifically.

High-yield savings accounts and money market funds are a great place to put half your emergency savings (the other half should be in your everyday checking or savings account). This is so your emergency fund can earn something while you're not in the midst of a crisis. Depending on current bond yields and your risk tolerance, it can also make sense to put a portion of your bond allocation into high-yield savings. That said, be wary of keeping too much cash around. It is human nature to want to keep money safe and shield it from risk. But without investing money for the long term, it will be difficult to build wealth.

Equity Compensation

The next section covers a type of employer benefit program known as an employee stock option (ESO). If you do not have ESOs, you might want to skip this section and jump to the next one, "Building Your Portfolio." We are going to get into the nitty-gritty details of this subject, and there are a *lot* of them, enough to be a bit overwhelming. If you do have employee stock options or want to learn something new, then keep calm and read on.

Restricted Stock Units (RSUs)

A *restricted stock unit (RSU)* is employee compensation in the form of company shares. RSUs are granted to employees but cannot be sold until after a certain time period, known as a "*vesting period*," has passed. When the vesting period is over, the market value of the vested shares is used to formally determine the taxable compensation.

Elsie works for ABC Company. In her contract, ABC grants her 100 shares of restricted stock units each year on her work anniversary, but they take another year to vest. On the date when the RSUs vest, the shares are worth $100. Elsie receives $10,000 ($100 x 100 shares) in ordinary taxable income in addition to her salary at ABC Company. In essence, Elsie receives $10,000 worth of stock as though it were cash.

Employee Stock Options (ESOs)

An employee stock option is another form of employee compensation in the form of options. Employees like to think of their options like cash. I caution you against this. Stock options, unlike RSUs, are not like receiving cash. An option represents the right to buy stock, not a stock position. Your company ESOs will give you the right to purchase company shares at a specific price.

Options have a lot of lingo. Your options have a "***grant date***," the date on which you receive them. They also have a "***strike price***" or exercise price, the price at which you can purchase your company's shares. Your company's share price may be above or below the strike price at any given time. Your options also have a vesting period, just like RSUs. Lastly, they have an expiration, a date after which your options lapse and you can no longer purchase company shares at your designated strike price (figure 24).

HOW AN EMPLOYEE STOCK OPTION WORKS

fig. 24

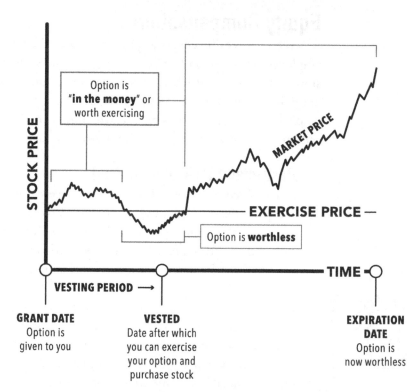

Exercising the option only makes sense if the strike price is below the market price of the stock. If not, your option is worthless; it would be cheaper to buy the stock directly in the market instead, unless the price goes back up.

One option gives you the right to buy one hundred shares. If, for example, you negotiate a compensation package entitling you to two hundred options, then you have the right to purchase twenty thousand shares. For successful companies with rapidly increasing share prices, employee options can produce sudden and unexpected millionaires, albeit millionaires with tax issues.

As there is the possibility of the option expiring worthless, having an option subjects you to more risk than simply owning RSUs.

There are two types of ESOs: non-qualified stock options and incentive stock options. The number one feature that sets these two types apart is their taxation.

Key Characteristics of Non-Qualified Stock Options (NQSOs)

Non-qualified stock options (NQSOs), like any options, give the employee the right to purchase company shares at a set strike price over a set time frame after a set vesting period. I am purposely being vague regarding the time frames that accompany NQSOs. Employers may grant you an NQSO on any terms, exercisable over any period of years. You must read your documentation and negotiate where possible! When you exercise your options, you are subject to W-2 compensation on the difference between the exercise price and the market price.

In addition to her RSUs, Elsie also receives one NQSO with an exercise price of $10. On the day Elsie's option vests, shares of ABC Company are worth $100. Since one option represents the right to buy 100 shares of stock, Elsie can exercise the option to purchase 100 shares of stock at $10 per share. Thus, she will receive $9,000 in W-2 compensation.

Mathematically: ($100 market price at exercise − $10 exercise price) x 100 shares = $9,000 ordinary income.

Elsie is responsible for income taxes and FICA payroll taxes on the $9,000. She can immediately sell the 100 shares for $10,000 or she can choose to keep them. If Elsie holds the shares, she will have the same tax treatment going forward as if she had purchased them in the market herself, without the options (see tax planning in chapter 13 on how capital gains taxation works). Going forward, her cost basis is $100 per share. This is because she already paid taxes on the difference between the $10 exercise price and the $100 market price as ordinary income.

Key Characteristics of Incentive Stock Options (ISOs)

Compared to NQSOs, *incentive stock options (ISOs)* are subject to many more rules. Your ISOs have an offering period, meaning you must use them or lose them within ten years, or they will expire worthless. This means if you are granted options on January 1, 2020, you will have until December 31, 2030, to exercise your options, after which they will expire and cease to exist.

The exercise price of an ISO cannot be less than the market price of the stock at the time of the grant. For example, if shares in Company X are worth $10 when you are granted your options, your exercise price cannot be less than $10. Then, you have ten years to exercise, and hopefully your company moves up and not down during that time.

ISOs must be exercised within three months from the date of retirement or termination, meaning if you are laid off or decide to retire, you had better exercise those options within three months, or you lose 'em!

If you have the cash to buy the stock at the time of *exercise*, then you will have a lot more flexibility as you evaluate the best strategy for exercising the contract. This is yet another reason to manage your savings levels: flexibility with ESO strategies!

In order to receive favorable tax treatment, you must hold shares at least two years from the date of grant and one year from the date of exercise. What is this favorable tax treatment? Drum roll, please ... you get long-term capital gains treatment on your profits rather than paying ordinary income taxes at a higher rate! You can see why having the cash on hand to buy the stock is super handy when it is time to exercise. Otherwise, the tax treatment of ISOs is the same as that of NQSOs, and you will pay ordinary income taxes.

Elsie is also granted one ISO on January 1, 2019, with the same exercise price of $10. Elsie's option vests and she is interested in exercising her option, because the share price is $100 on January 2, 2020. Elsie can purchase 100 shares of stock at $10 per share:

100 shares x ($100 market price at exercise − $10 exercise price) = $9,000 in income for Elsie.

How much tax will Elsie pay? It depends! If she holds the stock until January 3, 2021, she will receive favorable long-term capital gains treatment. If she decides to sell sooner, her option will be treated like an NQSO and she will pay ordinary income taxes on $9,000.

Paying the lower capital gains rate on your ISOs is great, but the IRS is not content to let your good fortune go completely unpunished! With this favorable tax treatment also comes a positive alternative minimum tax (AMT) adjustment. AMT is a tax that runs parallel to regular income tax. You only pay AMT when it exceeds your regular tax amount. Essentially, AMT is the IRS's way of recouping tax dollars when an individual finds a lot of deductions. Because Elsie's ISOs would give her a big tax break, she would likely owe AMT in the year she exercised. We don't really know what her AMT will be, because we don't know what the rest of her tax situation looks like.

Now, let's assume Elsie exercises the options, holds the stock until January 3, 2021, and the stock stays at $100. In the year of exercise, she would have a positive AMT adjustment of $9,000 that she would potentially pay tax on. After selling her stock, she would pay long-term capital gains on $9,000. When Elsie filed her taxes, she would have a taxable long-term capital gain of $9,000 and would get a negative AMT adjustment of $9,000 in the year of the sale (that is, she paid tax in the form of AMT at exercise and then had some tax deducted in the form of AMT at the time the stock was sold).

In short, with an ISO, the option holder will probably pay extra tax at exercise due to AMT but will pay less tax upon the sale of the stock later, due to getting AMT back. Note that the additional AMT tax does not apply if you exercise and immediately sell because, in that case, the options are treated like NQSOs.

Now that your head is ready to explode with all this information about AMT, NQSOs, and ISOs, let me give you some actionable steps that can help you manage your ESOs.

1. **Start with your goals**: What do you want to do with the income from your employee stock/option plan? If your goals are short-term in nature, the best approach is to sell the company stock or options as soon as the window opens. If your goals are long-term,

the best approach might also be to sell as soon as the window opens and diversify into long-term assets like stock mutual funds. It all depends on your overall financial situation, goals, and time horizon. Your ESOs must also be included in your overall asset allocation.

2. **Collect relevant information**: Often, the hardest part of dealing with NQSOs, ISOs, and RSUs is collecting accurate information. You may not even know what type of stock awards you have, so be sure to contact the human resources department if you have questions. You must find your original award agreement that governs your stock plan. Your custodian will also have relevant information about grants and vesting dates, strike prices, and current share values.

3. **Create a calendar**: Timing is critical with ESOs. Keep a calendar so you know when the blackout periods are, when your trading windows open, when the company's earnings are released, and when stock exchanges are closed for holidays. Now you know when to sell and diversify. Keep a copy of your grant dates handy if you own ISOs. For all options, you need a calendar of the expiration dates.

4. **Check your withholding rate on the sale of your RSUs**: With RSUs, most companies allow withholding of taxes through the selling of shares (known as *sell to cover*). The problem is that this withholding is generally set by default to the "supplemental wages" tax rate of 22 percent, even though 22 percent may not be your tax rate. Compare 22 percent with your effective tax rate and then notify human resources if you need more or less withholding.

5. **Set aside money for taxes** (and AMT) if your company didn't withhold enough!

That's it.

Employee Stock Purchasing Plans (ESPPs)

An ESPP allows a company employee to purchase the firm's stock at a discount. Contributions to the plan build over time through payroll deductions until a purchase date. When the stock is purchased, the discount can be up to 15 percent (your plan may differ; always check your plan documents for the particulars). If the stock is sold short-term, the discount is considered compensation income. If it's held long-term, there are special long-term capital gains treatments on the discount.

Timing: When Should You Sell RSUs or Exercise Options?

I typically ask clients this question: If you had the whole value of your RSUs in cash right now, would you invest all the money in your company's stock? The answer is generally no or that they would buy a smaller amount. So, why are you holding the stock? It likely comes down to energy. You haven't motivated yourself to act. Maybe you don't understand how the plan works. Or maybe there is an emotional attachment to the company for which you've worked so hard. Perhaps you believe you can influence the outcome of the company's stock because of your position, so why not hold on a little longer. While this sentiment is understandable, you may not be acting in your own best interest. Now that you have more insight into RSUs, more confidence (and the energy and will to take action), it is my hope that you will grab the reins and change your path as needed to accommodate your unique personal financial goals.

Regarding timing your options, you get to choose when to exercise, thereby choosing in what year you'll have a tax event. With incentive stock options, due to the special tax treatment rules, you should plan to exercise options and purchase most of your stock earlier in the year. This will give you more time to see the gain or loss in your company's stock before deciding whether to maintain ISO treatment or sell (assuming you have the cash to purchase the shares). If you're going to buy the stock in one calendar year and sell it in the next calendar year, make sure you hold for an entire year to take advantage of the ISO treatment. I know I sound like a broken record, but always remember that you must hold shares at least two years from the date of grant and one year from the date of exercise.

If you have a lot of ISOs, I highly recommend consulting with a financial planner and/or a certified public accountant (CPA) to discuss how to handle your options. If you're like Elsie, holding only $10,000 in RSUs, then paying an advisor might not be worth it. But if you have $100,000 in options, then even the small decisions you make will have profound implications, especially in terms of tax liability.

MY TAKE

Always keep your goals front and center. Remember, what do you want to do with the money? If you have a short-term goal on the horizon, you will want to diversify out of your company's options quickly (and not take advantage of preferential tax treatment). On the other hand, if your goals are more long-term or you have the funds available for your shorter-term goals, then you can take advantage of tax-favorable ISO treatment. It doesn't have to be all-or-nothing.

Building Your Portfolio

Now that you know about the different asset classes, it's time to build your portfolio! As you venture into this stage of planning, remember that you are a unique person with unique goals and time horizons. You must consider your risk tolerance and the results you want to achieve when creating your asset allocation.

Asset allocation is the process of picking the percentages in which you will hold all the different asset classes. Once you make your high-level asset class decisions, you can pick the specific investments that make up your asset allocation. For example, if you know you want to hold 5 percent of your assets in small-cap stocks, you can instantly achieve your asset allocation target by purchasing the Russell 2000 Index Fund to get exposure to this asset class.

There are rules of thumb to determine your optimal asset allocation. For instance, some investors believe in the "rule of 100," which says that your total stock allocation should be your age minus 100. So, if you are thirty-five you should keep 65 percent of your assets in stocks, and if you are sixty-five, you should have 35 percent in stocks. I'm not a fan of the rule of 100, because it doesn't tailor your investment strategy to who you are at your core. There are many factors to consider other than age.

My approach focuses on combining your risk tolerance with your investment time horizon, because we want to focus on funding your most fulfilled life. And we must do this in a way where you can stick to your plan through any market cycle. Love your portfolio unconditionally, rather than shunning it and rebooting it from scratch whenever it behaves badly.

Before we begin, let's review the difference between a short-term asset and a long-term asset (figure 25):

GRAPHIC

fig. 25

ASSET TYPE	VOLATILITY LEVEL	TIME HORIZON
STOCKS	High	Long Term
HIGH-QUALITY, SHORT- TO MID-TERM BONDS	Low	Short Term
HIGH-QUALITY, LONG-TERM BONDS	Medium	Mid to Long Term
LOW-QUALITY BONDS	Medium to High	Mid to Long Term
REITS	High	Long Term
GOLD	High	Long Term
BITCOIN	High	Long Term
CASH	Lowest	Very Short

Disclaimer: These volatility levels and time horizons are for guideline purposes only. Your risk tolerance and needs should be considered before building a portfolio.

The next few pages review hypothetical scenarios featuring people with different needs and risk tolerances. It shows how I would allocate their portfolios on a high level. The purpose of this section is to show you how to match your investments (assets) with your financial goals (liabilities).

CAUTION

These hypothetical scenarios are for illustrative purposes only and should *not* be construed as investment advice. Before choosing investments, you must evaluate your particular situation, risk tolerance, and objectives.

NOTE

For simplicity's sake in these hypothetical scenarios, I only show stocks and bonds in the portfolios. However, use your discretion when creating your own asset allocation. Any stock or bond position can be replaced with a similar asset in a lower proportion. For example, if you determine your allocation should be 60 percent stocks and 40 percent bonds, you can be more detailed in your asset allocation by deciding what you will hold within that 60/40 allocation. See the following example in figure 26.

%	ASSET CLASS	
15%	US Large-Cap Stocks	**60% STOCKS** (High Risk)
10%	US Mid-Cap Stocks	
10%	US Small-Cap Stocks	
12%	International Developed Stocks	
3%	Emerging Stocks	
8%	REITs	
2%	Bitcoin	
30%	Short- & Mid-Term High-Quality Bonds	**40% BONDS** (Low Risk)
10%	Long-Term High-Quality Bonds	

GRAPHIC

fig. 26

A basic portfolio asset allocation.

Disclaimer: This is for informational purposes only. Your asset allocation will differ based on your goals, time horizon, and risk tolerance.

Couple in Late Twenties with an Aggressive Risk Tolerance

Jim and Steph are a couple in their twenties with an aggressive risk tolerance for investing. They have three clearly defined goals: 1) buy a house in three years, 2) pay college tuition for their two children in twelve and fifteen years' time, and 3) retire in thirty years. Here is how they should allocate their assets, given their time horizons and goals:

» Buy a house in three years: 100 percent cash and short-term bonds
» Pay for kids' college in twelve to fifteen years: 80 percent stocks, 20 percent bonds
» Fund retirement in thirty years: 100 percent stock

Couple in Late Twenties with a Conservative Risk Tolerance

Let's assume a similar couple—Tom and Rita—are in their twenties, but they have a more conservative risk tolerance. Even though their goals are identical, their asset allocation will be less risky. Additionally, Tom and Rita will need to save more money than Jim and Steph to make up for the lower expected performance of their investments.

» Buy a house in three years: 100 percent cash and short-term bonds
» Pay for kids' college in twelve to fifteen years: 40 percent stocks, 60 percent bonds
» Fund retirement in thirty years: 60 percent stocks, 40 percent bonds

Couple in Late Fifties Planning to Retire in Ten Years

Henry and Rachel are in their fifties and their focus is building up additional savings and wealth to fund a comfortable retirement. They would also like to contribute annually over the next five years to the health care costs of their aging parents, both of whom are in their eighties. Finally, they want to update their outdated kitchen in two years' time. Each month they put 20 percent of their money into savings.

Assuming they have an aggressive risk tolerance:
» One to five years, health care for aging parents: 100 percent cash and short-term bonds
» Two years, kitchen renovation: 100 percent cash and short-term bonds
» Thirty to forty years, all other assets: 75 percent stocks, 25 percent bonds

Let's say Henry and Rachel have a more conservative risk tolerance:
» One to five years, health care for aging parents: 100 percent cash and short-term bonds
» Two years, kitchen renovation: 100 percent cash and short-term bonds
» Thirty to forty years, all other assets: 60 percent stocks, 40 percent bonds

Given their lower risk tolerance, why are we still so aggressive with the rest of their assets earmarked for retirement? Henry and Rachel are still young. They may live another thirty-plus years. The period known as retirement is a long time horizon, even if funds are being distributed regularly. We must protect them against inflation.

Couple in Late Fifties Planning to Retire in Ten Years, Aggressive Risk Tolerance and Trip Plans

One day Henry and Rachel decide that, in ten years, they want to take a three-month trip and see the world. The couple estimates that their budget for this adventure will be $75,000. While they may want to be more aggressive, we want to make sure they don't have to take a one-month trip instead of a three-month trip! As the time for the trip gets closer, we will decrease the amount of stock in the travel budget until we're at 100 percent cash and short-term bonds.

» Health care for aging parents: 100 percent cash and short-term bonds
» Kitchen renovation: 100 percent cash and short-term bonds
» Travel budget: 50 percent stocks, 50 percent bonds
» All other assets: 75 percent stocks, 25 percent bonds

Single Mom in Her Forties with Two Kids

Penelope is a single mom and has many responsibilities. In addition to putting food on the table for her two children, aged seven and ten, she wants to financially assist her aging parents, who are in their seventies. Penelope has an aggressive tolerance for risk. Her two children will presumably enter college eight and eleven years in the future. Her parents will need to go into assisted living in five to fifteen years, depending on their health.

» Eight to eleven years for college tuition: 75 percent stocks, 25 percent bonds
» Five to fifteen years for parents, depending on health: 50 percent stocks, 50 percent bonds
» Twenty to fifty years of retirement: 100 percent stocks

Here's what Penelope's portfolio might look like if she had a more conservative risk tolerance:
» Eight to eleven years for college tuition: 40 percent stocks, 60 percent bonds
» Five to fifteen years for parents, depending on health: 30 percent stocks, 70 percent bonds
» Twenty to fifty years of retirement: 60 percent stocks, 40 percent bonds

Widow in Her Seventies

Mildred wants to leave the bulk of her estate to her two adult children. She has enough income, thanks to Social Security and personal investments, to cover her living expenses, but she wants to tap into her portfolio occasionally to visit her children and grandchildren who live out of state.

If Mildred is aggressive, she might put the money for her adult children in funds that invest 100 percent in stocks.

» Ten to thirty years of retirement: 70 percent stocks, 30 percent bonds
» Ten-plus years for inheritance: 100 percent stock
» Visiting grandkids now: cash and short-term bonds

Here's what Mildred's portfolio might look like were she more conservative-minded:

» Ten to thirty years of retirement: 30 percent stocks, 70 percent bonds
» Ten-plus years for inheritance: 60 percent stocks, 40 percent bonds
» Visiting grandkids now: cash and short-term bonds

ON YOUR OWN

Set three financial goals and objectives and think about the asset allocation that best matches the time horizon of each goal as well as your tolerance for risk.

#12

Monitoring, Adjusting, and Rebalancing

My hope is that after digesting the section on how to build your portfolio, you will start contributing regularly to your investments. Your initial asset allocation becomes a "set it and forget it" endeavor. However, markets move. Goals change. Even risk tolerances change; you may become much more confident and comfortable in your ability to invest and therefore feel willing to take on more risk. As such, you may need to adjust your overall asset allocation or rebalance the investments back to their original percentage values.

You may be thinking, Are you kidding me, Morgen? I did all this work and now I have to monitor, adjust, and rebalance my portfolio?! Yes, I'm sorry. Unfortunately, building wealth and securing income from investments takes time and effort. However, hopefully you chose the passive, diversified index route, in which you will have much less to do than an active manager would. Yet another reason to be passive!

Monitoring

Monitor infrequently. During a crisis, don't look at all. The custodian Fidelity once did an audit on which accounts performed the best at their institution. Guess what they found? The accounts of the deceased or inactive performed the best. Play dead and don't look at your portfolio.

Adjusting

Only adjust your overall asset allocation when your goals, risk tolerance, or time horizon has changed. For example, you want to buy a house in ten years, so you chose a 50-50 stock-bond portfolio. But when you're three to five years away from the home purchase, it's time to adjust the allocation. You either move all the stocks into bonds or all future contributions to your savings plan go into cash and short-term bonds. By three years out, you should be 100 percent in cash and short-term bonds, no matter your risk tolerance.

Rebalancing

Rebalancing is also something you should do infrequently. I don't like rebalancing. It takes time. It costs money in transaction fees and taxes. Taxes and fees cause a drag on performance. I rebalance infrequently and only when the asset allocation moves well beyond the individual's tolerance for risk. The following are a couple of strategies for rebalancing:

1. **Calendar rebalancing**: You choose a set point in time (monthly, quarterly, or annually) when you will rebalance your portfolio back to its initial weights. You rebalance consistently. For example, say you choose to rebalance monthly. On the 8th of every month you rebalance back to your initial asset allocation. The advantage of rebalancing more often is that you're more likely to catch sudden market drifts that will be good rebalancing points. The disadvantage is that you incur taxes and transaction costs along the way, and you're likely cutting positions that are performing well and rotating into underperformers.

2. **Tolerance band rebalancing**: You choose a range, going outside of which triggers a rebalance. For example, you decide to hold 60 percent stocks and 40 percent bonds. You will tolerate a 10 percent change in position, which is a range of 54 to 66 percent stocks and 36 to 44 percent bonds. If your stocks or bonds go outside these ranges, you rebalance back to your initial positions. The advantage here is you will not rebalance as often, and you will also likely catch sudden market movements. The disadvantage is you will need to check your portfolio regularly to see if your positions have moved enough to warrant rebalancing.

That's it, folks! Now you can invest like a pro!

Financial Planners

If you're struggling to focus on and create a plan to achieve your life's goals, you may decide to hire professional help. Before you decide to forgo any assistance and do it all yourself, consider the following points:

» Attempting to plan and invest on your own can be difficult, time-consuming, and emotionally draining at times.

» Our natural instincts cause us to hoard cash or invest at the worst possible times; we often need extraordinary discipline to counter these instincts.

» A professional can give you the perspective, knowledge, and feedback you need to succeed.

Here are a few reasons you might hire a personal finance professional:

» You would like to reduce complexity and get answers that are personally relevant to your life.

» You need help taking action and want an accountability partner.

» You want to offload things that you find unpleasant, like doing your taxes or investing your money.

» You want to save time.

» It puts your spouse at ease to have someone else keeping an eye on things. And, in the event something happens to you, your spouse will be able to rely on a trusted party to help sort through financial matters.

» You would like to increase confidence in the financial decisions you make (generally, people who are more confident in their decisions have better results and do not spend time second-guessing).

» You want encouragement. Who doesn't like airing out a new investment idea and hearing a *heck yeah* every now and then?

» You would like to feel a sense of security and safety regarding your finances.

» You want help evaluating trade-offs and key decision points.

» And finally, you want to have someone to blame if it doesn't work out!

If you're going to hire a professional, there are a few types to choose from:
» A retail broker
» An independent advisor
» An independent, fee-only advisor

NOTE

Regardless of whether you choose to work with a broker or a fee-only advisor, make sure the person has a CERTIFIED FINANCIAL PLANNER™ certification. CFP® professionals have met training and experience requirements, including passing a series of rigorous exams, achieving a level of industry experience, and committing to a set of comprehensive ethical standards.

If the person is not an independent fee-only advisor, they can sell you products and will not be able to put your interests first. That's just how it is. They can call themselves a financial planner. They can even have CFP® marks. But if they're not a fee-only fiduciary, they have inherent conflicts between their interests and yours. A broker's duty is first to his firm, not to you. The advice they give you is incidental to the main business of generating commissions and trades. Likewise, an independent advisor who is not fee-only can sell you products for an additional commission. Here are a few key points to remember:

» Your broker's compensation increases in direct proportion to your trading activity. They have an incentive for you to buy and sell, in and out of various investment vehicles, thereby generating more commissions and fees.

» Your broker or advisor earns extra compensation for selling you certain investment or insurance products.

» Your broker is limited to selling you investment products approved by their firm.

I am a fee-only *fiduciary* and do not earn any money from commissions. I started my firm so I could be free to work with clients in objective pursuit of their best interests, with the least amount of conflict. I am legally obligated to put my clients' interests first, ahead of my own and my company's interests. I also do this because I love my clients and treat them like family!

You can go to a financial planner for guidance on pretty much any financial matter that is going on with you and your family. They will help you plan, save, and invest. They will also provide guidance on how to best pursue and achieve your financial aspirations. Who better to talk to about your hopes and dreams than someone who can make the money work?

Most of my discussions with clients initially center on their financial stress. Some have avoided confronting the reality of their financial situations, causing unease and lack of control. Some confront the necessity of change, and their stress stems from their anxiety and doubt—will they be able to create a long-term comprehensive plan and stick to it? Others inherit money without any knowledge of how to protect or grow it.

I have had clients so stressed about making the right investment decisions that they keep their cash deteriorating under the mattress. Other clients worry about their own or their family members' constant overspending.

But perhaps the most common source of stress I encounter in my practice is that experienced by those who are so busy they have no time to think about their finances at all, at least not in any long-term strategic sense.

More than anything else, I find my clients need a trusted advisor to help them focus, so they can take care of things one step at a time as they strive for control of their finances. That, to me, is the job of a financial planner—to help you prioritize what is important to you and create a plan to live your most fulfilled life.

We have emphasized this concept of your most fulfilled life throughout this book. Knowing who you are at your core and what you want to accomplish is crucial to your financial success. Humanizing personal finance was pioneered by George Kinder, the father of financial life planning. Kinder created the Registered Life Planning Program, which comprises a study of his book, *The Seven Stages of Money Maturity*, and a five-day intensive empathetic listening course. This, along with a six-month mentorship program, ensures all life planners can deliver a transformational experience for their clients. Working with a Registered Life Planner® is a great way to further your quest for financial freedom. A life planner learns about you and creates a vision of your most wanted future. They will encourage you to prioritize what is most important to you. They will support you as you thwart obstacles that arise. A Registered Life Planner® combines empathetic listening, coaching, and financial knowledge to help you achieve your most precious dreams.

Choosing a planner is more art than science. Financial planners come in all shapes and sizes, each with their own philosophies and techniques.

Interview as many as you need to before you find the one that feels right to you. Remember, the goal is to find someone who can help you create a great plan, one you will understand and be able to execute.

If you decide to work with a planner, pay attention to how you feel as you work through your sessions. You should feel like progress is being made. You should feel like you trust them. They should accommodate your needs and personality. You should feel more in control of your finances and less stressed about money.

Chapter Recap

» Asset allocation is the process of positioning a portfolio among different financial instruments depending on the individual's investment time frame and risk tolerance.

» Diversification is extremely important.

» Employee stock options are complicated and need to be considered within the context of your overall asset allocation.

» Financial advisors provide expertise and perspective, but at a cost. They can also help you be more objective (and successful) by insulating you from your emotions.

» CERTIFIED FINANCIAL PLANNERS™ CFPs® have passed a series of exams and are required to have a certain level of industry experience to earn the designation.

» Know whether your advisor, agent, or broker is fee-only or earns money through commissions.

SOLVING EVERYDAY CHALLENGES

PART II

SPELLING EVERYDAY CHALLENGES

| 8 |
Managing Debt

Chapter Overview
- » Good Debt and Bad Debt
- » Special Student Loan Programs
- » How to Assess Your Debt
- » Debt Reduction and Payoff Strategies

What can be added to the happiness of a man who is in health, out of debt, and has a clear conscience?

— ADAM SMITH

What is debt? In the financial world, debt is money owed to a lender from a borrower. It is everywhere around us—from the multibillion-dollar corporation issuing bonds to fund operations, to the 18-year-old that applies for his first credit card after landing a job at Hot Dog on a Stick at the county mall.

Debt often helps us achieve our most precious life goals. With debt, we can grow a business, improve our skills, or buy a home. We can live our most fulfilled lives by using debt as a tool to get us there.

Unfortunately, debt can also lead to an unfulfilling, stressful existence if you take on more than you can afford. When you look around, it seems normal to be either in debt or surrounded by those in debt. But is it normal? It is fine to want a house or a college degree. However, using debt to live beyond your means is crazy!

Debt is like investing, in reverse. Just as compound interest helps you build wealth dynamically, compound interest on debt deteriorates your wealth rather quickly. For example, if you borrow $10,000 at a 10 percent interest rate and agree to pay the money back with interest in a lump sum in thirty years, you are going to owe $191,943.42!

I liken debt to nail polish remover. It works great to take off polish, but too much will damage your fingernails permanently. Likewise, sometimes you need a little debt, but don't dump out the whole container of acetone all at once. When it comes to including debt in your plan, it is ultra-important to examine a) what aspects of your life are worth financing, and b) what interest rates are acceptable to you and your financial well-being.

Credit Scores

Building up good credit is one of the most important factors of personal finance. If you recall our discussion in chapter 3 on budgeting, it is your large fixed expenses that have the deepest impact on your overall budget and ability to grow wealth. This portion of your budget is often financed (think car, education, home). Financed purchases come with an interest rate. You will get the best possible interest rate in the current economic environment by building up good credit and having a high credit score. This will save you many, many dollars in interest.

Interest is an expense, often a necessary one. But unlike other household expenses, no one ever puts paying interest in their "must have, can't live without" column of their budget. Do what you must to have the best possible credit score and pay the least amount of interest on your big-ticket items. Here is how to build a good credit score (figure 27):

» Reliably pay off your credit cards and other debts; 35 percent of your credit score is based on your payment history.

» Use less credit than you are given; 30 percent of your credit score is based on how much you owe relative to how much you can borrow, known as your *credit utilization rate*.

» Have a long credit history; 15 percent of your score is based on how long you've been using credit. If you have just started out, there's not much you can do to improve this metric other than wait. If you've been using credit cards for a while, keep your cards with the longest histories open. And better yet, if you have teenage kids, add them to your credit card account so you can help them build credit early (more on kids and money in chapter 13).

» Rely less on new credit; 10 percent of your score is based on the number of loans you have. Too many new loans can drag down your credit score.

> » Have multiple types of credit, without turning into a debt fireball; 10 percent of your score is based on how varied your debt is. For example, lenders like to see that you can pay back both your credit card and your student loans at the same time.

BOOSTING YOUR CREDIT SCORE

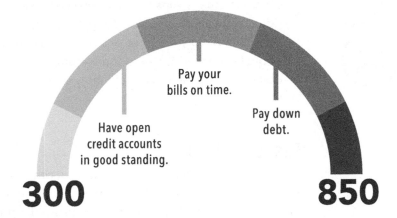

Pay your bills on time.

Pay down debt.

Have open credit accounts in good standing.

300   850

GRAPHIC

fig. 27

NOTE

Sixty-five percent of your total credit score is completely within your control. Pay your bills on time! Just do it! Set it on autopay! Additionally, you can make micro-payments on your credit cards to keep your utilization rate lower. You do this by paying your credit card bill more often than once per month. Ideally, you pay the full balance at the end of the month, as well. This is a good way to lower overall credit utilization for the purpose of improving your score. You can also ask for a credit limit increase, while keeping your spending the same. However, don't spend more just because they will lend you more.

These are great ways to significantly influence the 65 percent of your score that is under your control. The remaining 35 percent will come in time. Focus on what you can do right now.

Credit reporting agencies (CRAs) or credit bureaus collect all this information about you and your borrowing history and assign you a credit score somewhere between 300 and 850. Lenders pull your credit report and look at your score, along with your salary information and account values. They then decide whether they want to lend to you and at what interest rate. A higher credit score means a lower interest rate.

Your credit score does not reflect who you are or your value. I know you will make many good financial decisions in your lifetime that will not be tracked or measured by a credit rating agency and thus will not show up on your credit score. For example, do you return the favor when a friend picks up the check? Not tracked. When you moved in with your boyfriend and paid him half the rent every month, that wasn't tracked either. Putting away funds for retirement? Not tracked. Are you a genuinely good person who wants to pay off your debt? Also not tracked.

Slow and steady wins the race, and consistency is key. You will not get a credit score of 800 overnight. You must focus on what you can control to build your score over time. You can shout to the heavens about how unfair or stupid the system is. I'm with you! But don't obsess or lose sleep over it. Simply do what you must to build and keep a good score.

Reasonable Debt

Campfires are great. You can heat up a can of soup, roast marshmallows, or just hang out and tell ghost stories. The campfire provides warmth on a cold summer night. When you're done using the fire, you throw a bucket of water on it or you let it burn out on its own. Campfires are controlled fires. Conversely, wildfires burn uncontrollably. They damage property and make it difficult for us to breathe. To extinguish them, copious resources are brought to bear, like helicopters, trucks, and countless brave men and women. The cost of preventing a wildfire is nothing compared to that of containing one already set ablaze.

Fires are much like debt. Reasonable debt you want. It helps you achieve your most fulfilled life. You pay it off on a set schedule or throw a little extra its way when you have the means to do so. Both the interest rate and the amount of the debt are manageable. Conversely, *slippery-slope debt*—the kind that grows and seems to build upon itself like a snowball from hell—is unwanted. It deteriorates quality of life. It damages your credit over time. It causes fear and anxiety. It is difficult to repay due to the sheer size of the balance, the high interest rate, or both.

Any debt can be considered reasonable if it is not beyond your means to repay it and is used to improve your standard of living, increase income, or accomplish a short-term objective.

Student Loans

We make one of our single most important financial decisions as seventeen-year-olds: college. When I think back to my life at age seventeen, I cared about prom and hanging with my friends, neither of which was a particularly forward-looking endeavor.

Asking teenagers to plan for their future is a big ask. They're not neurologically wired for that kind of thing. Nevertheless, planning before college is vital. As a teenager, it is so important to think about the results you want to have from your college education. As parents, it is our job to guide our children through this decision, without trying to live vicariously through them. Furthermore, we must make the finances clear to our child. They will have difficulty understanding the long-term ramifications of the big decisions they are making in the short term. It is our job to either help them or find someone who can.

According to the College Board, in 2017, the average senior graduated with $32,600 in student loan debt. At a 5.3 percent interest rate, that's an expense of $350 per month for ten years, or $42,000. While this loan may be justified, the problem is that payments on student loans gobble up a good percentage of the graduate's starting wages. Worse, some cannot find jobs at all, and loan payments are typically due within six months of their graduation date. Additionally, interest has accrued throughout their school years.

Consider this: a newly minted graduate gets a job paying $50,000 per year. He needs a car to get to work. He also wants to save for an eventual wedding with his longtime girlfriend, pay off his student loan debt, buy a house, and save for retirement. Here's where his money goes (figure 28):

fig. 28

CATEGORY	AMOUNT
Taxes	$8,200
Healthy Savings	$8,300
Student Loans	$4,200
Rent	$15,000
Utilities	$800
Cell Phone	$800
Groceries and Household Items	$4,200
Car, Gas, and Insurance	$4,500
TOTAL	**$46,000**

With this minimal budget, our graduate only has $4,000 per year (or $333 per month) left over for everything else. If this recent grad spends $100 a week on going out to dinner and drinks with friends, he will save only 6 percent of his income instead of 20 percent. If he decides to take a vacation, he will have no savings left. If he buys random stuff on Amazon, he will rack up credit card debt.

We all occasionally want a night out, some new clothes, a new computer or phone, or a vacation. With conscious spending, it is doable; however, you can easily see why a recent grad would save less than 20 percent of after-tax income or, worse, accumulate additional debt after school.

The question to ask before borrowing heavily to pay for an education is whether the degree adds enough value to justify the loan amount. That is, what will my starting salary be like, and will my income increase enough to pay the loan off in a reasonable time?

For example, I worked with a psychologist who amassed $280,000 in debt to pursue his degree. He was a bit disappointed to find out that starting salaries in his area were around $90,000. However, it was his life's dream to become a psychologist. When you are deciding whether to go to school, you need to evaluate the trade-off between a profession that would make you truly happy and the potential debt you may amass to achieve it.

Ideally, the student loan amount should roughly match or be less than the expected salary of the first few years. So, if your student loan is $150,000 (and your interest rate is around 5 percent), then you should be pursuing a career that pays at least $150,000 per year.

NOTE

The Washington Post offers a handy calculator for comparing student loan balances, repayment schedules, and expected salary. It's simple: enter your student loan balance, loan term, and interest rate, and then you can see how your debt compares to the expected income of your chosen profession. The link to this and a multitude of other fantastic resources are catalogued in your Digital Assets at go.quickstartguides.com/personalfinance.

If your expected salary is equal to the amount of the loan, then 10 percent of your income will go toward paying off your loan under the standard term of ten years. Ten percent or less is an ideal scenario. It frees up cash for other important savings goals, such as retirement account contributions.

Through the power of compounding, money set aside for retirement in your twenties has astounding potential for growth over time. Don't let debt rob you or your children of this opportunity.

There are student loan programs that will decrease the payments to 10 percent of income but will increase the term. Some programs may also offer forgiveness. This is when the lender releases the borrower from repaying all or part of the money owed. Forgiveness may sound nice on its face, but depending on the program, you could be looking at a very long payoff period, well over ten years, and you may also incur a significant tax liability. The IRS considers your forgiven loan balance to be taxable income in the year the loan is forgiven.

There are many different student loan repayment programs with lots of rules. We will discuss income-driven repayment programs and public service loan forgiveness (PSLF). If you have additional questions about your specific loans, I highly recommend reaching out to a planner with the CSLP® (Certified Student Loan Professional) designation.

Public Service Loan Forgiveness Program (PSLF)

Public service loan forgiveness is earned by doing the following:

» You must work full time for a US federal, state, local, or tribal government or for a not-for-profit organization.

» You must have federal direct loans or consolidate your loans into a federal direct loan (that is, you must consolidate those FFEL or Perkins loans, or you won't get forgiveness).

» You must enter an income-driven repayment program.

» You must make 120 qualifying payments after points 1–3 are achieved.

If you do all four of the above, then you will get full loan forgiveness (minus the 120 payments you make) without any tax bill. If you miss any of the above points, you will not get forgiveness. Recently, I saw a news article about how many borrowers were rejected from the PSLF program. Almost all the rejections were because the borrowers did not have federal direct loans or they were not in an income-driven repayment program. It may seem ridiculous, but these are the rules.

If you want to work for a government or nonprofit and you have student loans, this is the program for you. I do not recommend working at one of these institutions solely for loan forgiveness. Rather than working somewhere you don't like, instead focus on changing your spending habits or generating more income.

Income-Driven Repayment Programs

Income-driven repayment plans help lower your monthly student loan payment. The program evaluates the income you make per year and lowers your payments accordingly. These programs extend the life of your loan from ten years to twenty or twenty-five years, depending on the program. They also promise loan forgiveness at the end of the loan's term, at which point any remaining balance will be wiped off the slate. Loan forgiveness will, however, come with a tax bill on the following April 15th. Despite the taxes, sometimes this can be a great option.

For example, Gerald recently graduated from his master's program with $125,000 in student loans. He finds a job making $75,000 per year. Under a standard ten-year payment plan, Gerald would need to pay $1,345 per month with an interest rate of 5.3 percent. Under an income-driven repayment program, he may pay $465 per month and much of his loan balance will be forgiven (if his income doesn't drastically increase). This frees up $880 per month for Gerald to save for his forgiveness tax bill, plus any other life goals he wants to fund. At the end of twenty or twenty-five years, roughly $100,000 of his loan will be forgiven. He'll owe around $30,000 in taxes.

Over the life of the loan, Gerald will in fact make $111,600 in loan payments and then also pay $30,000 in taxes. He will pay $141,600 in total, which puts his annual interest rate at 0.66 percent (super low!). Additionally, along the way Gerald will be able to save for retirement, for a home, or for any other goal he wants to fund with the money that didn't go toward his student loan payments.

Income-driven repayment programs are best when PSLF is not an option for you, and when you choose a profession with much lower long-term expected income than your loans allow you to afford—the teaching profession comes to mind. If you expect your income to increase significantly over the life of your career, then income-driven repayment programs will likely not end in any loan forgiveness. That said, if you start your career with a low salary and you can't afford anything else, then an income-driven repayment program may be your only option. Just know that your interest is compounding on interest (like a mega-compound!) while you make these reduced debt payments. It will make paying back the loan much more difficult later.

Advantages of Federal Debt Over Private Debt

I am often asked whether a student loan borrower should refinance their loans through a bank or a company like SoFi. It depends!

There are advantages to having a federal student loan. If you fall on hard times, federal loans allow for three years of deferment while you get your life back on track. You have access to loan forgiveness programs with federal loans. Your credit does not have to be as good as it would to secure low interest rates through private lenders. Federal loans also have forgiveness provisions for any of the following scenarios:

- » The borrower becomes disabled
- » The borrower dies
- » The school closes during the time of study
- » Identity theft was used to obtain the loan
- » Loan documents were falsified by the school

Refinancing privately makes sense when you have both good credit and stable, high income. This will allow you to pay off your debt much more quickly and move on with your life.

MY TAKE

Pursuing your dream career is admirable and inspiring, but sometimes the math forces you to acknowledge that your pursuit is not practical. And for some, practicality be damned, you're going to go after your heart's desire, even if it means slogging down a tough financial road. Then again, you may opt for the job that promises the larger salary. A big part of your most fulfilled life may be financial comfort. There are always trade-offs. The challenge posed by these crucial decisions is compounded by the fact that we are asked to chart our professional course at a very young age. I highly recommend taking a year off between high school and college. If nothing else, you'll get some life experience under your belt before you commit to taking on significant levels of student debt.

Mortgage

A *mortgage* is a loan taken to purchase a home. For most, this is the largest debt they will have. I'm all for buying a home that you love and want to live in for a long time. That said, do not confuse your home purchase with an investment. It is not. Your home is a consumption item, like everything else you use regularly.

I'm going to cover this topic in greater detail in chapter 9. A complete discussion about the different types of mortgages—and the pros and cons of buying versus renting—will be presented in chapter 9 as well.

A mortgage carries an interest rate and a term. For example, a $240,000 thirty-year mortgage with a fixed 4 percent rate would have a monthly payment of $1,500. In the early years of a mortgage, these monthly payments cover mostly the interest on the loan. For example, $1,400 of the $1,500 monthly payment may go toward the interest, whereas only $100 pays down the *principal*. As time passes, a greater percentage of each payment applies to the principal. By the end of the loan term, $1,400 may go toward paying down the principal, with only $100 going to pay the interest expense.

The specific ratios of interest versus principal allocations in each loan payment change over time; usually each successive payment on the loan allocates a bit more to the principal and a bit less to the interest. These precise allocations over the entire term of the loan are disclosed in the loan's *amortization schedule*, which the borrower receives from the lender. We will talk about the amortization schedule in chapter 9.

Amortization schedules apply to any loans where equal payments are made over a set period. Student loans, loans for equipment or property, and several other loan types are all defined by schedules where borrowers pay more interest per payment at the start of the loan and more principal per payment toward the end of the loan.

The monthly mortgage payment is not the only cost associated with owning a home. All the monthly expenses for your home, added together, should amount to no more than 20 percent of your pretax income. In addition to any maintenance, repairs, and improvements, homeowners must consider the following:

- » **Insurance:** Mortgage companies will require you to carry homeowners insurance. The monthly premiums are often included in the mortgage payment and held in an escrow account until the insurance policy is up for renewal. The costs vary depending on your home's location. If you live in an area prone to natural disasters like hurricanes or flooding, be prepared to pay a bit more.

- » **Property Taxes:** These are usually paid once per year, and the amount will vary depending on where you live and the value of the property. Property taxes can be added to your monthly mortgage payment and held in an escrow account until the bill is due.

- » **Homeowners Association (HOA) Fees:** The more amenities in your community (pools, landscaping, clubhouses), the higher the HOA fees. Some areas have no HOAs, while others have robust and active HOAs that cover things like internet service and snow removal.

Unless your only goal is to own a house at the high end of what you can afford, you should not spend what the bank will lend you. The bank will gladly lend you more, but it is your responsibility to borrow less, so you can achieve all the goals you listed in chapter 1. Therefore, if your combined annual household income is $100,000 ($8,333 per month), no more than $1,667 per month should go toward your monthly mortgage and other home-related expenses.

Car Loans

Cars are often a necessary fact of life. If you need to get around, you often need to own a vehicle. Because a car is a large purchase, it is usually financed.

There are a few issues with car loans. First, they tend to have high interest rates. Second, purchasers of cars tend to get longer loan terms to make the vehicle of choice more affordable. Third, as soon as you drive your new car off the lot, you are "underwater" on your loan. This is because your new car rapidly depreciates in value. All of these factors put car loans on the very edge of reasonable debt.

How do you get around this?

» **Buy Used Vehicles:** This will shave a lot off the sticker price and save you thousands of dollars.

» **Don't Stretch:** Keep your car expenses under 5 percent of total income.

» **Go for Lower Annual Percentage Rates (APRs):** You may end up with a shorter term and therefore a higher payment, but it will be financially sound over the long run.

» **Refinance:** If you already have a high-interest car loan and good credit, it may be a good time to refinance.

» **Sell:** If you are having trouble making ends meet, it may be time to sell your car and buy a cheaper one.

Business Loans

Leveraging a business loan, a line of credit, or a credit card is reasonable when your business has a legitimate investment opportunity. When evaluating a business loan, be sure to consider your payment requirements in relation to the anticipated proceeds from the business. For example, if your business sells electric bikes that require some tools and equipment to assemble and you need a loan to acquire this equipment, then you must calculate the number of bikes you'll need to sell in order to repay the loan *and* make a profit. We will talk a lot more about business planning and loans in chapter 14.

Slippery-Slope Debt

Debts with high interest rates are extremely difficult to pay off, due to compounding interest. At the end of 2019, total consumer debt was nearly $14 trillion. The average American household had more than $8,200 in credit card debt and $137,000 in total debt, according to Debt.org. The following categories of debt are ones that I consider to be "slippery slopes." As you take your first steps toward accumulating these kinds of debt, it often hampers your future decisions, making it easier to take on more and more debt.

Credit Cards

In some ways credit cards are like manna from heaven. You don't have to go to the bank to get cash. You have a little plastic card in your pocket that you can simply swipe, or enter the digits onto a web page, whenever you want something. Better yet, you can have completely frictionless payments by allowing a store you trust to keep your digits on file. The credit card company even gives you a nice short-term zero percent loan on your purchases if you pay off your balance at the end of each month. You can keep track of all your spending by importing the transactions into software or downloading them into an Excel spreadsheet. Plus, they offer you perks, like cash back.

Based on this, credit cards should be your best friend, right? Wrong. Credit cards have some downsides too. Miss a payment? Get ready to get hit with late fees and interest. Spend more than you earn? Too bad, pay it off over time with punitive interest rates. Someone steals your identity, opens credit cards and racks up debt in your name? While you may have limited liability, generally your credit score will get ruined, and it can take many years to repair the damage.

The main problem with most credit card debt is that, while monthly minimum payments are relatively low, the interest rates charged are often exorbitant. In early 2020, the average annual percentage rate on credit cards was roughly 17 percent. Compare that to the average rate on a savings account at a bank of just .1 percent!

While it may seem enticing to pay only the minimum payment due on your credit card, it is destructive for your overall financial health not to pay your balance in full. Ignore the "minimum payment." It's a scam. Pay your balance in full.

Here are the best practices for responsible credit card use:

1. **Use a credit card if and only if you can pay your entire balance every month. This is literally the most important rule of credit cards. If you can't follow this rule, then no credit card for you!**

2. Take precautions with your personal information and your credit card numbers. Don't save them on shopping websites just because it's convenient. Don't email sensitive information.

3. Line up your credit card payment due dates with your pay schedule.

4. If you miss a payment once or twice, call the credit card company. Ask them to reimburse your late fee because you're usually so good at paying on time. Also ask them to make sure it doesn't hit your credit report.

5. Negotiate a lower APR (interest rate) if you are currently paying off credit card debt. It doesn't always work, but it never hurts to ask. The best way to do this is to ask after you've paid more than the minimum balance for a few months.

6. Ask your credit card company to switch you to a card that doesn't have an annual fee. Unless you travel a lot or are using a card for business purchases, it doesn't make sense to have an expensive annual fee. There are plenty of no-fee credit cards out there offering good perks.

7. If you don't have any ongoing credit card debt, ask for a credit limit increase to lower your credit utilization rate.

8. Compare cards online, but don't open so many of them. I have a business card, a personal card, and a family credit card, and I honestly find it annoying to check even those three statements regularly. I can't imagine having more than that. Less is more.

9. Stick with cards whose benefits you understand.

10. Ignore all mailings inviting you to open new credit cards.

11. Stop doing the zero percent introductory transfer of balances. Unless you're going to pay back your debt in the next six months, you're kicking the can down the road.

12. Stop getting so excited about points and cash back. Honestly, how excited would you be if you went to a store and they told you that you could pay $99 instead of $100 if you used cash? That is the equivalent of cash back on your credit card. No one gets rich from their credit card rewards. Manage your cash flow and invest the difference—that is how you'll become wealthy.

You may be asking, but what if I am already in credit card debt? Keep reading! We have tips for you later in this chapter in the section called "Getting Out of Debt."

Personal Loans

Imagine you want a big, uproarious, expensive wedding. Unfortunately, your parents don't have the money to help you. And your future spouse has no savings. Heck, you barely have any savings yourself. But this is your life's dream! So, you decide to take out a personal loan, because you can get a lower interest rate than on your credit card.

Kudos to you for considering a personal loan over credit card debt. However, what results will you achieve by starting the next phase of your life with a hefty load of debt? Perhaps fights with your new beloved are on the horizon. Recent research from TD Bank shows that one out of every three couples fights about money. I'd hate for that to be you!

Personal loans are used for more than weddings. I often see them used to repay medical debts, take on home improvement projects, fund a vacation, or provide financing for consumer purchases.

The problem with this type of debt is that you're living beyond your means. You're establishing a pattern of wanting things you cannot afford and then using debt to get them. It completely erodes your ability to make behavior changes and build wealth. I highly recommend considering the ramifications of your purchases before taking on any personal loans.

IRS Debt

Owing money to the Internal Revenue Service is a common problem. Each year, Americans file tax returns and some owe money because they did not pay enough throughout the course of the year. The IRS requires that taxes be paid in full by April 15 and, if not, they charge penalties and interest. In addition, if you do not pay in at least 90 percent of what you owe prior to filing your taxes, the IRS will charge a penalty.

If an outstanding balance is not paid, and the individual does not have the funds to pay it, then the IRS typically allows that person to set up a payment plan and make payments each month. The penalties and interest are added to the amount owed.

NOTE

The Internal Revenue Service offers payment plans without question for sums less than $50,000. If you owe more than $50,000, watch out—they will definitely come after you and your assets aggressively! Also, states are even less friendly than the IRS. Depending on where you live, your state may be quick to start garnishing wages if you do not pay on time.

As a rule, it makes a lot more sense to pay taxes on time and avoid any interest and penalties. Accumulating debt with the IRS is usually the result of poor planning and spending in excess of your after-tax earnings. If it is a recurring problem, it might be time to adjust the amount of money being withheld from your paycheck, start making estimated tax payments during the year, or consult a tax professional or planner.

How Much Is Too Much?

> *Don't let your mouth write no check that your tail can't cash.*
>
> – BO DIDDLEY

What would it be like to live without debt? Have you ever imagined it? My husband and I have a mortgage. We followed all my financial planning rules when we bought a house. We underbought on purpose to keep our home expenses under 20 percent of our income. Despite that, I still don't like paying my mortgage. It would be glorious to live without a mortgage! I can feel freedom and excitement when I think of owning my home outright.

Perhaps the debt you have is more substantial. Feel what it would be like to live without debt. What could possibly get in the way of that glorious vision?

Maybe it's your spending. Maybe it's your income. Maybe it's both. I challenge you to live in the vision of being debt-free. Feel all the good feelings. Then start addressing all the obstacles that stand in the way of realizing your vision.

Guidelines for Taking on Debt

Lenders use ratio analyses to determine whether they will lend to you. Here are the ones I like to review with my clients when I advise them on taking on debt:

» **Total Debt/Total Assets:** Your total debt divided by your total assets. This should not be more than 50 percent. If you have high-interest debts, you will want this to be as low as possible. With the ten-year US Government Treasury at under 1 percent as I write this, I consider anything over 6 percent to be high.

» **Savings Rate:** Your annual savings divided by your annual pretax income. Ideally, this number will be 20 percent or more, but at a minimum you should be saving 10 percent or putting it toward high-interest debt.

» **Net Savings:** Your income minus your spending will give you the dollar amount you have to pay off debts or save for goals.

» **Debt-to-income:** All monthly debt payments and housing costs divided by gross monthly income. A bank will give you a mortgage if this number is less than 36 percent. Fannie Mae and Freddie Mac will lend to you if it is below 45 percent. *I* think you should keep it below 25 percent. If you want to build wealth, the best way to do it is to manage large fixed expenses.

#13

Add up all your payments to debt each month: car loans, student loans, credit cards, second home loans, Vinnie the bookie in Brooklyn— all of it. To compute your debt-to-income ratio, simply divide your debts by your gross monthly income. For instance, if you have $2,000 in monthly debt payments ($1,400 mortgage, $400 auto loan, and $200 student loan) and a gross monthly income of $6,000, your debt-to-income ratio is $2,000 ÷ $6,000, or 33.3%.

Your interests are not aligned with those of the banks and credit card companies. They want to lend you money. It is how they make money. This is known as *fractional reserve banking*. The bank receives deposits from its savers. In turn, it can lend out ten times the amount of cash it holds. For example, if a bank has one million dollars in deposits, it can make ten million dollars' worth of loans. Banks charge a higher interest rate to their borrowers and pay a lower interest rate to their account holders; this is known as a *spread*. They also make money on loan origination fees, usually on a percentage basis, thus they want to lend you more than you need. It is your responsibility to say no. You, not the bank, need to decide on the optimal amount of debt for yourself.

Here is how to find the right amount of debt:

1. Calculate your income after taxes.
2. Add up your total amount of fixed expenses, including debts you have and new debts you want to take on.
3. Subtract number two from number one and see if the amount left over supports other spending and savings goals.

Melanie and Todd make $75,000 per year. They each pay $300 per month in student loans. They want to take on a home that will cost them $22,500 per year in mortgage, property taxes, and other associated home expenses. They know they spend $1,000 per month on groceries and $1,000 per month on other necessary expenses (like insurance, cell phones, utilities, car payments, etc.).

After-tax income: $63,500 ($5,292 per month)

Fixed expenses: $53,700 ($4,475 per month)

Net: $9,800 ($817 per month)

This means they have $9,800 left over for anything fun they want to do and for savings. Given that they should also be saving 20 percent of their income, this doesn't leave them anything for an occasional night out, a home improvement issue that may come up, a vacation, or anything else that might add fulfillment to their life.

Conclusion: $22,500 per year for a new mortgage is too much.

This is the key to a healthy relationship with debt. It's okay to have debt if you can afford it! I am not here to put a wet blanket over your fun. I am here to give you perspective and help you evaluate trade-offs.

Getting Out of Debt

At this point, you might be asking yourself, what if I already have too much debt? While there are no easy ways out, there are actionable steps that can get you on the right path. The important thing is to take action and work on it a little bit every day.

If you were trying to get stronger, putting yourself on an exercise program where you worked out two times a day, seven days a week, indefinitely, would eventually lead to a lack of adherence. Personal finance is very similar. If you cut *everything*, you're likely to slip back into old habits, because the new ones are just too hard.

Paying It Down

The first step is to budget; this was covered in detail in chapter 3. There is no way around it. Sit down and look at what you spend money on—see what happened in the past.

Revisit the exercise you completed in chapter 3 called Where Does Your Money Go? Did your spending (the things that you purchased) line up with your values? Is your spending helping you live your most fulfilled life?

I love a 50/30/20 budget for helping folks get out of debt. Obviously, you can pay your debt off with maximum speed if you can cut all your expenses, couch surf for a while, and eat everyone else's food. However, your quality of life will surely suffer in the process. The 50/30/20 budget breaks down how to allocate your income on an after-tax basis. It's a great tool for anyone, but especially if you're in debt.

Fifty percent of your income will go to essential needs like housing, groceries, and insurance. Thirty percent will go to things that improve your quality of life but are not necessarily needs. Examples include travel, dining out, and subscriptions. The remaining 20 percent is for savings, investment, and paying down debt (figure 29).

GRAPHIC

fig. 29

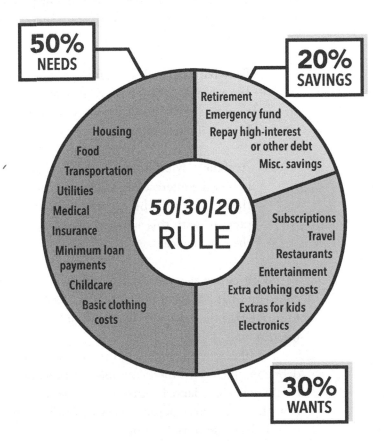

All percentages based on after-tax income

Sometimes it makes sense to use savings to pay down debt, particularly if your savings is not earning much interest. Before you make this move, you must consider how often you receive income, in order to make sure you have enough cash on hand. For example, if you are paid every three months, then don't take all three months of your savings and put it toward your debt. No matter how often you are paid, having at least one month's worth of emergency savings is essential.

A simple way to start paying down credit cards or other personal loans is to make more than the minimum payment each month. For example, start by doubling the minimum payment and, once you have done that successfully for a few months, see if you can triple it. There are a few other approaches to consider as well:

» **Snowball Method:** Pay off the entirety of your smallest debt first. For example, if you have three loans of $1,000, $3,000, and $5,000, then pay off the $1,000 debt first, no matter which one has the highest interest rate. The goal is to see measurable results quickly.

» **Avalanche Method:** Focus not on the balance of the credit card but on the interest rate. The goal is to pay as much as you can on the card with the highest interest rate. It may take longer to see progress with this approach, but from a financial perspective, it is the most logical.

With either the snowball or the avalanche method, you will want to calculate what 20 percent of your after-tax income is and put the full amount toward either the loan with the smallest balance or the loan with the highest interest rate.

Another way to tackle high-interest-rate credit card balances is through debt consolidation, which is simply the process of bundling multiple account balances into one large balance at the lowest rate possible. Debt consolidation is my least preferred method because, while it can help lower the interest rate on the debt, the consolidation does nothing to diminish the account balance and does not encourage you to change your behavior. Furthermore, it often comes with fees and extends the life of your debt, in which case you could be paying more than before!

Refinancing your home can also be a viable option to pay off debt. This is because you can get a much lower interest rate on your mortgage than on your credit card debt (or even a student loan debt). If you have equity in your home, you can do a cash-out refinance. If you don't have much equity in your home, you can do a rate refinance (if interest rates have declined) or a term refinance (where you extend the life of your mortgage). Like debt consolidation, this does not address any behavioral issues with respect to spending. It may also increase the amount of interest you pay. As such, refinancing must be combined with a 50/30/20 budget to ensure that you pay less interest and change your habits at the same time. We will discuss more about mortgage financing in the next chapter.

It may seem like tackling debt is insurmountable and that progress will be slow or painful. You may feel pleasantly surprised with the results you see after you make a commitment to right the ship. One positive change empowers and spurs on others; they build on one another, and the forward momentum persists. Remember, this change won't happen overnight. You didn't get into debt in one day. You won't be able to get out of debt in one day either. You're looking for general forward progress. It won't come in a straight line.

My son is two years old. I've watched him grow from a helpless little newborn into a crazy toddler that loves jumping in puddles, running across the lawn, and doing puzzles. The difference over the past two years is almost more than my heart can take. He has learned so much! Imagine who you can be ninety days, six months, or two years from now if you put your mind to it!

The less pleasant alternative you can choose is to take negative actions every day. You can continue to spend recklessly, ignore your financial position, and build negative momentum. Evaluate what you are doing wrong and what you are doing correctly, and make incremental changes a little at a time. Small efforts add up to big changes in the long run.

Here are some actionable steps you might consider right now as you begin (or continue) your quest to eradicate your debt:

>> Create a 50/30/20 budget.
>> Increase your income.
>> Work overtime.
>> Buy used items.
>> Accept hand-me-downs.

- » Sell things you don't need.
- » Stop spending on things that do not bring you real value.
- » Review Netflix, Hulu, and cable TV subscriptions.
- » Evaluate insurance deductibles and look for ways to save money on premiums.
- » Appreciate the things you have rather than shopping for new items you don't really need.
- » Downsize your home, your car, or any other large fixed expenses that are holding you back.

Dealing with Financial Crises

If you are really struggling or are already in financial crisis, I suggest you commit at least a few hours to rigorous introspection. Ask yourself (and answer) some tough questions. Why am I in financial crisis and what were all the steps that led me here?

Write down the answers that emerge. If you are feeling guilt or shame, allow yourself to have these emotions. Examine your thoughts as they come up, and let go of the negative ones as if you are letting a balloon float up to the sky. Forgive yourself (and, if married, forgive your spouse as well). We are all humans and we all make mistakes sometimes. There is no shame and no blame. Be focused on solutions rather than rehashing the past and dwelling on prior mistakes.

Now write down your new goals. What are two things you can do right now to get yourself closer to those goals? When can you do them? To whom will you be accountable? You're here because you spent more than you earned. Where can you cut spending? What would give you the most bang for your buck?

For example, selling a car and buying a cheaper (used) one is a very effective tactic to cut spending. Another idea is to move to a different house and/or location. Perhaps you committed to a too-expensive home. This does not mean you should sell your home at any price. However, it is time to number-crunch and see what makes the most sense in your situation.

Filing for **bankruptcy protection** is an option in worst-case scenarios, but if you go this route, then you will feel the repercussions. There are two types that people generally use: Chapter 7 and Chapter 13. Chapter 7 wipes out unsecured debts such as credit cards and medical bills without the need to pay back balances through a repayment plan. Chapter 13 is a reorganization of debt for those with higher income. It allows them to keep a lot of their belongings and get on a more affordable debt repayment program. A bankruptcy results in poor credit ratings (Chapter 7 stays on a credit report for ten years and Chapter 13 for up to seven years) and possibly fewer job opportunities—for many years or even decades.

Be open-minded, proactive, and creative. I know you can find ways to make the changes needed to get out of crisis and back onto the path of financial security.

Dealing with debt is challenging and exhausting. The good news is that all debt problems have solutions. Small steps in the right direction can make substantial differences, especially when they take place consistently over a considerable time frame.

If you are in crisis mode, separate yourself from the circumstances that led you there. Get rid of the thoughts and scripts that brought you to this state of crisis. Look toward the results you want to have.

Every day, as you make financial decisions, ask: Does this get me closer to the result I want, and is it getting me closer to financial security? If you already did something that is working against the result you want, acknowledge it and move on. Then, change your behavior to get closer to the results you want. As each day passes, try to make improvements, and then try again tomorrow.

The need to establish an objective view of the situation is challenging and one of the reasons people choose to work with professionals. A financial advisor, aided by his or her expertise and emotional distance from the situation, can often see what those in crisis cannot.

Chapter Recap

» Reasonable debt includes mortgages, car loans, and, in some cases, student loans.

» Taking out loans in order to live above your means and incurring debt from not paying taxes are examples of slippery-slope debt.

» Due to high interest rates and stiff fees, credit card balances can quickly get out of control; credit cards should only be used if you are capable of paying off the full balance every month.

» Ratios such as total debt/total assets, savings rate, and debt-to-income can help you assess your current debt levels and decide whether to take on new debt.

» The first step in reducing debt is to establish a budget. From there, there are various debt reduction strategies that can be used to chip away at and eventually pay off outstanding debt.

| 9 |
Buying a Home

An old man in a house is a good sign.

— BENJAMIN FRANKLIN

My client Elizabeth wanted a house so much. It was at the top of her mind during our first meeting. To Elizabeth, a home meant so much more than just a place to sleep. She was expecting her first child. She wanted to live somewhere permanently with her husband and new baby. She wanted birthdays in the backyard. She wanted to decorate a nursery. She wanted a space for more children to grow and run. She wanted a nest in which her family would blossom and thrive, and that she would fill with laughter, stories, and memories. To Elizabeth, a home represented family and connectedness. Perhaps this is something you feel as well.

Homeownership is often considered an important part of living the American dream: finish school, get married, buy a home, and start a family. Homeownership also presents with behavioral biases, thoughts, scripts, and other notions that are completely unfounded.

For example, we often think of our homes as investments. They are not. They are consumption items and much less productive assets than we choose to believe. Homes have mortgages, property taxes, maintenance, insurance costs, and homeowners association fees, most of which are unrecoverable costs. In addition, there are often ancillary expenses, such as when we find we need additional furniture or another car due to the home's location.

In chapter 1, we discussed a building wealth mindset. If we want to be financially successful, then we must tap into this mindset when choosing where to live. If we are careless financially, we can easily get carried away, feeling much like Elizabeth, where everything about our dream home is non-negotiable except for the rising sticker price.

When you purchase or rent a home on the edge of what you can afford, you are making a trade-off: short-term comfort over long-term ability to build wealth. This does not mean that you cannot have that desired place for your family to bloom. But you do yourself and your future vitality a great disservice if you fail to consider the immense financial ramifications of this decision. While your home may symbolize the emotional core of your family, you will surely pursue other dreams, aspirations, and ambitions, most of which will be more readily attainable if your household is on secure financial footing.

My goal in this chapter is to debunk some of these common myths (thoughts) and help you make better financial decisions (with facts) when deciding whether to rent or buy, what type of mortgage to take out, and when it makes sense to buy a rental home or vacation property.

Common Real Estate Myths

Decisions about real estate are emotional decisions. We think back to our childhood experiences. We want to give our kids what we had or did not have. We can envision the curtains blowing on a crisp spring day, our kids playing in the yard while we flip grilled cheeses for lunch. Maybe we remember the lines drawn on the garage wall at Uncle Fred and Aunt Gracie's house in Des Moines. Each line showed how tall we and our cousins had grown since the previous year. We reminisce about our summer visits there, playing in the yard, eating barbecue ribs on the back porch. These memories alter our ability to consider home-buying as just another business transaction, because it is not. Home is truly where the heart is.

In addition to the many emotions we feel regarding real estate, we also have deeply embedded scripts, much like the money scripts from chapter 1. Perhaps you heard your parents or a trusted friend say something like "renting is throwing money away" or "they're not making any more land." These off-the-cuff remarks can easily become lodged in our belief structures and distort our whole perception of home-buying.

In addition to our emotions and thoughts, our government has offered many incentives to compel its citizens to buy homes. These incentives often lead us to believe that owning is cheaper than renting, since mortgage interest and property taxes are deductible. However, deductible does not mean free, it merely means capable of lowering your tax rate.

Whether it's government-sponsored bias or a tidbit of "wisdom" overheard at a family reunion, the myths surrounding homeownership are rampant and have the potential to be destructive. Buying a home is one of the most financially consequential decisions you will make, so if there was ever a time to discard the myths and to focus on the facts, this is it.

Here are some of the most common real estate myths and why they should be put on a bonfire:

1. **"Renting is throwing money away."** This is a giant misconception. I often hear that you can't build equity in a home by renting, and you can't take advantage of the mortgage interest tax deduction, and therefore you're lighting money on fire. This is simply not true! For one thing, you can build equity anywhere, not just in a home. The cash you have set aside for a down payment on a house could just as easily—or more easily—be applied toward building equity in a long-term diversified asset. The house may or may not pan out as a good investment. There is a mortgage interest deduction, but there are also unrecoverable costs associated with purchasing a home. For example, your mortgage, which is comprised of principal and interest. The interest is an unrecoverable cost, and the remainder goes toward paying down principal. Additional unrecoverable costs are property taxes, homeowners insurance, and HOA fees. There is also regular maintenance on the property: gardening, cleaning the gutters, replacing window screens and furnace filters, etc. These are regular costs that do not increase the value of your property but are often not considered when you make a home purchase.

2. **"Your home is an investment."** A home is a consumption item, not an investment. You live there. There is wear and tear. You make changes to the property to please yourself, not because someone else may come along and buy it. The sooner you start thinking of your home as a consumption good rather than an investment, the sooner you will be able to make rational decisions about what you are and are not willing to pay. Additionally, you might buy a home and find that it doesn't appreciate in value. Say you buy one in a subdivision that is growing, but it turns out that the house you bought has some serious problems or defects. It is the "lemon" on the block and, when it comes time to sell, it is not worth nearly as much as the others.

3. **"Your home is a forced savings account."** Your home is actually a forced spending account. I see this over and over again with clients,

and I was not immune either. My husband and I purposely bought a new construction home, so we could walk in without needing additional remodeling. We still ended up spending $20,000 on home improvements and repairs! Among other things, we finished a storage unit, blew extra insulation into the walls, and resolved other odds and ends that the builder had missed. There is still a long list of improvements I would like to make, but on the other hand, we just want to be content to live in the house and enjoy it. You can spend every penny you have on your home, or you can decide to be content with what you have. If you don't know where to draw the line, buying a home is not going to yield any savings. The best way to save is to increase income, decrease expenses, or both. It is not by purchasing a home.

4. **"House prices only go up"** and **"They're not making any more land."** Since the financial crisis of 2008, I hear less often that house prices only go up. You *can* lose money on your home. Over long periods of time, people tend to make out all right, but it's more difficult to predict with shorter time periods. In addition, there are closing costs and commissions that make it hard to make money over the short term. My advice is to only buy a home if you're willing to stay there for a long time. And, yes, they're not making any more land, but there needs to be demand for the land and the home on it.

5. **"Mortgage interest deduction makes it cheaper to own."** I believe that markets are efficient, and therefore the mortgage interest deduction is baked into the price of both purchases and rentals. It may feel like you're getting a deal because you can see your taxes decline annually as a result of owning a home. But that does not necessarily make owning cheaper than renting. A rental property owner is also getting a mortgage interest deduction and can pass that through to a renter to make rents more competitive. That's how markets work.

6. **"Renovations pay for themselves."** We think if we spend $60,000 updating our kitchen, our home price will increase commensurately. More often than not, renovations cost more than the value they add. This does not mean that you should not renovate your home. But you must realize that renovations, like the home itself, are consumption items. You remodel because you want to, because you saved for it or planned for it. Sometimes renovations maintain the value of a

home rather than increasing it. For example, perhaps that $60,000 kitchen renovation simply updates your thirty-year-old kitchen, and the home would decline in value without it. Renovations don't always pay for themselves; sometimes they do, but it is not an expectation you should have.

7. **"Location, location, location."** This one is not a myth! Being in a good location generally makes properties more expensive. They can also retain their value because of it.

8. **"Buy at the maximum of what you can afford, because you are using other people's money by taking a loan from the bank."** More debt on your balance sheet does not guarantee that more equity will follow. I sometimes hear from clients that businesses have an optimal level of debt that allows them to grow, and therefore they should, too. However, you're not taking on debt to grow your business, you're doing it because you want to buy a specific house. Debt only magnifies risk, that's all. I do think it makes sense to take out a mortgage to buy a home, especially in today's interest rate environment, but debt must always be used thoughtfully.

9. **"Buy at the maximum of what you can afford, because your income will increase."** This is just a flat-out no. Do not do this. You don't know that your income will increase. If you are unsure, you can always rent until you are making the income to justify the home you would like to purchase. As a reminder, I recommend spending 20 percent or less of your income on all home-related expenses. This is so you're not clipping coupons and worrying about every latte you buy. I don't want you to be "house poor," where house-related expenses overwhelm your budget and make it nearly impossible to save. I don't want you to worry about every penny you spend. Do yourself a favor and buy less house than you can "afford," as this will afford you more savings and flexibility. The less you spend on large fixed expenses, the easier it will be for you to save and spend on whatever brings you joy.

10. **"You need multiple streams of income to become wealthy, and owning a rental property will give you that."** Not so fast. Investments in general can create multiple streams of income, but owning and operating a rental property is a *business*. It is not passive income, and it is not free money. As with all businesses, owning a rental property

involves receiving income, paying for expenses and, hopefully, achieving a net income. You pay taxes on that income. You have to want to be a landlord. You can get multiple streams of income by investing, but it doesn't have to be in real estate.

The number one reason to buy a home is because you love it, you can afford it, and you want to live in it for a long time. None of these other myths matter.

Buy or Rent?

Say you buy a home for $300,000, pay $10,000 in mortgage expenses, spend $40,000 to add a pool, and do $50,000 worth of remodeling. If you sell the home for $400,000 after one year, you are merely breaking even, even though it might feel like you're coming out $100,000 ahead because you are selling for $400,000 rather than the $300,000 that you paid. In addition, we don't consider all the little items we purchase specifically for the home that add up over time, many of which would become new expenses after a move.

NOTE

There are added fees and costs associated with buying and selling homes that folks do not factor in, but they can add up fast as well.

Cars are depreciating assets, we all know this, but a house can be like that too—we're faced with this when we need to replace a carpet, fix a wall, or update the kitchen. For example, if my child rips a large section of the carpet with a toy sword, fixing the carpet does not add value to the home. This is different from an investment in shares of a company trading in the stock market; stock can increase in value without requiring additional expense.

In other words, if you hold a mortgage, you pay down principal each month and you build home equity over time. But it is not a savings account, because homeownership also comes with other costs such as maintenance, taxes, and insurance.

Moreover, the money used to remodel, improve, and provide for general upkeep is money you could have invested elsewhere if you were renting. So, if you are renting, all is not lost—you simply need to build wealth with other types of real estate, stocks, or other investments. When evaluating whether to buy or rent, there are a myriad of factors to consider:

> » Do I love the home and want to spend ten-plus years there?

» Is the cost going to be more than 30 percent of my pretax income when I factor in the mortgage payment, insurance, taxes, HOA fees, maintenance, repairs, and improvements? Twenty percent or less is ideal.

» Do I live in an area where it makes sense to buy a home, or should I rent? You might find a high-paying job in New York or California where property values are too high, and it makes more sense to invest elsewhere while you rent.

» Do I like do-it-yourself projects? If you like fixing things and making home improvements, it might make more sense to buy a home. On the other hand, if you need to call a plumber or electrician for every little problem, the bills can pile up. A lot of care and maintenance is required with 2,500-square-foot houses.

Do the Math

Are you convinced that buying is not always better than renting? Let's break down the cost of renting versus buying, using real numbers.

1. First, the easy part. Write down your monthly rent (or an estimate of monthly rent for a prospective property).
2. Second, make a list of all homeowner's expenses:

    » **Property Taxes: 1.7 percent** (could be higher or lower depending on where you live; adjust accordingly)

    » **Maintenance Costs: 1 percent per year** (this is what most people agree to be the standard maintenance cost for a home, but it generally ranges from 1 to 3 percent, depending on how old the home is and how much money you want to put into it)

    » **Cost of Capital: 2.6 percent** (two components: the interest on 80 percent borrowed money and the opportunity cost of putting down 20 percent to buy the home; see the following note for an explanation of these components)

When we total the percentages in this example, we see that the cost of owning is roughly *5.3 percent* per year. For the home you are considering, multiply the value by 5.3 percent, then divide by twelve months. If you can rent for less than that, then renting is a sensible financial choice. Therefore, on a $1 million home, if you can rent for less than $53,000 per year ($4,417 per month), then it is cheaper to rent.

I'm going to give you a basic walk-through of my cost-of-capital calculation. By putting 20 percent down, you've decided to make an investment in real estate rather than continuing to rent and investing in the stock market (easy example of another long-term investment). You are thereby creating an opportunity cost. According to the Credit Suisse Global Investment Returns Yearbook, the estimated expected return for real estate (1900–2017) is 3 percent. The estimated expected return for stocks (1900–2017) is 6.9 percent. That difference of 3.9 percent is the opportunity cost of buying real estate rather than investing in the stock market.

Now, had you invested in the market, you would not likely be holding a portfolio of 100 percent stocks in a tax-favored, transaction-free account, so let's be realistic and say you have a portfolio of 60/40 stocks and bonds and an expected rate of return of 5.8 percent. Subtract 3 percent from 5.8 percent; our new opportunity cost is 2.8 percent. The cost of debt is our mortgage interest rate adjusted for tax deductibility. Next, we compute the weighted cost of capital (for the 20 percent down payment and the 80 percent borrowed money), which leads us to the total cost of owning versus renting: weighted cost of capital = 0.80 x 2.5% + 0.20 x 2.8% = 2.6% (.80 for 80 percent borrowed money and .20 for 20 percent opportunity cost of making a down payment).

How to Buy a Home

Here is my step-by-step process for evaluating a home purchase that will leave you content and with savings:

1. **Favor Rational Over Emotional**: If you find yourself making excessively quick decisions, you may be reacting on an emotional level rather than rationally assessing facts. A lot of our money decisions have an emotional component to them. Buying a home is one of the most emotional decisions you'll make. Knowing this, you must appeal to your rational side by pausing and taking time to distinguish what you know to be true from what you are feeling. Give yourself the greatest gift you can by detaching from emotions and weighing the facts.

2. **Calculate Your Budget in Advance**: If you know what you can spend, then you will not look for houses outside your price range. Here is what to do:

    •   Multiply your pretax income by 1.7.
    •   The result is roughly the mortgage balance you can assume, while keeping home expenses affordable.
    •   Divide the mortgage balance by 0.8, to arrive at your home purchase budget.

»   **Then Check Your Math:**

    •   Multiply your pretax income by 20 percent. This is the annual maximum you should spend.
    •   Use an online mortgage calculator to estimate your monthly mortgage payment.
    •   Determine the property tax percentage in the area where you would like to own and multiply it by your home price.
    •   Calculate approximate homeowners insurance (0.85 percent of the home value is a good starting point)
    •   Calculate home maintenance of 1 to 3 percent of the home price.
    •   Add in HOA fees if applicable.
    •   Throw in a couple hundred per month for utilities.
    •   Add up the numbers and compare it to 20 percent of pretax income.

You make $105,000 per year; you can spend $21,000 per year (or $1,750 per month) on a home.

»   **Mortgage balance:** $105,000 x 1.7 = $178,500
»   **Home purchase budget:** $178,500 ÷ 0.8 = $223,125
»   **Check your math:**
    •   **Annual mortgage amount:** $9,619 (3.5 percent, 30 years)
    •   **Property taxes:** $4,463 (2 percent)
    •   **Homeowners insurance:** $1,897 (0.85 percent)
    •   **Home maintenance:** $4,463 (2 percent)
    •   **Utilities:** $2,400 (estimated)
    •   **Total:** $22,840, therefore you know you can spend around $223,000 or less on a home, since $22,840 is greater than $21,000 (or 20 percent of pretax income)

I like using 1.7 times pretax income as a starting point for mortgage balances. Rather than picking a number out of thin air, you have something to go on! Based on the example, you can assume if your mortgage rate is higher than 3.5 percent for 30 years, you'll need to lower your budget. Conversely, if property taxes are only 1.5 percent in your neighborhood, you can increase your budget.

3. **Assess Location**: Given your budget, you will want to pick your location. Perhaps the neighborhood you've always dreamed of is completely out of your price range. Or perhaps it makes sense to rent in that location while you save money to buy something there. Once you know your budget, it will be much easier to decide where to live. Ask yourself lots of questions regarding what is important about location. Do you want to be close to shops or a grocery store? Does the school district matter? Do you want to be near parks or a community center? What is available to you in that location? All of these questions will help you narrow down what is important.

4. **Rent versus Buy**: After you've arrived at your budget, do a rent-versus-buy calculation to make sure it still makes sense to buy. If it is less expensive to buy or you still want to buy despite it's being more expensive, move to the next step.

5. **Fixer-Upper versus Move-In Ready**: This is similar to the rent-versus-buy question and will be determined by a number of factors. Are you looking in an expensive area where the only option within your price range is a fixer-upper? Are you capable of doing some repairs yourself? Are you willing to be selective about what truly needs repairs? Can you be patient through the process and live with some flaws while you fix the home?

6. **Small versus Big Details**: Have you ever walked into a home and gotten a bad feeling? Sometimes our instincts can be trusted, but other times we're responding to something easily fixable, like a stain in the carpet or old-looking cabinets. It is much more important to pay attention to the details that matter, rather than getting bogged down by the little stuff. For example, when we chose our lot in Texas, we knew we would experience hot summers. We did not want any big windows facing the western sun that would make our home difficult to cool in the summer. We bought a home where the back, and all the large windows, face east. Details like these

are important; they cannot be changed once you've purchased the home. Having our windows on the east side of the house saves us thousands of dollars in energy costs per year.

NOTE

You may also want to do an "energy audit" before purchasing a home, in which you inspect past utility bills, lighting, windows, insulation, and other features of the house that will affect your energy-related expenses after you move in.

7. **Seasonality**: Depending on the market in which you are looking, you may find some seasonality in pricing. For example, a home in a beach community will likely sell for a lower price in the winter than in the spring or summer, and the opposite will be true for a ski chalet. If you are willing to be patient, you can learn the ebbs and flows of your market and may be able to get a great deal on a home.

That's it! Happy hunting!

ON YOUR OWN

Calculate 20 percent of your pretax income. This is your housing budget. Are you above or below 20 percent right now? Are you currently saving at least 20 percent of your after-tax income? If not, what changes can you make to get to a healthy financial position?

#15

Finding the Right Mortgage

Once you have decided that buying is better than renting, the next question is, how do you pay for it? Unless you have an extra few hundred thousand dollars sitting around, you will probably borrow money to buy a home, using a mortgage.

NOTE

Some mortgages have fixed interest rates and some have variable rates that change over time. Since mortgage rates have been at historically low levels in recent years, fixed rates have been the way to go because the buyer is essentially locking in an attractive rate for a period of fifteen or thirty years.

If you're looking for a home, chances are you have thought about how to finance it. If you google "mortgage rates," the quotes will show an interest rate based on a 20 percent down payment. This is the industry standard. However, it is not set in stone. You can put down as little as 3 percent, depending on your lender's requirements.

I caution you against putting less than 20 percent down. Generally, when people want to put less than 20 percent down, it is because they are purchasing a home at the maximum of what the bank will lend. I want you to be successful in your financial endeavors; therefore, I do not want you reaching to purchase a home that you cannot afford, even if the bank thinks you can. When you're considering your home budget and down payment, you must be honest with yourself about why you want to put less than 20 percent down.

A 20 percent down payment will earn you a lower mortgage rate. Lenders will compete for your business, and you may have access to a more competitive rate. A 20 percent down payment also waives the requirement for **private mortgage insurance (PMI)**. When you put down less than 20 percent, you are considered a riskier home buyer. Therefore, you must pay PMI to protect your lender from your potential default on the mortgage. The amount of PMI you pay will vary based on lender PMI tables. These tables account for how much you put down, your debt-to-income ratio, and your credit rating. Typical PMI ranges from 0.4 percent to 2.25 percent of the total loan amount.

Let's say you want to purchase a $400,000 home. To avoid PMI, you will need $80,000 in savings for your down payment. PMI can be exceptionally expensive if your down payment is 10 percent or less—between $120 and $675 per month. I typically advise clients to save for the full down payment and not pay PMI, as it is a completely unrecoverable cost.

However, there are times when putting down less than 20 percent and paying PMI conforms to your goals. For example, one of my clients purchased a real fixer-upper. Prior to closing, they spoke with architects and contractors and estimated that the home would need $300,000 in work. To conserve funds for construction, it made sense to put only 10 percent down at closing and pay PMI. After construction was complete, they had the house appraised and, because the home's value had been so greatly improved, the PMI requirement was removed. The best decision is not always the most obvious and always depends on the situation.

The more money you put down, the lower your mortgage balance will be and the more equity you will have in your home. The equity builds over time with each mortgage payment, as you pay principal and interest.

MY TAKE

The more you put down on a home, the less you have to invest elsewhere, so the ideal amount to put down depends on what your goals are and where you are in your life. For example, when you are younger and accumulating assets, putting 20 percent down and financing the remainder with a mortgage is likely the right approach. On the other hand, when you are retired and living off your assets, the math may be more favorable if you pay for your home in cash. It is important to assess your particular situation and number-crunch to determine what is best for you.

Understanding Amortization

As noted in chapter 8, a mortgage has an interest rate and a term. Thirty-year mortgages are the most common, and interest rates are constantly changing based on a myriad of economic factors, which are difficult to anticipate or predict. In early 2020, the rate on a thirty-year fixed mortgage was less than 3.45 percent.

A mortgage is amortized over the term of the loan, which means that the payments are put on a monthly schedule, with a slice going toward interest and a portion going toward principal. In the early stages of the loan, the bulk of each payment is applied to interest. As the mortgage enters its final year, nearly the entire amount is applied to the principal balance (figure 30).

MONTHLY PRINCIPAL AND INTEREST REPAYMENTS
ON A 30-YEAR FIXED-RATE MORTGAGE

—— Interest Payments   —— Principal Payments

fig. 30

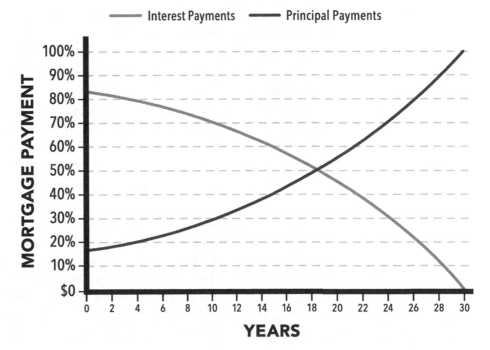

Fifteen-Year vs. Thirty-Year Mortgage

A client of mine was interested in purchasing a home that would cost only 15 percent of his pretax income. We got quotes from a mortgage lender for both fifteen- and thirty-year mortgages. The fifteen-year mortgage had a much lower interest rate. Although the payment was $800 per month higher than that of the thirty-year mortgage, we decided to go for the lower rate and lower term. This saved $150,000 in interest over the life of the mortgage. Though there was an opportunity cost to not investing that $800 per month somewhere else, the client felt that the fifteen-year mortgage payments were affordable, and he could still save for other goals. This is a great reason to stay below 20 percent of pretax income when considering a home purchase or a rental. It will afford you choice.

Buying a home with a thirty-year mortgage is a substantial commitment. Think about how much has changed in your life over the past thirty years. People burn out on their jobs after ten years or get laid off. Couples get divorced. People fall ill or go on disability.

The nature of life is that the unexpected will occur. Since buying a home is a relatively illiquid investment and a long-term commitment, it might be difficult to sell the property if something occurred that forced you to move. For that reason, if you are unsure whether you will live in your home for at least ten years, I recommend considering renting rather than buying until you are certain of where you would like to be. Buying a home with the intention of selling it in four or five years is an exercise in market timing, and there is no guarantee that a house bought today can easily be sold several years from now. Furthermore, I often see clients who want to "trade up" their home a few years after purchase. This is risky. For one thing, prices may have lowered since your initial home purchase. Also, you may not be able to sell your old place after committing to a new one. I have seen clients end up floating two mortgages because they expected their smaller place to sell as easily as the larger one they purchased.

I happen to like fifteen-year mortgages because I see clients feel complete freedom after their mortgage loan is repaid. However, it is important to note that there is an opportunity cost. By taking on a higher payment, you are building equity in one home rather than building equity in a diversified way outside your home. Because interest rates are low as I write this—and longer-term mortgages incur less overall interest expense than they have in the past—it may make more sense for you to take advantage of the lower payment afforded by a longer-term mortgage and to invest elsewhere with the money you save. As a rule, you should not allocate so much of your income to a fifteen-year mortgage that you are unable to save and invest in other assets.

NOTE

You can do a quick comparison of fifteen- versus thirty-year mortgages using Bankrate's mortgage calculator. This resource is listed with several others in your Digital Assets and can be accessed at go.quickstartguides.com/personalfinance.

ARM vs. Fixed Rate

An adjustable-rate mortgage (ARM) is one in which the interest rate changes over time, and fixed-rate mortgages have an interest rate that is set when the loan is taken out and does not change. With an adjustable-rate mortgage, the interest rate is reset periodically and may go up or down.

Many ARMs start with interest rates that are lower than those offered by fixed-rate mortgages. These lower rates may stay the same for months or a few years. After the introductory period is over, your interest rate will change depending on where mortgage rates are. Rates adjust based on a benchmark or index rate. Some ARMs limit how much rates can move and, if rates decline, there is no guarantee that the interest on the ARM will move lower as well. That's why it is essential to understand the key details of the loan:

» When is the introductory rate period over?
» When does the ARM adjust?
» How often does it adjust?
» How high can your interest rate and monthly payments go after an adjustment?
» How soon might your payment increase or decrease?
» Is there a cap on how high the interest rate can go?

In a lower interest rate environment, it usually makes sense to lock in a fixed-rate mortgage. However, if you don't think you will be in your home for a long time, an ARM may make sense. If you plan to move in the next five to seven years, then you don't need to be as concerned about how the rate may change. Moreover, if you are going to move in five to seven years, then you may not want to buy at all. Be sure to do some calculating. When you include closing costs and selling costs, it may not be worth the hassle of buying a property, regardless of the rate type.

Cashing In on Home Equity

Over time as you pay down your mortgage, and as progressively larger portions of your payments go toward paying down the principal, you build equity in your home. In other words, the extent to which the asset belongs to you increases; your claim on the asset gradually grows stronger relative to the claim of your lender. That's equity in a nutshell. Equity is an asset.

New lenders will solicit you, inviting you to take out a loan on the equity you've built, essentially reconverting the equity back into the debt from whence it came.

I want to approach this section with caution. Generally, when someone wants to take equity out of a home, it is because they want to do something beyond their means. I don't suggest using any "cashing out" options to buy the red Porsche you always wanted, or to pay for your dream vacation to Orlando. And I certainly don't recommend cashing out on a home to cover your daily living expenses.

There are times, however, when it makes sense. For example, you can use your home's equity to finance home improvements that will create value for your property. And if you are in debt and willing to make significant spending changes, using home equity can save you thousands in credit card interest.

If you're considering borrowing against your home equity, then it's important that you be honest with yourself. Why do you need the money, *and* does the math line up with your goals?

» **Home Equity Loan**: Also known as a second mortgage, it is a lot like your first mortgage, but the interest rate is usually higher. You use the equity in your home as collateral for the new mortgage. You pay it back the same way you paid your initial mortgage. You have a set term and an interest rate. Like your initial mortgage, the loan is amortized. While interest on second mortgages is often tax-deductible, there are other costs to consider. Credit checks, appraisals, and other closing costs can easily add up to thousands of dollars. This includes the origination fee, which is the up-front fee charged to process the loan and is typically around 1 percent of the total loan value.

» **Home Equity Line of Credit:** The HELOC is a line of credit that homeowners can draw upon as needed. It requires bank approval and usually no funds are issued. The HELOC often comes with a book of checks or a debit card. As money from the line of credit is used, it must be paid off at the end of the term, with interest. Periodic payments are required as well. Think of it as a credit card but with your home equity as collateral. The advantage of this approach is that, unlike mortgages and second mortgages, there are no closing costs. Note, however, that HELOCs often begin with a lower interest rate than home equity loans, but the rate is adjustable, or variable, which means it rises or falls according to the movements of a benchmark. That means your monthly payment can rise or fall, too.

» **Cash-Out Refinance:** You probably know somebody who refinanced their home for a larger amount than their current mortgage balance and took the difference in cash. That's known as a cash-out refinance and often comes with high closing costs.

» **Rate Refinance:** Homeowners can sometimes save money by refinancing home loans after a drop in mortgage rates. This type of refinance may be optimal if costs of originating the new loan are less than the money saved from refinancing at a lower rate. Generally, origination fees and other expenses equal 1 percent to 3 percent of the balance of the loan. The best way to see how this works is to consider an example. Say your current mortgage has 25 years left, a balance of $500,000, and a rate of 3.75 percent. Your current payment is $2,570 per month. You could refinance to 3.25 percent and keep the term the same. Your new payment would be $2,437 per month. You would save $133 per month, or almost $1,600 per year. Let's say the refinancing costs are 2 percent of the loan, or $10,000. It will take you 6.25 years to break even on the refinancing. If you don't stay in the home longer than 6.25 years, it's not worth doing. This is why you *always* start with your goals.

» **Term Refinance:** As the name implies, you are basically extending the term of the mortgage in order to lower your monthly payment. For example, if you have twenty years left on your mortgage but you refinance to a thirty-year term, you will pay less monthly, but this also means you're starting from scratch, and, since mortgages are amortized, a higher percentage of each mortgage payment will go toward interest rather than principal.

NOTE

Rate and term refinances are often combined into one.

» **ARM to Fixed Rate**: Recall that an ARM has an interest rate that adjusts over time. Suppose you took an ARM because your original intention was to live in your home for only a few years. Then your plans changed—you love your home, and you decide to stay for many more years. Depending on where rates are, it is likely prudent to refinance into a fixed-rate mortgage and remove the risk of a rate spike.

» **FHA to Conventional**: If you are paying PMI, it is a good idea to refinance if the equity in your home is worth 20 percent or more. If the real estate market is heating up and home values are rising, then you may find yourself with 20 percent in equity without having to make payments in excess of your required mortgage amount. In short, even though it involves paying origination fees, refinancing to end PMI requirements can make a lot of sense when the homeowner wants to stay in the home for many years.

Your best option for tapping into your home equity will depend on your credit score, income, and what you want to do with the money. If you want a lump sum amount to consolidate debt, put a down payment on a vacation home, or cover some other large expense, a second mortgage or a cash-out refinance might be better for you. If you are simply looking for additional funds to do home improvements or better manage cash flow, then a HELOC is probably a preferable option.

MY TAKE

Like most financial decisions, always start with results. What results are you looking to have? What feeling do you want to generate? Why do you need more cash? Maybe you want to renovate your kitchen and the math indicates that financing it is the best approach. Or maybe you are stretched financially and need a helping hand. It is hard for me to know without knowing you, but I suggest that you be honest with yourself about why you're doing what you're doing. Know and understand what your goals truly are. Are you kicking the can down the road because you don't want to deal with your bad habits now? Or is there a purpose to refinancing that will lead to your most fulfilled life?

Is a Vacation Home Right for You?

Many people dream about having a cabin in the mountains or a home on the beach somewhere. Owning a vacation home is certainly a worthwhile and rewarding financial goal. But, just as with buying a home, there are many other expenses to consider beyond just a mortgage payment: travel to and from, utilities, taxes, and insurance, to name a few.

I do not recommend buying a vacation home unless it's possible to keep the total costs of the existing home and the vacation home below 25 percent of pretax income. Lenders will lend you up to 36 percent of your pretax income. Therefore, if you already spend 20 percent of your pretax income on your primary residence, would you spend an additional 16 percent of income on vacations? Probably not, as it would leave little left over for savings and other pursuits. Therefore, in most cases, unless you have a lot of disposable income, a vacation home is not worth it.

Consider an example: you and your spouse make $115,000 per year. You spend $25,000 per year on your primary home (22 percent of income). You finance a vacation home and spend an additional $16,100 per year (14 percent of income). You make $94,000 after taxes. That leaves $52,900 left over for everything else, including savings (46 percent of income). Having a vacation home will make it difficult to save $18,800 (20 percent) per year. Additionally, let's say you and your spouse get two weeks' vacation every year and you only go to your vacation home one additional weekend per month. That's thirty-eight nights in your vacation home, meaning you're spending $424 per night on your vacation. Is the home worth $424 per night? Perhaps you would be happier staying somewhere for $300 per night, saving $4,712 per year, and not worrying about maintenance. When a client asks me about a vacation home, I ask them the following questions regarding their preferences:

» How much vacation time do you have, and do you like staying in the same place every time? If you vacation less than four weeks per year and like seeing different places, then a vacation home is not for you, unless you have a lot of income.

» Are you willing to own the property for many years to justify the investment? If not, then the costs likely outweigh the benefits.

» Will you possibly retire in this location? If so, it is worth considering, as you can have a home fully paid for in retirement.

» Will buying this property make your life better or be a financial drain?

In terms of more specific financial considerations, I review the following with a client as well:

» Does the property add diversification to your assets, or does it lead to greater concentration in real estate holdings? No more than 40 percent of your net worth should be in real estate.

» Do you have a sufficiently stable income to take on a second mortgage? It would be quite hard if you qualified for a mortgage in a higher income bracket, only to lose that income later.

» Do you already have $750,000 in mortgage debt? If so, additional interest will not be tax-deductible.

Vacation homes, like primary residences, are typically thought of as investments. They are not. They are consumption items. While you do build equity in the home, it is important to consider that this equity could be built in other less costly ways, like investing in a highly diversified, low-cost portfolio of stocks and bonds that matches your risk tolerance. There is no guarantee that the vacation home you purchase will rise in value. Keep in mind that a vacation home is subject to the same costs and maintenance needs as your primary residence. Unless you really like gardening and upkeep, I highly suggest segregating vacation spending and home purchases, so you can relax and enjoy yourself on your time off and not worry about house maintenance.

Multiple Streams of Income – Rental Properties

Do you want to be a landlord? This is the most important consideration when it comes to rental properties. You must want to be in the property management business.

Often when people think of multiple streams of income, they envision themselves sipping margaritas by the pool while the money is deposited directly into their bank account. There is no work involved. Ahh, the good life. This is a complete fantasy. No one is going to give you income for nothing.

Earlier in this chapter we debunked Real Estate Myth #10 by acknowledging the reality that a rental property is a business. Even if you hire a property management company to do the landlord work for you, you are still running a business. Your business will have income from rent. Your business will also have expenses like a mortgage, property taxes, utilities, maintenance costs, homeowners insurance, HOA fees, and property management fees if applicable. Your business will have net income on which you will pay taxes. You will also have more complicated accounting, which will cost you additional money. While you may not receive the 3:00 a.m. plumbing call if you've hired a manager, you still get to write all the checks.

If being a landlord is super exciting, an endeavor that you view as fulfilling and worthy of your time, then you must do the math to ensure that your prospective rental property is worthwhile. I had a client who purchased a rental property during the financial crisis of 2008. This should have been a slam dunk, yes? No! She did not want to be a landlord, so she rented the property to someone she knew well to ensure she would not have any tenant issues. Because it was a friend, she charged her a below-market rent. In addition, the area in which the rental property was located did not appreciate in value, unlike nearby neighborhoods. She was losing a lot of money every year holding the property and could not deduct rental losses against income because she made too much money.

This is more common than you might imagine. You may be thinking, Well, I would never rent to a friend. Sure, maybe you wouldn't, but the rents in the area still need to justify the cost of the rental property. In this example, if my client wasn't renting to a friend, it would have allowed her to ask for $150 more per month in rent. Assuming she was able to keep a new tenant on for a year, she'd have made an extra $1,800 for the year. That would *not* have been enough to remove the rental losses. You must consider this when you are number-crunching. What kind of rate of return will I get in this area, given what I can charge for rent and what I will pay for the property? Don't forget to include 2 or 3 percent per year in maintenance costs, as your tenant is not likely to care for the property as well as you would if you lived there.

Q: When can you deduct rental losses?

If you are single or married filing jointly and you don't earn more than $100,000, then some of the expenses of owning a rental property can be used to reduce taxable income, up to $25,000. As always, the IRS loves their phaseouts. You can deduct progressively less when income is between $100,000 and $150,000. Once you earn more than $150,000 in income, you will not be able to take any deduction, but you can carry losses forward.

Only you can decide if a rental property is right for you. I encourage you to throw out the "multiple streams of income" mindset and absorb a "building wealth" mindset instead. The numbers will tell you whether it is possible, not the dream of passive income. As always, think of the results you want to have. If you are only seeking passive income, there are many other ways you can get it without owning a rental property. If you want to be a landlord, great! Do your homework and find the right property. There's a forthcoming ClydeBank Media book by real estate investment coach Symon He that will help you on your path. It's called the *Rental Property Investing QuickStart Guide*. Check it out.

We all think about debt and mortgages differently. For example, I have a client who always wants to use his extra income to pay down his mortgage. This client introduced me, by way of referral, to a couple that has a big mortgage for their home and another for their rental property, sending their debt-to-income ratio through the roof. The point is that what is financially right for one family is not always so for another. Your friends and family members may be very comfortable doing something that would cause you great stress. This is why I keep emphasizing your most fulfilled life and the results you want to achieve. Keeping results in the forefront of your mind will lead you to where you want to go. When you are unsure of what to do next, your fallback question should always be, Which choice brings me closer to my most fulfilled life?

Risk tolerance for debt is often vastly different than risk tolerance for investments. You must evaluate the two separately. While you may be perfectly content to own 100 percent of your assets in bitcoin and emerging market stocks, you may feel entirely uncomfortable with a large mortgage. Risk tolerance often depends on experience, scripts, and people we've learned from throughout our lives. As such, it is important to distinguish what is right for you.

Chapter Recap

» The government encourages homeownership by offering tax incentives, like the ability to deduct mortgage interest. Nevertheless, the choice to buy or not to buy a home should be considered carefully through the weighing of all advantages, expenses, and opportunity costs.

» Homes should not be viewed as investments but as consumption items.

» Equity can be built, often with less cost, through assets other than homes.

» Several factors determine how much it costs—monthly—to own a home: the interest rate, the term of the mortgage, and any expenses related to owning the property.

» Purchasing a vacation home is usually not a good decision for those without excess disposable income.

| 10 |
Insurance

Perhaps the best cure for the fear of death is to reflect that life has a beginning as well as an end.

– WILLIAM HAZLITT

Insurance is a tool used to protect yourself and your family in a world of uncertainty with hidden risks. Different types of insurance abound, from policies covering individuals who get sick to those covering homes against floods and earthquakes.

Some insurance policies are pitched as investments because they have a component that can increase in value and offer a cash payout after a period of time. I typically do not recommend insurance products as investments. Instead, the best approach is to obtain reasonable coverage so that one's family is well protected in the event of the unexpected. The goal is to have the best protection available while minimizing costs.

Insurance is a for-profit business. The insurance companies cleverly price policy premiums to pay claims, employees, and all other expenses while also turning a profit. This may sound self-evident, but I think it is worth repeating. More often than not, you will pay in more than you get out of your insurance policy.

The point of insurance is to cover losses that you could not otherwise afford. When considering insurance, you must think, What is the risk, and can I self-insure?

I also recommend keeping your results in mind. I doubt that you enjoy paying insurance premiums, and I'll bet you like having savings. Lower insurance premiums mean more money in your pocket. More money in your pocket means more savings. More savings means more flexibility to fund future goals and buffer against potential catastrophes. This does not mean you should stop paying for all insurance. However, you should evaluate the insurance you have, what risks you are willing to take, and whether you can self-insure.

NOTE

Keep in mind that your ability to save increases your ability to self-insure. And your ability to avoid paying insurance premiums on policies you don't need increases your ability to save.

What Is Insurance?

When I was an adolescent, my father explained insurance to me. He said, "Every year, I make a bet with the insurance company that I'm going to die. In turn, they bet me that I will not die." I remember saying, "Why don't you just save that money instead? You're not going to die!" He said, "Because if I do actually die, you'll need more than the savings of the premiums."

That is insurance in a nutshell. You make a bet that you will die, have a catastrophic illness, or that all your stuff will be destroyed, and the insurance company says, "No, not likely. We know thousands like you and it only happens to a small percentage."

Insurance is a contract. In exchange for premiums, the insurance company will pay for whatever is in that contract. If you buy a twenty-year term life insurance policy and die in year nineteen, they will pay out the value of the contract. If you die in year twenty-one, they will not. If you stop paying premiums, the contract will cease.

We don't know what the future holds for us. Therefore, the number one rule when choosing insurance is to cover catastrophic losses and let the little stuff go. What are the most valuable assets in your life?

1. **Your Income**: Unless you are living on your assets, your income is the most important thing you have to build wealth and afford future flexibility. If you are the primary earner in your family, then you may need life insurance and disability insurance. If you are a business owner, then you may need to protect your business against lawsuits.

2. **Your Health**: "Health is wealth" may sound cliché, but it's true: we don't have much without good health. Health insurance exists for

this very reason. There is also long-term care insurance to cover long nursing facility stays later in life.

3. **Your large purchases:** Unless you have a huge amount of savings, you will want to cover catastrophic losses related to your home or car through property and casualty insurance.

It may be tempting to buy insurance or warranties for little things that are more likely to occur. Over the years, insurance companies have crafted a variety of different policies to cover travel, credit card balances, electronics bought through retailers, and a myriad of other things. For example, you purchase a couch with an electronic footrest. When you talk with the cashier, he tries to sell you a warranty because the electronics can fail. Rental car insurance is often covered by the individual's standard auto policy, or sometimes by the credit card company used to book the reservation. If you take your child to the dentist twice per year for cleanings, then dental insurance may seem worthwhile. However, if you do a little math, you'll often find it cheaper to plan and save for these types of expenses rather than to take out insurance on them. If they won't create catastrophic losses for you, then usually self-insuring is the wiser financial decision.

On the other hand, if you died tomorrow, and you only had $10,000 in the bank and your family was relying on your $75,000 of income per year, that would be a catastrophic loss.

To repeat the fundamental inquiry that should govern your insurance decisions: What is the risk, and can I self-insure?

Make a list of your most valuable assets. If something happened to any one of them, could you cover the loss?

#16

When to Buy Life Insurance

Does anyone depend on you financially? If something were to happen to you, would you want their financial needs taken care of after your death?

Perhaps you are the breadwinner in your family. Life insurance will protect you during your working years. Or perhaps you are a stay-at-home parent and childcare costs would be high without you. Life insurance can help protect your family when your children are young.

I recommend life insurance to those with children, anyone with a business, anyone with a taxable estate, and those who want to leave a legacy.

Determining how much life insurance you need takes a little math. Begin by assessing your liabilities and your assets. The greater your liabilities, the more life insurance you will need. Generally, as your assets grow, your need for life insurance will decline.

#17

Determine how much insurance you need: 1. What are the assets that you want covered for your loved ones if you die? 2. What income do you need to protect in case of your incapacitation or death? 3. What burial costs need to be covered? 4. What assets do you currently have to offset these costs? (Hint: refer to your net worth on your own assignment back in chapter 5.) Given your goals, is there anything else you need to add to this list?

A lot of insurance companies offer the ability to put part of your life insurance money toward medical bills if you get a terminal illness. On one hand, this sounds very appealing. Why not use life insurance proceeds to cover your illness? However, the amount of insurance you calculated was to meet your family's needs *after* you pass away, not in addition to your medical bills. If you want to dip into life insurance proceeds for a terminal illness, then you must over-insure; otherwise, you won't leave your family with the amount they need to survive without you. If you die without appropriate coverage, then your surviving spouse will need to figure out how to make more income, spend less money, or both. This can result in a financial crisis that could have been avoided with the correct amount of life insurance.

Generally, you will not need life insurance forever. You will only need it until you have accumulated sufficient assets to self-insure.

Term Life Insurance

Most life insurance policies fall into one of two categories: term and permanent.

Term life insurance is the simplest kind, because it offers death protection and nothing else. It is more affordable than other policies, especially if you are young and in good health.

The typical term life insurance policy is in effect for a specific length of time (thus the name), which can be as short as five years or as many as thirty, or even longer.

A term life insurance policy usually has a fixed premium that remains the same throughout the life of the policy. At the end of the term, the policyholder needs to requalify for a new policy if they want the insurance to remain in effect. This often requires a review of their health and age, and it often entails rising premiums. In some cases, the insurer may prohibit the policyholder from renewing the policy at all.

If you are considering a policy of thirty years or more, then you are looking for permanent insurance, not term. If that's you, then it is important to ask yourself why you think you need permanent insurance. It's much more expensive than term and could hinder you from achieving your savings goals. As you approach retirement, if you find yourself worrying that you have not saved enough to accommodate the needs of your spouse or other dependents if you died prematurely, then permanent insurance is not the answer. Saving more now is. Term insurance is cheaper because you are unlikely to die between the ages of twenty and sixty. In addition, if you're saving money and investing, then you will not need insurance later in life because your nest egg will cover any future catastrophic losses. The goal with term insurance is to insure what you cannot self-insure right now, knowing you will save for the future and eventually no longer need life insurance. Generally, term life is there for you when you're young, "poor," and trying to accumulate assets.

Permanent Life Insurance

Permanent life insurance has both death benefit protection and a cash value component. The cash value is a type of savings vehicle that can be used to obtain loans, withdraw cash, or pay policy premiums. These policies require fixed premiums, of which a portion covers the insurance premium, and the rest is deposited into a separate cash value account, which earns a rate of return.

Permanent policies are typically more expensive than term because of the cash value account. In addition, permanent life differs from term insurance in that it exists until the policyholder passes away (or stops paying premiums)—there is no fixed term. There are a few different types:

Whole Life Insurance

Whole life is the most basic type of permanent life insurance. The premium is fixed and remains the same during the lifetime of the policyholder. If you buy a policy at a young age, the premium stays the same as you age, even if you have health problems after purchase.

Money in the cash value component of a whole life insurance policy grows on a tax-deferred basis, which means any gains are not taxed until the money is withdrawn. Importantly, these plans have commissions (for the insurance agent selling the product) and other costs, which means that the cash value account will grow slowly in the beginning. However, once these expenses have been paid, the money can begin to grow tax-deferred.

The owner of a policy can take a loan against the total cash value of the policy without paying any taxes on the difference between the growth of the policy and the premiums paid. However, if the loan is not repaid and the policy owner dies, the death benefit will be reduced.

Some whole life policies pay dividends, which are not taxed because they are considered a return of premium to the policyholder. Dividends can be an important source of growth in the cash account, but they are never guaranteed.

You can create your own whole life policy. An insurance company takes the premiums you pay and invests them on your behalf, and they have access to the same investments you do. My suggestion is to get a whole life quote and a term quote and then purchase the term insurance, which will always be cheaper. Invest the amount of the difference between the two quotes to create your own self-insurance account. You can withdraw funds or take a loan against your funds later in life, just like you could with a whole life policy.

My main issue with whole life policies is that they are often used as "forced savings" accounts. If you can easily save money, you don't need a whole life policy to save for you. You will do better with a diversified asset allocation that matches your needs and risk tolerance. However, if you have trouble saving and decide to purchase a whole life policy to help you, you'll be very likely to let your policy lapse when income runs out, and then you will lose all coverage. If you have cash flow problems, this is not a solution for you. Instead, work on your cash flow issues to create savings.

Universal Life Insurance

Universal life insurance is a second type of permanent life insurance. It also provides a cash value component and a death benefit. Any returns generated in the cash account grow tax-deferred.

Compared to whole life, universal life is more flexible because the policyholder can usually decide, based on specific guidelines, how much of the premium goes to the cash value and how much goes to the death benefit.

A universal life plan can make sense for some people because the premiums can be applied to the death benefit portion throughout the life of the policy, which may be longer than the length of time a term policy will give you. However, the premiums increase as you get older, so the decision usually involves some number crunching to see if the plan makes sense or whether buying a less expensive term policy (while also investing) is more cost-effective.

As with other permanent life policies, money in a universal life cash account can be withdrawn for any reason—to pay down debt, cover living expenses, or even take a vacation.

Variable Life Insurance

With variable life insurance, the policyholder has a variety of investment options using the cash account, including investing in stocks. Most variable life policies have a floor under which the cash value is guaranteed not to fall. Even with the floor, there is almost never a good reason to carry one of these policies. You can do much better by simply investing independently (self-insuring) and buying term life insurance to cover immediate catastrophic losses.

Variable Universal Life Insurance

Variable universal life combines the features of a universal life and a variable life policy. The policyholder can invest the cash in their policy in different types of investments, but there is no guaranteed minimum cash value.

Annuities

An annuity plan is an insurance or investment that provides steady (often annual) payments in exchange for a lump sum investment. An immediate annuity begins making payments as soon as the investment is made, and a deferred annuity provides a payment stream in the future.

Fixed Annuity

Fixed annuities guarantee an income stream after an individual makes an initial investment. Most fixed annuities invest money in US Treasury bonds, highly rated corporate bonds, or other short-term debt deemed "safe." As a result, the returns from fixed annuities are often lackluster and will generally not keep pace with inflation. Fixed annuities can be either immediate or deferred. The longer the time until the payments begin, the greater the risk that the future payouts will lose purchasing power due to inflation.

Variable Annuity

Compared to fixed annuities, variable annuities, which can also be immediate or deferred, are designed for more aggressive long-term investors, because the money is invested in different types of mutual funds that are selected by the owner of the annuity. Since variable annuities offer investment options like stock funds, the overall performance of the investments will determine the amount of the final stream of annuity payments. In other words, an investor assumes greater risk when investing in a variable annuity in exchange for growth potential and the greater probability of keeping pace with increasing costs of living (inflation).

I avoid all annuities. I have yet to see an annuity product that delivers a superior stream of income relative to the assets held in the contract. You can create a stream of payments with investments, just as an insurance company can do for you via an annuity. Annuities have large expenses, from commissions to rider fees to investment expenses. You can avoid these expenses by investing on your own. That said, if you have really good genes and expect to live to 105 or beyond, then you may want to consider investing a small portion of your assets in an annuity to guarantee a lifetime stream of income.

Disability Insurance

In today's age, you are much more likely to become disabled than you are to die. Modern medicine has made it possible to save many lives.

What would happen to you if a disability occurred? The outcomes are highly dependent on what you do for a living. For example, I can do my job as long as my brain works. Were I to break both my legs, it might be difficult for me to get new clients, since I would be less mobile. However, I would be able to maintain my current client load. Not every profession is like that. If you are a dentist or a surgeon, you need your hands. If you fell and broke your hands while skiing and could no longer operate, then your income would significantly decrease. If you work in construction, it would be extremely difficult to be on-site if you were confined to a wheelchair or had severe back pain.

Therefore, your profession (and love of your profession) is the most important thing to consider when you decide on disability insurance. Here are some questions to ask yourself before purchasing disability insurance:

- » Would my income be at risk if something happened to me?
- » Could I work and generate income if something happened to me?
- » How badly would I need to be injured to no longer work in my profession?
- » Would I be content doing something else if I were hurt?
- » Could I find a similar-paying job that I would also enjoy?
- » Do I have enough assets to self-insure?

If you answer these questions honestly, then you will know whether you need to buy disability insurance.

Disability policies can be purchased for short or long terms. Short-term plans typically only pay benefits for up to two years. A long-term policy will usually pay until age sixty-five, and you can collect Social Security thereafter.

Sometimes employers offer these benefits at very reasonable rates. You use pretax income to pay a portion of the disability premium through payroll. Since both you and your employer are using pretax dollars to purchase the contract, you will pay taxes on any benefits you receive through your policy. However, if you purchase a private policy, you will pay with after-tax dollars and receive benefits tax-free. Policies often cover 60 percent of income; therefore, with a private policy your after-tax benefits will likely look similar to your after-tax income pre-disability.

Another consideration is the "elimination period." This is the amount of time you must be disabled before the insurance company starts to pay benefits. A longer elimination period will decrease the premiums of the policy. If you are able to manage your cash flow well and create a good emergency savings fund, then you can choose to have a longer elimination period in order to lower the cost of premiums.

The last consideration is whether you want an "own-occupation" plan. These plans provide benefits if you become unable to work in your chosen occupation. For example, say you're a highly paid baseball pitcher. You have an accident and can no longer pitch; however, you can coach. An own-occupation plan will pay disability benefits to you despite your being able to continue working in a different capacity.

Property and Casualty, Health, and Umbrella

If you manage your income and your spending, you will build savings. If you do this consistently, you will build wealth. If you build wealth, at some point you will be able to self-insure.

Home and auto insurance are typically forced expenses. You can't get a mortgage or a car loan without them. And we purchase them because we can't afford the consequences. For this reason, I like high deductibles on home and auto insurance. It reduces premiums, allowing you to save more for a day when you need a landing pad. If you have a good emergency savings fund, a high deductible will be no problem for you. If you do not, then you will need to pay higher premiums in order to cover a littler fender bender or a small housing issue. As usual, savings give more freedom and flexibility.

I think similarly about health insurance. When you are young and healthy, it's good to have lower premiums and higher deductibles. Unless your company is completely covering your health insurance cost, this will save you a lot of money. In addition, high-deductible plans often come with a health savings account (HSA). HSAs are tax-advantaged medical savings accounts. After you turn sixty-five, your HSA becomes a retirement account that you can use to pay any expenses, not just medical ones.

However, if you know you are going to incur high medical expenses, it is worth taking a lower deductible plan. For example, you're pregnant and are going to incur some high costs for office visits and a hospital stay. This is a great time to increase coverage.

While I do not specialize in health, auto, or home insurance planning, the topic of umbrella insurance often comes up in my practice. It can cover many events that are not covered or provide coverage beyond what your existing home or auto policies will. Maybe you caused a ten-car pileup, or a group of toddlers developed food poisoning from the cake you served at your three-year-old's birthday party.

In short, an umbrella policy is designed so that you never have to live a nightmare. Maybe your dog gets loose, bites your neighbor in the buttocks, and you get sued. An umbrella policy can help pay the legal and/or medical bills.

The coverage from umbrella policies can be expansive. The best time to shop for coverage is typically when your income or net worth reaches a certain level. Generally, I recommend shopping for plans when you are making more than $100,000 annually or have $1 million in assets. I also suggest getting at least the amount of insurance that you have in assets; that way, in the rare event that you're sued, you have the insurance to cover the legal bills without dipping into savings.

Long-Term Care Insurance

Did you know that Medicare does not cover things like nursing home stays or in-home health care? Since staying in a nursing home can cost up to $100,000 per year, extended health problems can quickly deplete retirement savings. Long-term care insurance can help solve the dilemma, and the policies provide quite a range of coverage:

» In-home skilled nursing care
» In-home occupational or physical therapy
» Expenses associated with assisted living facilities, nursing home facilities, and adult day care
» In-home help with personal care
» Alzheimer's care facilities
» Assisted living facilities
» Nursing home facilities
» Accessibility modification for the home, such as wheelchair ramps or grab bars
» Hospice care

The downside to long-term care insurance is that plans can be expensive and are not suitable for everyone. For my clients in their mid-fifties and older, I typically suggest shopping for long-term care insurance if they are finding it difficult to save for a health event on their own and need a policy to force them to save. Sometimes I tell clients to consider long-term care plans that are designed for couples to share benefits, which often makes sense (depending on the price of the premiums). It can backfire, however, if both people on the policy need long-term care for a long time. Still, in many cases, the joint long-term care plan is the way to go for married couples.

Self-insuring is better for two reasons:

1. You likely won't need all the insurance you have. You bought it because it would be catastrophic if something happened at the time of purchase. Insurance companies have reasons for how they price their premiums. They know most of their policyholders will not ever need the insurance they purchase. I hope you never need any of your insurance.

2. Insurance policies cover only what they say they do in the contract. You have a myriad of goals. Self-insuring will enable you to use the money for whatever you want, rather than for only what the policy allows.

My hope for you is that you can save, invest, and self-insure.

Life Insurance Strategies

I am a wife and a mother. I want to make sure that if I die, my family is protected. So, I bought both a twenty-year and a thirty-year term policy (this is known as laddering life insurance policies). The twenty-year policy is there to cover short- to medium-term needs if something were to happen to me. I have the longer thirty-year policy to cover our mortgage and because I want more kids and don't want to apply for more insurance later. For many people, a twenty-year policy is long enough, because the children should be grown and financially independent by then.

Laddering is a great tactic. It provides more coverage in earlier years and less coverage in later years. You pay higher premiums in the initial years when savings are lower and then pay lower premiums in later years when you can mostly self-insure.

Another way to develop an insurance strategy is through the use of **withdrawal rates**, or the amount of income generated annually from a lump sum life insurance payment. Say your family's living expenses are something like $80,000 a year. If you want your spouse to be able to spend $80,000 a year after you die, then you would need $2 million in coverage, which implies a 4 percent withdrawal rate (2,000,000 x .04 = 80,000). That's the maximum you would need in coverage. Any assets you have can offset the amount of insurance you need.

Calculate the right amount of life insurance for your situation. If you are single and in your twenties, you might not need any. A stay-at-home mom or dad will probably need coverage because, if something happens, there will be childcare costs to consider. If you are a breadwinner in the family, use the withdrawal-rate formula.

Let's consider some hypothetical examples of people with differing insurance needs:

Couple in Late Twenties

Jim and Steph are a couple in their twenties. Jim makes $75,000 per year and Steph makes $60,000. Their annual spending is $80,000 per year. They have $65,000 saved in retirement accounts, $80,000 saved for a down payment, and $35,000 in a joint checking account. They want to buy a $550,000 house in three years, pay for their children's college in twelve and fifteen years, and retire in thirty years (figure 31).

Insurance needs:

» **Jim:** $1.7 million: $1 million twenty-year term with $700,000 thirty-year term

» **Steph:** $1.5 million: $1 million twenty-year term with $500,000 thirty-year term

fig. 31

NEEDS ANALYSIS FOR LIFE INSURANCE:				
JIM			**STEPH**	
EXPENSE	**AMOUNT**	**EXPENSE**	**AMOUNT**	
Funeral	$10,000.00	Funeral	$10,000.00	
Present Value of Future Income Needs	$1,103,136.14	Present Value of Future Income Needs	$882,508.91	
Present Value of Retirement Needs	$260,210.44	Present Value of Retirement Needs	$260,210.44	
Present Value of Children's College	$421,960.55	Present Value of Children's College	$421,960.55	
Present Value of Down Payment	$103,655.46	Present Value of Down Payment	$103,655.46	
EXPENSE TOTAL: $1,898,962.59		**EXPENSE TOTAL: $1,678,335.36**		
INCOME OR ASSETS	**AMOUNT**	**INCOME OR ASSETS**	**AMOUNT**	
Less: Joint Checking	$35,000.00	Less: Joint Checking	$35,000.00	
Less: Retirement Accounts	$65,000.00	Less: Retirement Accounts	$65,000.00	
Less: Down Payment Funds	$80,000.00	Less: Down Payment Funds	$80,000.00	
INCOME/ASSETS TOTAL: $180,000.00		**INCOME/ASSETS TOTAL: $180,000.00**		
Total Life Insurance Need **$1,718,962.59**		**Total Life Insurance Need** **$1,498,335.36**		

Couple in Late Fifties Planning to Retire in Ten Years

Henry and Rachel are in their fifties, and their main focus at this stage in life is building up additional savings and wealth to fund a comfortable retirement. One day Henry and Rachel decide that, in ten years, they want to take a three-month trip and see the world. They estimate that their budget for this adventure will be $75,000. Henry makes $190,000 per year. Rachel makes $110,000 per year. They have $2.5 million saved and want to spend $200,000 per year in retirement.

It might be difficult for them to get life insurance at their age, unless they are in superior health. In any case, they have a shortfall in savings and it could make sense to have a ten-year term policy for the following amounts (figure 32):

> » **Henry:** $1.2 million
> » **Rachel:** $600,000

GRAPHIC

fig. 32

NEEDS ANALYSIS FOR LIFE INSURANCE:

HENRY		RACHEL	
EXPENSE	**AMOUNT**	**EXPENSE**	**AMOUNT**
Funeral	$10,000.00	Funeral	$10,000.00
Present Value of Future Income Needs	$1,439,586.25	Present Value of Future Income Needs	$833,444.67
Present Value of Retirement Needs	$2,233,579.11	Present Value of Retirement Needs	$2,233,579.11
Present Value of 3-month Vacation	$46,043.49	Present Value of 3-month Vacation	$46,043.49
EXPENSE TOTAL: $3,729,208.85		**EXPENSE TOTAL: $3,123,067.27**	
INCOME OR ASSETS	**AMOUNT**	**INCOME OR ASSETS**	**AMOUNT**
Less: Joint Checking	$2,500,000.00	Less: Joint Checking	$2,500,000.00
INCOME/ASSETS TOTAL: $2,500,000.00		**INCOME/ASSETS TOTAL: $2,500,000.00**	
Total Life Insurance Need **$1,229,208.85**		**Total Life Insurance Need** **$623,067.27**	

Single Mom in Her Forties with Two Kids

Penelope is a single mom with many responsibilities. In addition to putting food on the table for her two children, aged 7 and 10, she wants to financially assist her aging parents, who are in their seventies. Penelope makes $70,000 per year and spends $55,000 annually. She estimates that care of her parents will cost around $12,000 per year and will be required for roughly ten years. She has $85,000 saved in retirement and savings accounts.

Penelope needs $1.2 million in life insurance and only needs a fifteen-year policy, because if she dies she will have no retirement needs, doesn't have to leave anything for a spouse, her kids will be grown, and her parents will likely have passed away by then (figure 33).

GRAPHIC

fig. 33

NEEDS ANALYSIS FOR LIFE INSURANCE:	
PENELOPE	
EXPENSE	**AMOUNT**
Funeral	$10,000.00
Present Value of Future Income Needs	$707,693.74
Present Value of Parents' Health Costs	$97,330.75
Present Value of Children's School Funds	$534,922.00
EXPENSE TOTAL: $1,349,946.49	
INCOME OR ASSETS	**AMOUNT**
Less: Savings	$85,000.00
INCOME/ASSETS TOTAL: $85,000.00	
Total Life Insurance Need **$1,264,946.49**	

Knowing the right combination of insurance coverage is a matter of personal preference, risk tolerance, and current savings levels. Having insurance should help you sleep better at night knowing you and your family are financially protected. It should not be an added source of stress. My recommendation is to envision the results you want for your family in case of your untimely demise or any other catastrophic occurrence. You will know what you need when you take the time to think about it.

Chapter Recap

» Insurance should be used to limit the financial risks posed by catastrophic events. For more moderate risks, self-insuring should always be considered.

» Term life insurance is less expensive than whole life but only provides coverage for the duration of the specified term.

» Some life insurance plans, in addition to providing coverage, act as a vehicle for increased savings and investment. These plans may be useful for those who struggle to save on their own.

» Annuities provide ongoing payments in exchange for a lump sum investment but are often riddled with commissions and other expenses.

» Various insurance contracts may be used to insure against the onset of disability, long-term care expenses, health care expenses, and liabilities you incur as a property owner.

» An umbrella insurance policy insures against a broad range of adverse, unpredictable events. This type of insurance may be useful for high-net-worth individuals.

| 11 |
Taxes

I hate paying taxes. But I love the civilization they give me.
— OLIVER WENDELL HOLMES

My client Kitt always worries about taxes. Every year, he gets a 1099 for his taxable investment account and laments to me about all the taxes he owes because of our investment strategy. In fact, Kitt worries about taxes so much that I once asked him, "You make a really good living and you are earning a great return on your investments. Why do you hate paying taxes so much? Isn't it better than losing your income or taking losses on investments?" He replied, "Because I don't have a choice."

As human beings, we like to feel that we have freedom to choose and make our own decisions. When we feel forced to do or pay for something, we take extreme displeasure in it. And sometimes it seems like the act of paying taxes is not a choice we have, but rather something we must do in lieu of facing jail time.

I don't see it that way. I pay taxes because I choose to, and I recognize it as a choice; it's the price I pay to live in America with the freedoms it affords, and it's the dues I pay in exchange for the many things this country has to offer. That's the final point I want to drive home: you can choose to do anything you want to, and once you recognize it as a choice, it's not such a bad or stressful thing.

Taxes are inevitable, but there are some methods you can deploy to lower your overall tax burden. This chapter digs into the basics of tax planning and offers a few tax tips. Keep in mind, whole books have been written about tax planning; we're just hitting the highlights.

Tax Facts

Your 1040 tells a story. You may look at it and think it is wildly confusing, upsetting, and anxiety-provoking. I invite you to look at it with curiosity. There are a few really important numbers in there. Your total income earned as an employee is on line 1. There are various lines for income earned through investments, income from a business, adjustments to income, and then your adjusted gross income (AGI). The IRS taxes you based on your adjusted gross income less any deductions.

Everyone likes to focus on deductions: What deductions can I take to pay less in taxes? Some common deductions are mortgage interest, property tax, business expenses (if you have business income), medical expenses above a certain threshold, and charitable contributions. For most, the standard deduction ($12,400 in 2020) is high enough that they will not itemize. To itemize, you need to find more than $12,400 worth of deductible expenses if you're a single filer and $24,800 if you file jointly.

As of this writing, the highest tax rate is 37 percent for individual taxpayers filing as single. The tax rate is on a scale; those who earn less pay a lower percentage of their income. The lowest rate is 10 percent, for single individual filers with income of $9,875 or less. Income tax tables for the 2020 tax year are shown in figure 34.

fig. 34

2020 FEDERAL INCOME TAX BRACKETS		
TAX RATE	**SINGLE**	**MARRIED, FILING JOINTLY**
10%	$0 to $9,875	$0 to $19,750
12%	$9,876 to $40,125	$19,751 to $80,250
22%	$40,126 to $85,525	$80,251 to $171,050
24%	$85,526 to $163,300	$171,051 to $326,600
32%	$163,301 to $207,350	$326,601 to $414,700
35%	$207,351 to $518,400	$414,701 to $622,050
37%	$518,401 or more	$622,051 or more

A common misconception is that you pay taxes at the rate of whatever bracket your income falls into. This is not the case. You pay more tax on each additional dollar that you earn above each threshold. Therefore, if you are a single filer with $150,000 in AGI, you will not pay 24 percent on all your earnings. You will pay 24 percent only on the additional income earned above $85,526. Check out figure 35 to see how the math works (for simplicity, I removed the standard deduction, which would normally apply):

» **10 percent bracket**: ($9,875 – $0) x 10 percent = You pay $988 on the first $9,875 of income

» **12 percent bracket**: ($40,125 – $9,876) x 12 percent = You pay $3,630 on the next $30,249 of income

» **22 percent bracket**: ($85,525 – $40,126) x 22 percent = You pay $9,988 on the next $45,399 of income

» **24 percent bracket**: ($150,000 – $85,526) x 24 percent = You pay $15,474 on the remainder of your income

fig. 35

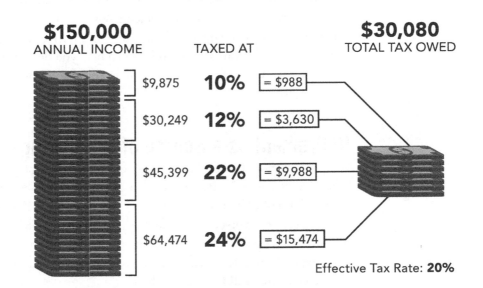

$150,000
ANNUAL INCOME

TAXED AT

$30,080
TOTAL TAX OWED

$9,875 **10%** = $988

$30,249 **12%** = $3,630

$45,399 **22%** = $9,988

$64,474 **24%** = $15,474

Effective Tax Rate: **20%**

It is important to understand that, if you are a W-2 employee working a normal full-time or part-time job, then your estimated taxes are withheld from your paycheck. You are paying taxes with each paycheck you receive throughout the year. Whether you owe more or receive a refund the following year depends on how much is withheld from each paycheck. If you owe a lot, then you did not pay enough over the course of the year. If you get a large refund, then you paid too much and effectively gave the IRS an interest-free loan. You might like the big refund check, but your overall financial gain would have been greater had you not overpaid throughout the year but instead placed the money in an interest-bearing or investment account.

NOTE Business owners, the self-employed, and freelancers often have tax considerations and challenges that are quite different from those of individuals with W-2 income. If you fall into this category, don't fret. We cover tax strategies for business owners in chapter 14.

NOTE If you consistently owe tax or get large refunds, you might want to adjust your withholding amounts. This is usually done through the human resources or accounting department at your workplace. For example, if you receive a $12,000 tax bill at the end of the year, you'll want to withhold an extra $500 per paycheck if you get paid twice per month. Conversely, if you get a refund of the same amount, you should decrease your withholding by increasing the number of allowances you claim.

Since this is a book on personal finance and not income tax planning, there are many topics I cannot adequately cover in one chapter—such as the earned income credit (EIC), and the alternative minimum tax (AMT). Reputable tax software like TurboTax can help you determine what situations apply to you. A smart accountant can also help you understand why you pay what you pay.

Retirement as a Source of Tax Savings

Saving money affords you the capacity to deploy a retirement tax reduction strategy. I often hear from clients, "What can I do to lower my tax bill?" I reply, "Nothing—you don't save any money!" If you live paycheck to paycheck, or worse, are in debt, then you will not be able to capitalize on available opportunities. Good saving habits put you in position to take advantage of the right strategies for your situation and can tremendously reduce your final bill from Uncle Sam.

401(k)s and Other Qualified Retirement Plans

Many companies today offer qualified retirement plans such as 401(k)s or, for government and nonprofit employees, 403(b)s. Since contributions are made with pretax dollars and returns accumulate tax-deferred, individuals who participate in these plans stand to benefit on their tax bill, especially those in higher income tax brackets.

The money placed in these accounts needs to remain in them until you reach age 59½, at which point it can be withdrawn without penalty. The penalty for withdrawing early is 10 percent, plus taxes owed on the withdrawal.

Money in qualified retirement plans is not taxed until the funds are withdrawn, which often occurs after the retiree has left the workforce, is earning less, and is subject to lower tax rates. Retirees are required to begin withdrawing the money at a certain age. As of 2020, the age for these *required minimum distributions* (RMDs) is 72.

The contribution limits for qualified retirement plans—which also include 457s and the federal government's Thrift Savings Plan (TSP)—is $19,500 for 2020 (as shown in figure 36). The number increases by $6,500 for those 50 or older—this amount is called a "catch-up" contribution limit, because it is designed for those who have not yet accumulated enough in retirement savings.

GRAPHIC

fig. 36

ACCOUNT	2020
401(k), 403(b), 457 Elective Deferral Limit	$19,500
401(k), 403(b), 457 Catch-up Contribution Limit	$6,500
IRA Contribution Limit	$6,000
IRA Catch-up Contributions	$1,000

REMEMBER

If you are living paycheck to paycheck, then you will not be able to take advantage of a retirement account to lower income taxes.

How does it work? Let's say you are a single person with a $100,000 salary. After you take the standard deduction, you have $87,600 on which you will pay an effective rate of 15.3 percent in federal taxes and an additional 7.65 percent in payroll taxes. If you put $10,000 into your company retirement account, your taxable income is reduced from $87,600 to $77,600, on which you will pay 13 percent in federal taxes and the same 7.65 percent in payroll taxes. This saves you nearly $2,300.

Individual Retirement Accounts

If you do not have a qualified retirement plan through your employer, then you are probably eligible for an individual retirement account (IRA). Taxpayers can deduct contributions to a traditional IRA from their taxable income. (The advantages and disadvantages of traditional IRAs and Roth IRAs are covered in more detail in the next chapter.)

For 2020, individuals can make contributions and thereby take deductions of up to $6,000—or $7,000 if they're 50 or older—to traditional IRAs (not Roth IRAs). The money can generate returns over the years and penalty-free withdrawals can begin at age 59½. Like qualified retirement plans, RMDs for IRAs begin at age 72.

If an individual or couple has retirement plans through work, then IRA contribution amounts might not be deductible or may be only partially deductible. For example, a 35-year-old single person with a retirement plan through work making less than $65,000 (adjustable gross income) can deduct the entire $6,000, but if that person is making $75,000, there is no deduction available (figure 37):

GRAPHIC

fig. 37

2020 IRA Deduction Limits		
IF YOU ARE COVERED BY A RETIREMENT PLAN AT WORK		
FILING STATUS	**MODIFIED AGI**	**DEDUCTION**
Single or head of household	$65,000 or less	Full deduction up to the amount of your contribution limit
	More than $65,000 but less than $75,000	Partial deduction
	$75,000 or more	No deduction
Married filing jointly or qualifying widow(er)	$104,000 or less	Full deduction up to the amount of your contribution limit
	More than $104,000 but less than $124,000	Partial deduction
	$124,000 or more	No deduction
Married filing separately	Less than $10,000	Partial deduction
	$10,000 or more	No deduction

Source: irs.gov

Your IRA deduction is determined by single filing status if you file separately.

Mortgage Interest Deduction

Ah, the beloved mortgage interest deduction, the reason people like to buy homes! The mortgage interest deduction lowers your overall interest burden on purchasing a home, if and only if you itemize rather than taking the standard deduction.

At the end of 2017, the Tax Cuts and Jobs Act doubled the standard deduction and also decreased the loan value on which a taxpayer can take a deduction. On any loan originated before December 15, 2017, you can deduct the interest on up to $1,000,000 in mortgage debt. On any loan originated after that date, you can only deduct interest on up to $750,000 in mortgage debt.

Since the standard deduction was doubled, interest rates are at all-time lows, and the amount of deductible interest is lower, many more taxpayers are no longer itemizing. Therefore, even if you purchase a home, it is not a guarantee that you will have enough deductible interest to justify itemizing. Let's look at some examples:

1. On January 1, 2020, Calvin and Leena purchased a home for $900,000 and put 20 percent down. They took out a thirty-year $720,000 mortgage at 3.5 percent. The standard deduction is $24,800 for 2020. In year one, they will have $24,980 in interest to deduct and therefore will itemize. In year two, they will have only $24,488 in interest to deduct, which is less than the standard deduction; thus, they will not itemize.

2. On January 1, 2020, single mom Jessica purchased a home for $300,000 and put 10 percent down. She took out a $270,000 mortgage at 4.5 percent. She also pays $113 per month in PMI, which is currently deductible (however, the government has an on-again, off-again relationship with this!). In year one, she will have $10,721 in interest and another $1,356 in PMI, for a total of $12,077, and will therefore take the standard deduction of $12,400 instead of itemizing.

It is possible that you can take on enough mortgage debt and have a high enough interest rate that your mortgage interest will be deductible; however, I caution you against putting too much stock in this. Stick to the rules I laid out in chapter 9 about buying a home. Financially, it is much more beneficial to keep your home affordable than it is to take the mortgage interest deduction.

Health Savings Accounts (HSAs)

If you are enrolled in a high-deductible health plan, you may have access to a health savings account (HSA). In this account, you can save up to $3,550 per year for yourself, or $7,100 for your family, on a pretax basis for medical expenses. Individuals 55 or older can make a catch-up contribution of an additional $1,000. The HSA funds can help you meet your deductible or pay any other out-of-pocket medical expenses that you may incur. Any money you do not use for medical expenses will be rolled over to future years. In addition, you can invest the money in a wide variety of mutual funds, depending on who provides custody for the account. HSAs are also known for being "triple tax-free," meaning you put pretax dollars into the account, the funds can grow without taxation, and if used for medical expenses there is no tax when funds are withdrawn.

HSAs can also act as nice little savings accounts for retirement! When you're young, typically you are in good health, seeing doctors less often and incurring fewer medical expenses. Choosing a high-deductible health plan with an HSA option will lower the health care premiums you pay throughout the year, making it easier for you to save. In addition, you are not likely to need the funds and can leave them in the account for future use. When you turn fifty-nine and a half, you can withdraw the funds for any use, not just medical, without paying the 10 percent penalty, although you will owe taxes at your ordinary income tax rate.

HSAs offer a unique level of flexibility. If you pay for medical expenses out of pocket, you have the option of waiting to submit your expenses and withdrawing funds from your HSA until such time that you need the cash, assuming you've saved your medical receipts.

You open an HSA in 2020 and plan on using it to boost your retirement savings. After you turn fifty-nine and a half, those funds are yours, penalty free. You funded the HSA every year with the maximum amount and paid your minor medical expenses out of pocket. In 2030, your business has a hard year and you are short on cash. Provided you saved all your medical receipts from 2020 onward, you can submit those expenses and get your funds out of the account penalty free, despite several years having passed since you paid those medical bills.

Capital Gains vs. Dividend Income

Capital gains and dividends are treated differently than income. When you go to work and earn income, you are taxed on a different schedule than if you take gains on your investments or receive dividend income. To make matters more confusing, some investments pay ordinary income through interest or "ordinary dividends," which is taxed the same as the money you earn at work—your "ordinary income"—without being subject to payroll taxes. The dividends that receive more preferential tax treatment are known as "qualified dividends." Moreover, short-term gains, which are profits from the sale of an asset held for less than one year, are taxed as ordinary income, while long-term gains, the profits from a sale of an asset held longer than a year, are taxed on the same schedule as qualified dividends. The IRS loves all its little rules. Here is a handy chart to help you remember the differences (figure 38):

Ordinary income tax rates are higher than *qualified dividends and capital gains* tax rates.

fig. 38

TYPE OF INCOME	TAXATION RATE
W-2 Income (your paycheck)	Ordinary Income + Payroll Taxes
Schedule C Business Income	Ordinary Income + Self-Employment Taxes
Interest from Bonds or Savings Account	Ordinary Income
Ordinary Dividends	Ordinary Income
Qualified Dividends	Qualified Dividends + Capital Gains
Short-Term Capital Gains	Ordinary Income
Long-Term Capital Gains	Qualified Dividends + Capital Gains

Long-term capital gains and qualified dividends get special treatment. They are taxed at 0 percent, 15 percent, or 20 percent, depending on your taxable income and filing status.

The best way to see how this works is to revisit some hypothetical examples. Please note, these examples have been simplified for the purpose of demonstrating tax brackets. Actual taxes would include many other factors. Our main objective in the following scenarios is to depict the steep contrast between ordinary income and long-term capital gains tax rates.

Couple in Late Fifties Planning to Retire in Ten Years

Henry and Rachel are in their fifties, seeking to fund a comfortable retirement. Henry makes $290,000 per year. Rachel makes $210,000 per year. They have $2.5 million in savings and investments.

» Total Income Including Salaries: $579,085
» Qualified Dividends: $28,765
» Ordinary Dividends and Interest: $11,251
» Tax-Exempt Interest: $6,289
» (Taxable Income is $579,085 - $6,289 or $572,796)
» Capital Gains: $32,780

Henry and Rachel take the standard deduction of $24,800, reducing taxable income from $572,796 to $547,996. Their marginal tax bracket is 35 percent. Their qualified dividends and capital gains are taxed at 20 percent and they pay an additional 3.8 percent for *net investment income tax* (NIIT).

Single Mom in Her Forties with Two Kids

Penelope is a single mom with many responsibilities. She makes $70,000 per year. She has $85,000 saved in retirement and savings accounts.

» Total Income Including Salary: $75,166
» Qualified Dividends: $1,058
» Ordinary Dividends and Interest: $877
» Capital Gains: $3,231

Penelope takes the standard deduction of $12,400, reducing taxable income to $62,766. Her marginal tax bracket is 22 percent. Any qualified dividends and capital gains will be taxed at 15 percent.

FIRE Couple in Their Forties

Jerica and Jansen are recently retired after years of compulsive saving. They quit their jobs and will live off their $1.75 million nest egg.

» Total Income: $70,102
» Qualified Dividends: $21,152
» Capital Gains: $48,950

They take the standard deduction, lowering income to $45,302. Since their income is entirely from qualified dividends and capital gains, they pay zero percent in taxes, as their total income is below the $80,000 limit. Note that they would be in the 12 percent marginal tax bracket if all their income were through ordinary income.

The point I want to drive home is that you are not necessarily better off receiving ordinary income from investments, because of the tax considerations.

Tax-Loss Harvesting

Imagine a world where you thought losses on investments were glorious! I think that way, most of the time. It gives me great pleasure to see declines in the market, as it provides me an opportunity to create tax savings for my clients by doing something called *tax-loss harvesting*.

Under IRS rules, an individual or joint filer can deduct up to $3,000 per year of losses without itemizing. Any losses in excess of $3,000 can be carried forward to subsequent tax years. For example, Kayla suffers a $40,000 loss on a mutual fund and she decides to sell the fund. She also sells a mutual fund with a $5,000 gain in the same year. The net loss is $40,000 minus $5,000, a $35,000 loss. Therefore, $3,000 can be deducted on her tax return and $32,000 can be carried forward to offset gains or to be deducted in later years. This is a great strategy for several reasons:

1. You get a deduction, or ongoing deduction, without needing to itemize.
2. Gains in subsequent years can be offset by a loss taken in a previous year, reducing your overall tax burden.
3. You get to experience a nerdy euphoria when stocks are going down, because harvesting losses will help your plan later.
4. You can stay invested by purchasing a similar investment with the proceeds from the sale of your asset with losses.

You may be asking yourself, Why is this lady telling me to sell investments, when she's been telling me all along to stay invested no matter what? Great question!

The idea *is* to stay invested. You sell your asset with a loss and purchase a similar investment or investments with the proceeds. For example, you own shares of the SPDR S&P 500 Trust (SPY). SPY declines in value and you decide to tax-loss harvest. You sell your SPY shares and immediately purchase a large-cap growth ETF and a large-cap value ETF with the proceeds. That is tax-loss harvesting. You stay invested the entire time, with the same assets, while harvesting your losses for tax purposes.

An asset must be sold for it to formally count as an investment loss.

The rule on tax-loss harvesting is that you cannot buy something identical to what you already own. In the SPY example, you can't sell SPY to purchase iShare's ETF version of the S&P 500. You can, however, purchase a US large-cap growth and value ETF, because it will be indexed differently than SPY. The idea is that, if you take a loss by selling out of a highly diversified fund, then you immediately buy into that fund's components. It won't be an identical investment, but it will be very similar. Alternatively, if you took a loss when selling out of the fund's components, then you can buy right back into them through the purchase of the fund itself. This way you are staying invested, leaving your asset allocation unaltered, all while getting a tax break.

It is important to be mindful of the *wash sale rule*, which says that you cannot buy the same investment within thirty days (from the time the investment was sold) if you want to deduct the loss from taxes.

While the IRS does not allow you to offset gains with losses from a wash sale, the amount of the loss can be added to the cost of the new purchase and increase the cost basis of the new position, which will result in less gain in the future if the position is sold at a profit. For example, you buy 100 shares of ABC Company for $10 and you sell it when it declines to $8. You decide to buy back 100 shares of ABC Company fifteen days later at $7. You will not be able to deduct the $200 loss, but your new cost basis will be $9 per share rather than $7 per share.

The IRS does not want you day trading just so you can take losses. Therefore, in order to deduct losses, you must not purchase any asset you sold in the past thirty days. If you want to reinvest immediately, your only option is to purchase something similar. Your goal is to stay invested the whole time, not to have a thirty-day hiatus from the market.

Investment Asset Location

Where you put your invested assets matters! Hopefully, as you're reading this book, you're making changes to your financial life and you are saving and investing your income as you earn it. As such, you may start to accumulate accounts, like a savings account, a retirement account through your employer, or a taxable investment account for other goals.

You will also notice that some of your investments have an income component. Some stocks pay dividends. Bonds, savings accounts, and CDs pay interest. You may even have a partnership that sends you an annoying K1! You may also rebalance your investments or make changes to your asset allocation due to changes in your circumstances.

The IRS says that taxes are owed when income is earned. Therefore, as your investments earn income, or you sell something you own—assuming this activity is not taking place within a retirement account or an HSA—you will incur a tax liability. At the end of the year, you will receive a form called a 1099 from any investment or interest-bearing account you have, showing all the dividends, interest, and capital gains you earned. The information on the 1099 must be reported on your tax filings. If your 1099 shows income, then you will pay taxes on that income. If the 1099 shows losses, then you will deduct them from your reported income, up to $3,000 per year.

Paying attention to your investment asset location—the particular accounts in which you keep various asset types—can help you save money at tax time. Here's a handy rule of thumb: if it pays dividends or interest, it is more tax-efficiently held in a qualified retirement account, Roth IRA, or HSA. If it does not pay dividends or interest, then you can hold it in a taxable account. Eventually, you will pay taxes on your capital gains, but you get to choose when you sell those assets, thereby choosing when you pay the taxes.

When you construct your asset allocation, always start with your life's goals and risk tolerance to help you make investment decisions. You can then tweak these decisions to apply asset location principles, saving yourself from excessive taxes.

You and your spouse want to buy a house in two years, save for your retirement (twenty years from now), and have money for an antique car collection in retirement. The funds for the house should stay in a high-yield savings account or a short-term bond fund, and there is not much you can do about asset location. Regarding retirement, you can put all the dividend-paying stocks and taxable bonds in qualified retirement accounts, Roth IRAs, or HSAs. You can save for your antique cars with growth-style assets in a taxable account. Your overall asset allocation should match your risk tolerance, even if the allocations in each individual account do not.

Tax Thoughts

I hear this all the time: What can I do to pay less in taxes? What can I do to avoid taxes? Unfortunately, unless you are satisfied with very low income, you cannot avoid taxes.

While most people understand that taxes are a fact of life, the way we deal with the process can vary widely. In the book *The Millionaire Next Door*, authors Thomas Stanley and William Danko explain that the people who are most worried about taxes are the big spenders. A chapter called "Time, Energy, and Money" details a case study about two doctors, Dr. North and Dr. South.

Dr. North is what the writer calls a Prodigious Accumulator of Wealth, or PAW, and Dr. South is considered an Under Accumulator of Wealth, or UAW. Both are high-income-earning physicians. What the authors found is that, over time, UAWs are much more concerned with their tax rate than PAWs earning the same amount. While they have similar marginal tax rates, Dr. North (PAW) pays a much lower tax rate as a percentage of his net worth than does Dr. South (UAW). As a result, Dr. South spends a lot of his time and energy worrying about tax rates.

Jessica A made $144,763 in total income and paid $20,861 in federal taxes. Her net worth is $550,000. Therefore, her federal tax rate is 14.4 percent and her tax rate as a percentage of net worth is 3.8 percent. Jessica B has the same income, federal taxes, and federal tax rate, but her net worth is $20,861. Therefore, her tax as a percentage of her net worth is 100 percent. Which Jessica is having a cow when taxes come due: Jessica A or Jessica B?

Having more savings can reduce this wasted mental energy and allow you to live your life, rather than worrying about every little thing the government is doing or asking you to do.

I think of it this way: I like living in America. I feel safe in America. I grew up here. I can start a business and be an entrepreneur in America. I get access to beneficial retirement accounts, and I can make strategic investments in stocks, bonds, funds, and even innovative financial instruments like bitcoin. There are laws that allow me to put my money where I want to.

There are many good reasons to live in America and, to do so, I must pay taxes. Just as I pay dues to go to the gym, buy premiums for an insurance policy, and get subscriptions to Netflix, I pay taxes in exchange for benefits.

But when you really think about it, essentially you are choosing to pay taxes because you want to live here.

Adopting the attitude "I choose to pay my taxes" rather than "I must pay my taxes" puts us in a much better frame of mind and gives us freedom to use our time, energy, money, and talent to work on other, more productive concerns.

#19

- Take out your 1040 from last year.

- Write down the amount you see on line 7b, "total income." This is the income you accumulated through wages, business income, dividends, capital gains, and interest.

- Next, write down the amount you have on line 16, "total tax."

- Calculate your actual tax rate: line 16 divided by line 7b.

- Finally, gather your net worth from the exercise we did in chapter 5 and calculate your tax rate as a percentage of net worth.

Chapter Recap

» Taxes are a fact of life and, like other expenses, are connected to specific benefits that can be identified and appreciated.

» Taxes owed on April 15 are typically based on net income over the previous calendar year. The amount owed is affected by how much money was withheld and the individual's marginal tax rate.

» One's tax bracket doesn't determine the taxation rate on every dollar of their earnings, but applies only to those dollars earned beyond a certain threshold.

» Contributing to IRAs or qualified retirement plans is an effective tax strategy that can lower taxes owed and build savings in a tax-deferred manner.

» The mortgage interest deduction has long been touted as a boon for taxpayers, but increases to the standard deduction and limitations on the amount of interest that can be deducted blunt the advantage.

» Long-term capital gains and qualified dividend income are taxed at a lower rate than ordinary income, short-term capital gains, and ordinary dividend income.

» Losses from bad investments can be written off one's taxable income through the process of tax-loss harvesting.

| 12 |
Retirement and Saving for It

You can retire from a job, but don't ever retire from making extremely meaningful contributions in life.

– STEPHEN COVEY

I had coffee with my client Bruno last year, a casual financial checkup. If you met Bruno, you would never know he was retired. He is type A, physically fit, and working on his headset up to the last minute before his next meeting. He runs a successful business with many employees. After graduating college, Bruno worked in sales for a medical device company for fifteen years. He worked his way up quickly and found himself making a lot of money at a young age. Unlike many of his colleagues, he saved more than 50 percent of everything he made. However, something was not right. Despite his growing wealth and his status at the company, he recalled feeling like an ant marching into a building day after day, wondering if this was all there was to life. He started thinking about retirement and all the things he could do outside work. One day, he went into his boss's office and handed in his two weeks' notice. He had accumulated enough in savings to retire at age thirty-seven. He went on a long series of vacations around the world. He traveled for many months, meeting new people and seeing new sights.

The popular FIRE movement (Financial Independence, Retire Early) encourages saving and investing aggressively, living below your means, and retiring in your thirties or forties. Millennials are hastily abandoning their nine-to-fives and seeking out a life of personal fulfillment. I'll give you my personal take on FIRE later on in this chapter.

What's important for people to understand is that our need to be needed doesn't vanish with retirement. Whether you're a young or old retiree, the desire to make a difference, be productive, and live life with purpose doesn't disappear when you stop working.

My client Bruno had a blast traveling the world, but he confided that this time was special only because it was limited. He felt that if he continued to travel, he would lack direction in his life. He returned to America and decided to start his own business as a professional mentor. He didn't do it for the money. He did it so he could make a difference in other people's lives.

I talk with clients about retirement all the time. Everyone has different reasons why they want to retire: "I hate working" or "I want to spend more time with my kids or grandkids" or "I love golfing, sailing, hiking, (fill in the blank)." Everyone wants to spend their time meaningfully. Similarly, I have clients who *never* want to retire, because they find so much joy and purpose in their work that they cannot imagine living without it. I think we all want to feel needed on this earth and find significance in how we spend our time.

Yet the day will come when you feel tired and ready to stop working. You will need money so you can spend your golden years without care. This chapter will help you determine what you will need and what income will potentially be available.

Retirement Basics

When I first meet a client, I ask when they would like to retire. I always get jokes like "Yesterday!" The number one question people have about retirement is, How much do I need to retire?

This question is not as simple as it seems. It depends entirely on how much you want to spend while retired, what income sources you will have, and what your taxes will potentially be in retirement. Retirement is about distributing the assets you spent your life saving. Distributions taken in retirement must accommodate your regular spending and be used to pay taxes.

I have joked about how nearly everyone can retire if they are willing to cut spending. An unemployed thirty-five-year-old living in his mom's basement playing video games is technically retired. With minimal savings, you could move to a place like Vietnam and be retired for a long time, due to the low cost of living there.

However, most Americans want to live in the United States when they retire. In fact, they usually want to have a lifestyle pretty similar to the one they had before retirement. Shocking!

Here are some basic retirement rules:

1. The less you want to spend in retirement, the less you need to save for retirement, and the earlier you can likely retire.

2. If you want to live in a place with high costs of living (like California or New York), then you will need to save more.

3. For every $40,000–$50,000 you make in income while retired (after age sixty-five), you can save $1,000,000 less.

4. You need to save twenty-five times your spending to retire before age sixty-five. This is known as the 4 percent safe withdrawal rate.

5. There is something called "sequence of returns risk," whereby someone who retires right before a market decline will have worse outcomes than someone who retires at the beginning of a bull market.

We will expand further on the last three points as we continue through the section. The caveat to point number 4 is that your savings must be invested in a diversified stock and bond portfolio. If you save $1,000,000 in a savings account earning 1 percent, you will not be able to spend $40,000 per year without running out of money, as your assets will not be able to keep up with inflation.

Income Sources at Retirement

As retirement approaches, you will trade your paycheck or business income for other income sources, like your investments and Social Security. We discussed diversification of investments at length in chapter 7. Diversification of income is equally important. You will want to balance lifetime income with income from dividends, interest, or even a paying job!

Lifetime income is available through Social Security, pensions, retirement assets (when distributed according to a lifetime table), and any annuities or permanent life insurance policies you may have. Dividend and interest income are available through stock, bond, and real estate investments. Each plays a role in preventing you from running out of money while retired. Stocks and real estate protect you from inflation. Bonds mitigate volatility and give you somewhere from which to draw income when times are hard. Social Security, pensions, and annuities protect you from outliving your resources.

As a reminder, I do not like annuities. However, they do provide lifetime income.

Working in Retirement and Withdrawal Rates Explained

For every $40,000–$50,000 you make in retirement, you can save $1,000,000 less. These numbers are based on a withdrawal rate of 4–5 percent per year. If you're bringing in $40,000–$50,000, then you're basically earning the amount you would have withdrawn.

Whether you withdraw 4 percent or 5 percent depends on when you retire. Someone retiring at age thirty-five can only spend 4 percent of what they accumulate, while someone retiring after age sixty-five can spend 5 percent. There is less chance of running out of money over a shorter period of time.

The 4 percent safe withdrawal rate is based on the Trinity study. In this study, William Bengen looked at the highest possible withdrawal rate in the worst-case scenarios throughout history, going back to 1926. The conclusion was that a 50 percent stock, 50 percent bond portfolio could withstand a 4 percent distribution 100 percent of the time over a thirty-year period. The common misconception about the study is that you pick a withdrawal rate at the beginning of your retirement period and continue to withdraw that amount no matter the subsequent asset pricing. Instead, withdrawals look like this (figure 39):

GRAPHIC

fig. 39

DATE	TOTAL ASSET VALUE	4 PERCENT SAFE WITHDRAWAL IN NEXT YEAR
12/31/2019	$1,000,000	$40,000
12/31/2020	$1,100,000	$44,000
12/31/2021	$980,000	$39,000
12/31/2022	$880,000	$35,000
12/31/2023	$1,000,000	$40,000

Note how each year's withdrawal is based on the previous year's total asset value on December 31. The most important thing to recognize about withdrawal rates is that we are human beings and we can adapt.

I often hear pundits complaining about how financial rules don't work, especially regarding distributions of money from investments. Great— if they don't work, we will adjust! If you're retired and you know your assets are declining in value, it will be pretty easy for you to take a lower withdrawal rate, assuming you didn't commit to high fixed expenses (like a home, car, or boat).

Additionally, working part time in retirement can help for a number of reasons:

» You may find that you need work to feel content or useful in retirement, or you may want to work in some capacity because you enjoy it.

» You don't need to save as much to retire.

» There is less of a chance you will run out of money, as you will not withdraw as much from your portfolio during hard times.

Social Security

In 1935, President Franklin Roosevelt signed the Social Security Bill into law as a safeguard "against the hazards and vicissitudes of life." Eighty-five years later, workers continue to contribute 7.65 percent of their paycheck, up to $137,700 in 2020, into the program. Employers contribute another 7.65 percent.

Social Security is a "pay-as-you-go" system. Current workers pay payroll taxes. The federal government uses these payroll taxes to provide income to retirees who previously paid into the system. Essentially, Social Security is a contract between generations. By working, Gen Xers, millennials, and Gen Zers agree to pay the retirement benefits of the baby boomers, the silent generation, and those remaining of the "greatest generation." In addition to payroll taxes, the federal government has nearly $3 trillion in reserves, currently invested in Treasuries (perhaps they need to read this book to learn about asset diversification).

You become eligible for benefits based on your age. The full retirement age (FRA) is sixty-five for those born in 1937 or earlier, sixty-six for those born between 1943 and 1954, and sixty-seven for people born in 1960 or later.

If you are at least 61 years and 9 months old, then you can call the Social Security Administration at 800-772-1213 or go online to ssa.gov to submit an application for retirement or spousal benefits that start as early as age sixty-two. You can opt to begin getting benefits before you reach your FRA, but this comes at a cost. Benefits are reduced by 5/9 of 1 percent for every month before your FRA. If benefits are received earlier than three years before your FRA, they are reduced by only 5/12 rather than 5/9. For example, Belinda's FRA is sixty-six. She decides to take benefits at age sixty-two, which is forty-eight months before her FRA. She will receive only 75 percent of her original benefits (1 − ((5/9 x 1% x 36 months) + (5/12 x 1% x 12 months))).

If you wait until after your FRA, you get additional benefits. This is a nice tactic for those who want to retire before their FRA and have savings on which they can live. Yes, yet another benefit to having savings is that you can delay Social Security income, thereby increasing your payout. Yes, there is yet another complicated formula for this one. If you were born in or before 1940, you get a 7 percent increase for every year you wait beyond FRA. If you were born between 1941 and 1942, you get a 7.5 percent increase. If you were born in or after 1943, you get an 8 percent increase. For instance, Janet was born in 1950. She decides to wait until she is 69 and 9 months old to file for benefits. Her FRA is sixty-six. Having delayed her benefits for four years, she gets an increase of 32 percent.

How much can you expect? Well, that depends on how much you made during your working years, how many years you worked, and when you decide to take benefits.

In December of 2019, Social Security payments to retired workers averaged roughly $1,475 monthly. The average spousal payment was about half that amount, and widows and widowers receiving survivor benefits averaged $1,200 per month. While these amounts may not completely support a retiree in retirement, the lifetime income helps manage asset withdrawals. On average, Social Security benefits replace 38 percent of past earnings.

Some people fear that, with the US government running trillion-dollar deficits each year, entitlement programs like Medicare and Social Security will be scaled back or even eliminated. If Social Security is still around when we retire, your monthly benefit will be anywhere between $1,200 and $3,700 in today's dollars, depending on the number of your working years, when you decide to collect benefits, and potential cost-of-living increases. Depending on your income in retirement, up to 85 percent of those benefits might be taxable.

I'm concerned that Social Security will not exist when Gen Xers and millennials are eligible for benefits—or if it does exist, that benefits will be reduced. For that reason, I do not include estimates for Social Security benefits in retirement calculations for anyone under the age of fifty. If it is still around, great; the extra income will be icing on the cake. One other consideration for Social Security: you must check the benefits you receive to ensure accuracy. I see over and over in my practice where benefits are doled out in the wrong amount or are reduced in error.

Retirement Plans

Retirement plans are an essential source of income for many retirees. Why is this considered income? Great question! If you put assets into a retirement plan from which you took a tax deduction, you are required to take a minimum amount out of the account each year after you turn seventy-two. This is known as a required minimum distribution (RMD). RMDs are a significant source of taxable income for retirees. Remember in chapter 11 when we discussed saving on taxes via retirement accounts? Well, the government wants their tax money!

In addition, you may have put funds into a Roth IRA or a Roth company plan. When you contribute to a Roth, you are using after-tax dollars. Therefore, the government allows these funds to grow tax-free without any RMDs, since you already paid your taxes on the funds. While Roth distributions will not be counted as income on your tax return, the money from these accounts is still available to you.

Broadly speaking, employer-sponsored retirement plans are divided into two categories: defined benefit pension plans and defined contribution plans. One of the key differences between the two is who—employer or employee—bears the investment risk associated with the money in the plan.

Defined Benefit

When an employee works for a company and accumulates "defined" retirement benefits, the employee has a defined benefit plan. These plans provide a specified payment at retirement. They are often considered synonymous with pension plans; however, pensions are simply one type of defined benefit plan.

Defined benefit plans are costly, complex, and require actuarial assumptions to determine how much the employer must contribute to the plan. Furthermore, employers must contribute additional funds to the plan if the investments do not perform as expected. As such, these plans are not widely offered and are only available from firms willing to do more to attract and retain quality employees.

The employer is responsible for the investments in the plan and is also in charge of making the distributions at retirement. The payout typically depends on the employee's salary and years of employment. At retirement, the money can usually be taken out as a lump sum or annuitized into monthly payments over the individual's retirement years.

Often, retired employees want to take a lump sum rather than a lifetime stream of income. I think whether you take an annuity or a lump sum depends entirely on your specific situation. If you are unsure how to invest the funds from your pension and how to take distributions to ensure that the funds last, it is probably better to stick with the annuity. However, if you are concerned about the likelihood of the pension existing throughout your retirement, then it is better to stick with a lump sum and find the resources you need to manage it.

Defined Contribution

While a defined benefit plan provides you with a specific amount in retirement, a defined contribution plan provides you with a specific amount up to which you can contribute.

Does your employer offer a 401(k) match program? If so, you have the option to participate in a defined contribution plan. Under this arrangement, the employer and employee both contribute to the retirement plan. Payments are typically deducted through payroll on a tax-deferred basis. Some examples are 401(k)s, 403(b)s, employee stock ownership plans, and profit-sharing plans.

Employers have shifted toward defined contribution plans because they are less costly to manage and the employee shoulders the investment risk associated with the plan. The employee makes a contribution, which is then invested in mutual funds, stocks, or other investment options.

Defined contribution plans often have vesting schedules, meaning for every dollar your employer contributes there is a period of time over which you must continue to work for them before you receive said dollar. These schedules vary from employer to employer. Some vest matching contributions immediately, and others vest on a longer timeline. Typically, companies like to have longer vesting schedules in order to retain employees.

If you have access to a 401(k) with a match program, you should feel an obligation to pick up this money and put it in your 401(k) pocket! Let's say you have a 4 percent match on your plan, and you make $100,000 per year. If you contribute 4 percent, or $4,000, your employer will deposit another $4,000 into your account. I don't know about you, but I would love an extra $4,000 per year for minimal work!

IRA vs. Roth IRA

An individual retirement account (IRA) is another tax-advantaged retirement plan that can be used to build savings and invest money for retirement. Once the IRA is opened with a bank, broker, or other financial institution, the investor can invest in different types of securities like stocks, bonds, and mutual funds. Individuals have until tax day (typically April 15) to contribute for the prior year.

Tax-free withdrawals begin at age 59½ and required minimum distributions at age 72 with IRAs, but there are no requirements for Roth IRA distributions, which can be useful for four reasons:

1. You are not required to take RMDs in your lifetime, which is extremely helpful if you have several retirement plans that are subject to required minimum distributions.

You have three 401(k)s from previous employers, a 403(b) from the year you worked in the nonprofit sector, and a SEP IRA from the two years you ran your own business. You also have a traditional IRA and a Roth IRA. How many accounts do you have to take RMDs from? One from each 401(k), one from your 403(b), and then you can aggregate your SEP IRA and your traditional IRA to get one amount. Your Roth would not be aggregated, no RMDs there. Therefore, you would take five different distributions. (Crazy, right?) Note also that if you had two different 403(b)s, those could be aggregated, but your 401(k)s cannot.

2. There is no age limit on contributions to a Roth IRA, as long as you have earned income.

3. You can pass the assets tax-free to your beneficiaries (though they do have to liquidate the accounts within ten years under the SECURE Act that was enacted in 2019).

4. As long as the account is over five years old, you can take withdrawals of your contributions before age 59½. The ability to withdraw money without penalties is nice if you retire early or you're really in a bind!

REMEMBER

Tax considerations and retirement plan options for business owners are covered in chapter 14.

The main difference between a traditional IRA and a Roth IRA is the timing of the tax advantages. You deduct contributions now and pay taxes on withdrawals with a traditional IRA, but you pay taxes on contributions now and get tax-free withdrawals with Roth IRAs. It is important to note that if your tax rate stays the same, it does not matter into which account you contribute. However, if you expect your tax rate to change in the future, then you have decisions to make!

» **Traditional IRA**: Deduct contributions made to the plan now and pay taxes on withdrawals in retirement. If you expect your tax rate to be lower in retirement than it is today, then this account will provide more benefit to you. Retirees generally expect their tax rate to decline in retirement, since they are no longer working and therefore have less income. However, this is not always true and needs to be evaluated based on your situation.

» **Roth IRA**: There is no tax benefit to making contributions now, but there are tax-free withdrawals in retirement and no RMDs. If you expect your tax rate to increase in retirement, then this account is your best bet. Your tax rate can increase after retirement in the following situations: 1) Congress raises taxes, or 2) you save and invest so much money that you have more income in retirement than when you were working.

You can contribute a combined total of $6,000 per year into IRAs (traditional, Roth or a mix of both). You can contribute a total of $7,000 if you're 50 or older. It is important to note, however, that Roth IRAs have income limits for eligibility. If you earn above a certain threshold, eligibility is limited or eliminated. The income limits are adjusted from year to year.

For example, in 2020, the income thresholds for a single person are $124,000 and $139,000. If you earn between $124,000 and $138,999, your contribution will be reduced. If you earn $139,000 or more, you cannot contribute to a Roth IRA. The thresholds for those married filing jointly are $196,000 and $206,000. If you earn $200,000 as a couple, then your contribution is reduced, and if you earn $206,000 or more, you cannot contribute (figure 40).

Also, you cannot contribute an amount greater than your income. For example, your 16-year-old works at an ice cream stand on the boardwalk and makes $3,000 during the summer. He can contribute up to $3,000 to a Roth IRA. This is a great way to teach your kids about the time value of money and long-term investing plans!

The general guidelines for investing in IRAs and Roth IRAs (and most qualified retirement plans) are the same:

» Start participating as soon as possible. (Refer to chapter 4 for a reminder of when the right time is for you!)

» If you know you are under the income limit, contribute to an account evenly throughout the year. If you're not sure whether you'll be under the income limit, save throughout the year outside of your IRA and wait until you have your final income numbers before contributing.

» Consider your risk tolerance and a diversified long-term asset allocation plan for your retirement assets.

» Don't put money into retirement accounts that you might need in three or six months, as there are penalties for early withdrawal.

» Despite tax benefits, don't keep all your savings in retirement accounts, as it reduces future flexibility in how you use your savings.

GRAPHIC

fig. 40

ROTH IRA INCOME AND CONTRIBUTION LIMITS FOR 2020

FILING STATUS	MAXIMUM INCOME	MAXIMUM ANNUAL CONTRIBUTION
Single, head of household or **married filing separately** (if you didn't live with spouse during year)	Less than **$124,000**	$6,000 ($7,000 if 50 or older)
	$124,000 up to **$139,000**	Contribution is reduced
	$139,000 or more	No contribution allowed
Married filing jointly or **qualifying widow(er)**	Less than **$196,000**	$6,000 ($7,000 if 50 or older)
	$196,000 up to **$206,000**	Contribution is reduced
	$206,000 or more	No contribution allowed

Conversion to Roth IRA

My client Kitt was sixty-five years old when we met. He came to me with nearly 95 percent of his assets in traditional 401(k) and IRA accounts. He wanted to know what options were available to him to lower his future tax bill with distributions. He said, "I have never been good at saving, only at saving in a retirement account. If money goes into my checking account, I spend it. I even tried to trick myself with a brokerage account, but because I knew there were no penalties for accessing the money, I would inevitably spend what I saved. Very early on, I started putting the maximum into my company retirement plans. By doing this I was finally able to save, and I also had money to retire with; however, I think I'm going to owe Uncle Sam a lot of money now!"

It was true, Kitt's RMDs were substantial and put him in a high tax bracket. He planned to retire at age sixty-seven and wait until age seventy to receive Social Security benefits. This gave us a perfect window in which to do Roth conversions!

Converting a traditional IRA to a Roth IRA makes sense when you've accumulated many of your assets in traditional retirement plans, thereby creating a high-income tax rate for yourself in retirement.

There are no income restrictions or limits on the amount that can be converted. You could convert $1 million in one year if you really wanted to! The downside is that you would pay income tax on that $1 million in the tax year you converted it, as though you had earned it. For this reason, people typically convert IRAs in smaller chunks to reduce the tax burden in any given year.

Jerry is sixty-four years old and ready to retire. He has most of his assets in his company retirement plan from years of hard work and diligent savings. To maximize his Social Security benefit and not spend too much of his nest egg, he decides to wait until he is sixty-six years and four months old to claim his Social Security benefits. In the meantime, he has little income, as he is no longer working. It would be ideal for him to convert portions of his retirement plan to a Roth IRA at some point over the next two years.

It is smart to convert funds from a pretax traditional account into an after-tax Roth account when you expect a high tax bracket in retirement and any of the following also apply to your situation:

»   You are still in your working years but report much lower than usual adjusted gross income
»   You decide to retire before you must take required minimum distributions (RMDs)
»   You decide to retire before you attain the full retirement age for Social Security benefits

Finally, do not over-contribute to retirement plans simply for tax deductions. A lot of folks come into my office with all their assets in retirement plans because that is what the accountant said to do. In a way, the accountants are right: you pay them to get you the lowest possible tax bill, not to be your financial planner. But having assets outside of retirement accounts or in Roth accounts gives you more flexibility to use your money when you want to. Your most fulfilled life likely involves much more than waiting for retirement. Give yourself permission to save the way you need to in order to live that vision.

Backdoor Roth IRA

Sometimes converting a traditional IRA to a Roth makes sense because it allows high-income earners who want to participate in Roth IRA benefits (tax-free growth and withdrawals) to sidestep Roth IRA income-based restrictions. Called the "backdoor" method, this approach often makes sense for high-income earners that do not qualify for Roth IRA contributions. Here is how to do a backdoor Roth IRA:

Do not use this approach if you have any money in a traditional IRA, SEP IRA, or SIMPLE IRA. It will confound the accounting of the strategy and is generally not worth the hassle. Only use this approach if you have funds in 401(k), profit sharing, or 403(b) style plans.

1. Open a traditional IRA and make a "nondeductible" contribution. You will need to file a special form (8606) or involve your CPA when doing this.

2. Convert the funds into a Roth IRA, while leaving the traditional IRA open for future "backdoor contributions."

If you do not have funds in any of the aforementioned IRA accounts, then this contribution can occur tax-free. If you do, then the aggregation rule (another complicated IRS formula beyond the scope of this book) applies and you will pay taxes on the conversion. You want to avoid this, so follow step 1!

Finally, if you're considering a backdoor Roth contribution, you should know that although the IRS accepts this as a strategy, it technically circumvents the rule. The backdoor Roth was created because the IRS has one rule putting income limits on contributing to a Roth IRA and another rule that says there are no income limits on doing conversions. In addition, there are no rules against making nondeductible traditional IRA contributions. If you put all this together, a high-income earner can make a nondeductible IRA contribution and convert it. If the separate steps of making the contribution and converting it are done in rapid succession, there is a risk that the IRS will consider it an impermissible

Roth contribution and thereby disallow it. Therefore, I suggest that clients wait a month or longer between contributing to a traditional IRA and converting it to a Roth IRA, to show each step as occurring separately. On the other hand, I know accountants more aggressive than I who think waiting is silly, so I will leave it up to you how to handle your backdoor Roth!

How Much Should I Save?

Retirement planning is challenging for many people because of uncertainty: When do I want to stop working? How much money will I need each month? How long will I live?

Planning for retirement is a balancing act between what you would like to accomplish with your money now and in the near term, and ensuring you have enough for when you no longer want to work. This is yet another results-first conversation: what would bring you the most satisfaction in your life? And when do you want to do it?

Your answer to these questions will dictate your path. The savings recommendations for someone looking to retire at age fifty are quite different than those for someone who wants to work until it is physically impossible. The former will need to save a much higher percentage of their income early in their career to afford a longer period of distributions. The latter may be able to save very little for retirement, assuming good health throughout life.

There are some rules of thumb concerning retirement savings:

1. Save early. Remember our discussion about compounding in chapter 6? The earlier you commit to saving, the less you will need to save later.

2. If you want to retire in roughly twenty years, you must save at least 22.5 percent of your pretax income and be willing to spend the same or less than what you spend today.

3. If you save at least 10 percent of your pretax income, including employer matches, you will most likely be able to retire at age sixty-seven.

4. Assets should equal roughly twenty to twenty-five times spending when you are ready to retire. If you want to retire on the early side, you should aim for twenty-five times spending.

Why all the "probably's," and "most likely's"? Great question!

» Your investment returns may vary. You are unlikely to get 6–7 percent every single year on your investments, but over a long period of time, your returns should average this amount, given historic overall market performance.

» You may experience something called "sequence of returns risk" around the time you decide to retire. If you retire and the market tanks, unless you cut spending, then you are more likely to run out of money. If, when you retire, the markets see year-over-year double-digit returns, you may die with quite an inheritance. Again, there is no way to know what the outcomes will be when you decide to retire. I like to err on the side of saving a little too much so I have wiggle room!

Some like to look at their salary to help them understand how much they need to have saved for retirement at any given time. Here are some salary guidelines:

» By age 30: 1x salary
» By age 40: 3x salary
» By age 50: 7.5x salary
» By age 60: 14x salary
» By age 67: 25x salary

You may be thinking, Whoa, Morgen, what is with the huge jumps from age fifty to sixty and from sixty to sixty-seven? I'm glad you noticed! The asset values need to rise this high so that you have the same purchasing power in the future that you have today. This is less frightening than it seems. Remember the Rule of 72 from chapter 6? If your assets earn 7.2 percent annually, then they should double every ten years. For example, if you earn $60,000 per year, you will want to have $60,000 saved for retirement by age thirty, $180,000 by age forty, $450,000 by age fifty, $840,000 by age sixty, and $1.5 million by age sixty-seven. With the Rule of 72, even without contributions, your assets should double from age fifty to sixty and from sixty to seventy. The key is ensuring you save 10 percent of pretax income for retirement in those early years so your assets can grow over a long time. Note also that if you want to retire *before* age sixty-seven, I don't recommend following these guidelines, because you will not save enough, early enough.

A Most Fulfilled Retirement

What is the plan? I ask this question regularly of my clients looking to retire, especially those who want to retire early. If your only plan is to travel for a while until you figure out what you want to do, then retirement may not be your best bet. Perhaps you need to use all your vacation days to take the trip you want, and then see where you stand thereafter.

I also hear things like, I want to spend more time with my kids. Or, I don't have enough time to pursue my hobbies. I hear you. You want to do something meaningful with your time. What is stopping you from doing those things right now? We often blame work, but work isn't always the reason.

I say this because retirement covers a long period of time. When you have a good plan for what you will do, you will be successful. I know it seems hard to believe, but those without a plan often feel directionless. They don't find purpose in their days. They often live in ways that are opposite to how they imagined they would live.

It is the nature of work that makes this so. Work gives you a reason to get up in the morning, brush your teeth, and put on presentable clothing. It gives you a reason to use your mind, to improve your skills, and to continue connecting with others.

This doesn't mean you need to work forever. It simply means that you need to find the elements in retirement that will make your life most fulfilling, the elements that will get you out of bed in the morning to brush your teeth and put on something other than pajamas.

If you are married and considering retirement, then you have more to think about than yourself! Do you want to retire together? Or will one of you continue to work? It is important to formulate a plan together for your most fulfilled life, as you are a team!

My Take on the FIRE Movement

A few years ago, a close friend of mine was getting married in Bermuda. We decided to extend our trip beyond the wedding weekend and take a well-earned, eight-day vacation to Bermuda. It was everything you'd expect from a Caribbean vacation: beautiful sights, warm weather, great snorkeling, the feeling of getting away, and plenty of rest and relaxation. On day five, we were out on the beach under the sun, just as we'd been on days one through four. I looked over at my husband.

"Do you feel rested?" I asked him.

"Yeah, you?"

"Yeah."

"..."

"Are you having a good time?" I asked.

"Eh, it's ok. You?"

"Yeah, but I'm ready to go home."

It turned out that five days of R&R in Bermuda was all we required. The rest quickly turned into boredom, as we both love the challenges our work provides. We missed our home, our routine, and our careers. Being away for eight days was a nice reprieve, but we didn't want to do it for much longer, let alone forever. The purpose of a vacation is to relax and enjoy the moment. Once that purpose has been achieved, it is time to move on to other endeavors.

If your dream is to retire early, that's great. Go for it. But before flipping off your boss and living off your savings at age thirty-five, it is incredibly important to evaluate the reasons why you want to retire. Simply disliking your job is not a good enough answer. Perhaps there is something else out there that you can do to earn money that would be truly fulfilling. If you find you long for more time to do whatever is meaningful to you outside of your work, maybe there is a way to find those hours now, rather than waiting until you retire.

Your plan for your post-retirement life is just as important as your plan for your savings and investments. It will help to explore your post-retirement life before you fully retire. Whatever it is you see yourself doing as a forty-year-old retiree, start doing it in your thirties with the time you have outside of work.

A most fulfilled retirement is not made of money alone. What will you do to fill your time that will give your life purpose?

Retirement Math

Here is your chance to see how much you personally need! Below is a three-step process by which you will discover how much you need to retire and what you need to do to get yourself there.

Step 1: Compute Your Expenses

What will your lifestyle be like in retirement? How much do you want to spend in retirement? What do you want to do in retirement?

I work with a couple who want to be snowbirds in retirement. They decided they will continue to work and live in their northern home in the warm months and travel to warmer climates in the winter. They will have some income in retirement through part-time work. They will accumulate travel costs during some months of the year. We worked out a way for their income to cover their travel expenses so that they can be partially retired in their golden years.

Results first: what is your goal in retirement? What would make it feel meaningful and special for you? Once you can feel the energy of your sought-after results, then do some calculating. What does spending look like now? How will spending be different in retirement? Be realistic.

Some costs, like commuting and health insurance (when eligible for Medicare) might go down in retirement, but others—such as prescription drugs and travel—could go up. My research has found that, at age seventy-eight, spending has typically decreased by approximately 17–24 percent, depending on the sample/category. However, do not assume your spending will decrease when you reach retirement. If you've worked for many years, you'll likely want to take advantage of your seventies, when you are still young enough to do everything you put off while working. In addition, since interest rates have declined for quite some time, many still have mortgages going into retirement, due to refinances. In short, it is better to err conservatively and assume your expenses will resemble what you spend now, unless something in your situation says otherwise.

Retirement income and spending needs depend completely on your goals and anticipated lifestyle. *Only you know what you really want and need.*

Step 2: Calculate Your Retirement Income

Your income in retirement depends on the following:

1. Are you old enough to collect Social Security?
2. Do you have a pension or any other income in retirement?
3. Are you planning to work part time in retirement?
4. What assets have you accumulated on which you will live?

In general, I recommend that anyone retiring before age sixty-five spend 4 percent or less of their total assets, including taxes they pay. If you are older than sixty-five, depending on the rest of your financial situation, you can spend between 5 and 5.5 percent of your funds. As you get older, this number can increase, depending on a multitude of factors.

For example, if a fifty-five-year-old decides to retire with $500,000 in savings, she should not spend more than $20,000 per year, including her taxes from her portfolio. If she also gets $25,000 in royalties per year, then her total spending can be as high as $45,000 per year, including taxes. If a seventy-year-old decides to retire with $1,000,000 in savings, he can likely spend between $50,000 and $55,000 per year depending on his situation. If he also has $28,000 from Social Security, his total income is $78,000 to $83,000 per year.

The idea is to keep the majority of your assets invested, take a small amount of income from dividends, interest, and some principal, and let your assets continue to grow. If you are invested in a diversified mix of stocks and bonds, then you will be protected against both inflation and market volatility.

To calculate your total retirement income, add the income you will receive from your investments to any other income you will receive outside your investments.

Step 3: Do the Math

Once you have a clear idea about how your future expenses stack up against your income needs in retirement, you can determine if you're on the right track.

If your future expenses are less than your projected income, congratulations, you are on the right track.

The biggest mistake I often see is not accounting for inflation. If your plan is to retire in thirty years, saving enough in assets to support today's spending will not be enough. Inflation typically increases 2 to 3 percent per year, meaning for every dollar you spend today, you will need $1.80 to $2.50 more thirty years from now. Therefore, if you want to be able to spend $65,000 per year in retirement thirty years from now, you will need at least $2.34 million in assets to support $117,000 in yearly spending for twenty years, if you assume an average inflation rate of 2 percent.

If you see yourself having a substantial shortfall, then you have a handful of options:

» Reduce your spending now
» Lower your expectations for spending in retirement
» Increase your savings rate
» Attempt to attain higher returns on your investments (within reason)
» Plan on retiring later
» Find additional sources of income during retirement

Let's plug some real numbers into all three steps:

Step 1
Sandra and Elvis are both forty-five. They calculate their current expenses to be $6,758 per month, including their thirty-year mortgage of $1,809 with twenty years left on the term. Sandra and Elvis want to retire at sixty-five and spend an extra $10,000 per year traveling. They also want to make sure they have a heath care self-insurance fund of $5,000 per year. Though they rarely dine out now, they want to treat themselves in retirement by adding $100 per week into their dining-out budget.

» Current expenses: $81,096
» Expected expenses at age sixty-five: $79,588 in today's dollars (mortgage is paid)
» Adjusted for inflation: $120,000 per year (at 2 percent)

As you can see, though their retirement expenses will be similar to their current expenses, they will be higher in twenty years due to inflation.

Step 2
Sandra has a side business making soap and wants to continue it in retirement. She nets $1,500 per month from her artisan soaps and expects this to continue and grow with inflation until she is seventy-five years old. Elvis likes working on old cars and metal projects, as a hobby, not a

business. They currently make a combined $125,000 per year. They have $225,000 in assets. Between savings and investments, they expect to have $1.6 million saved by the time they retire, not including their home.

» Current income: $125,000
» Expected income in retirement:
  • Soap business: $26,750 (assuming inflation)
  • 5 percent withdrawal in retirement on $1.6 million: $80,000
  • Total income in retirement: $106,750

Step 3
At 2 percent inflation, the couple expects $120,000 in expenses and $106,750 in income. Sandra and Elvis are short, and especially so because we used the lowest inflation expectations. If they receive Social Security, they can make ends meet. Otherwise, they should save more, reduce spending in retirement, or try to make more income in retirement. They can delay retirement to save additional money and raise distribution rates.

CAUTION

Finding part-time work is an option for many, but it is not always possible if the job market is lackluster or health does not cooperate. Therefore, assuming you can continue working into your mid-seventies or beyond involves some risk.

ON YOUR OWN

Using this three-step process, imagine your retirement and what you think is a realistic plan given your income, your spouse's income, and your current rate of retirement savings. Consider how much you would want to spend, how much you need to save to support that spending, and what it would take to accomplish it. If you fall short, identify three key areas that could use improvement.

#20

As you think about this chapter and the suggestions given, do not beat yourself up if you're not hitting all the numbers yet. It doesn't matter what you did in the past, even if it included a lot of stupid spending. We have all done it. We all make mistakes, experience bad investments, fail at a business, or make ill-advised career moves. No blame, no shame. Accept it and move on.

I have a client in his mid-forties, Jeremiah, who makes a lot of money but had very little saved. When we spoke about his situation, he told me that he loves the feeling of being a provider for his family and he has a hard time holding back when it comes to spending money on them. He also told me that he loves problem solving; give him a good problem and he just cannot wait to solve it. I could see that, despite his shortcomings as a saver, there was a lot that was going well in his life. For one thing, his problem-solving skills seemed to have given him a knack for generating a lot of income. Surely, I thought, we could figure out how to get him onto a more secure financial footing.

On the spending side, Jeremiah confessed that spending money on his family gave him a sense of pride, and he also saw it as a way to prove to others how accomplished he was financially. This was ironic, considering he wasn't saving or building real wealth. Despite his blind spots, I could see that Jeremiah's motivations were innocent: lavishing his family with gifts and conveniences was the only way to show them he loved them and to show the world he'd made it.

There were, however, negative consequences of Jeremiah's spending behavior, which is why he'd decided to pay me a visit. Spending so much money was causing him immense anxiety about his future. How would he retire, and would he have anything to leave behind? Together, we had to change how he thought about his spending. We had to open his eyes to the reality that he could be an even better provider for his family by saving instead of spending. I wanted to put his problem-solving acumen to good use, to solve the puzzle of saving for a future goal. Once we established his goals, he focused like a laser on reducing his unnecessary spending. We found ways for him to feel that same sense of pride that comes from being a great provider for one's family, but we were able to do so without derailing his plan. And though Jeremiah is not perfect, he has made meaningful changes that give him a provider's satisfaction and abate his anxiety about the future, all while moving steadily toward his goals for savings, investment, and retirement. If it's possible for Jeremiah, it's possible for you, too!

Chapter Recap

» Social Security is one source of retirement income but is typically not enough to allow most Americans to sustain their pre-retirement lifestyles.

» Retirement savings levels should be determined by age and income.

» Individuals should try to contribute at least 10 percent of pretax income to retirement plans and max out defined contribution plans when possible.

» A Roth IRA makes the most sense when a person expects their tax rate to be higher during retirement.

» Retirement savings should be calibrated with expected retirement expenses. Don't forget to account for inflation.

» To succeed with your retirement planning you need to stay focused, not compare yourself to others, and begin today!

| 13 |
Weddings and Family

Chapter Overview
- » Tie the Knot
- » Partnerships
- » Teaching the Kids

Ninety-five percent of young adults' future happiness is going to depend on two choices that they'll be making: who to spend their lives with and how they'll earn a living.

— MITZI PERDUE

Family financial planning is incredibly important. It solidifies your relationship with your partner and fosters faith and trust in each other. It teaches your children good habits and "results first" thinking. It creates a foundation upon which you can provide for and protect those you love most.

I am a huge believer in the family team. Families with team spirit work together to create the life they want for each other. I highly recommend naming your family team something other than your last name. My husband and I have a family team name and we refer to it often to accomplish our goals!

In addition, I love the family meeting. The family meeting is a weekly time together where everyone appreciates the others for something good they did that week. It is also a time to say what is bugging them and bring up any other important family topics, like finances, health, vacations, family reunions, or anything significant. For families with young kids, I suggest having a shorter family meeting to correspond with their attention spans. As your children age, you can extend the meeting and include more mature topics that are relevant and appropriate. If you have no children, then the family meeting is a great time for you and your spouse to connect and speak freely about important issues at hand.

I truly hope you live a long, happy, healthy, connected family life. Being open and honest about the family finances aids in that endeavor.

How Much Wedding Can I Afford?

My client Delilah had a vision for her wedding. She wanted a beautiful outdoor ceremony with a priest and a long white dress with a train. She insisted on a large band, lavish decorations, a sit-down dinner, an open bar, a raw bar, a photographer and a videographer, fancy invitations, and posh gifts for her large wedding party. She and her fiancé, Jacob, wanted to invite nearly 400 guests. After some quick on-the-fly math, I said, "Your wedding in New York City will cost $200,000. Your budget is $40,000. What do you want to do?"

Starting the next chapter of your life with the right person is incredibly important and worth celebrating. I know this because I married the love of my life. I am happy to be married to him every single day.

How you go about celebrating this milestone is entirely up to you. If you're reading this book, I imagine money matters, and you can't go balls to the wall with spending. Here is my motto: prioritize what is most important and let the rest go.

If Delilah could do it, anyone could. She had been dreaming of her wedding since she was three years old. She cut her expenses from the projected $200,000 to $50,000. Her parents and soon-to-be in-laws pitched in a combined $10,000. Delilah and Jacob prioritized the following: photographer, outdoor ceremony with a priest, and sit-down dinner. They decided to get married outside New York City to decrease costs, and they cut their guest list in half. They created an open bar by purchasing wine and beer outside their venue. Delilah found a used wedding dress. They had a DJ instead of a band. They simplified the flowers. Delilah made many of her own centerpieces and favors and used leftover items from other friends' weddings. Delilah's parents paid for the raw bar because they knew how much she loved oysters and shellfish. Delilah was willing to cut it!

It is possible if you are willing to be creative. The important point is that you and your soon-to-be spouse are starting your lives together. Planning your wedding is a great way to create your team and make responsible financial decisions. Prioritizing what is important to you both will ensure that you start your lives exactly how you want to. I imagine you do not want to begin marriage with wedding debt!

Here is the rule of thumb for wedding budgets: 10 percent, not to exceed 15 percent, of your total liquid savings, not including retirement assets or home equity, can be spent on your wedding. For example, a couple has $75,000 in retirement accounts, $35,000 in a brokerage account, $35,000 in an emergency savings fund, and $100,000 in home equity. They should only consider 10 to 15 percent of $70,000 (the emergency savings and the brokerage account). That's enough for a nice $7,000–$10,000 wedding.

I highly recommend starting at 7 percent, rather than 10 to 15 percent, when you begin wedding budgeting. You will go over budget—almost everyone does. Starting at 7 percent will ensure that you end up in the right place.

One important note: your rings, engagement and wedding, are included in your total budget. There is no separate ring budget! If a ring is a priority for you, that's fine, you simply need to decide what else is *not* a priority. If you are paying for your child's wedding, the 7 percent to 15 percent number still applies, but consider your retirement first.

MY TAKE

I wear a fake diamond ring because love ain't a ring (and because I lose everything).

Finally, if parents are willing to pitch in, that's great, but large weddings are costly. I just hate to see couples start their lives together by wiping out their savings and causing financial strain on an otherwise beautiful relationship. My question is always, At what cost? As an engaged person, of course you want all these things. You may need immediate gratification. *But at what cost?* You can avoid many, many financial fights in your future with a little prioritization and budgeting up front. Things can still be nice for less; you just need to think outside the box!

Combined Finances

Some couples prefer that one person make all the financial decisions, and other couples like to make combined decisions. There is no right or wrong way to do it.

However, I happen to think that either totally separate or fully combined is the way to go, because trying to mix the two gets *very* messy. That said, if you want to go the full combination route, there is going to be a period of partial combination, and that can be stressful. Tip: share passwords on accounts while you're in partial combination to make life easy until things are fully combined.

If you want to keep things separate, keep them separate. But you still need to think of your family as a team. I am a huge believer in the power of a strong family unit, so however you split things up, it's really important to always consider your family one unit that is working together for a common goal (figure 41).

OPTIONS FOR COMBINING FINANCES		
TYPE	**ACCOUNTS**	**HOW TO**
SEPARATE FINANCES	• Keep all assets separate • Open one joint checking account	• Leave everything as is • Use the joint checking account to pay joint expenses and deposit gifts • Adjust direct deposit at work to send funds directly to the joint account to cover rent/mortgage and utilities, as well as any other joint expenses • Or send funds to the spouse that covers the bills • Have the remainder deposited into personal accounts; excess savings is separate
PARTIAL COMBINATION	• Keep all current assets separate • Open one joint checking account and joint credit card • Open one joint savings account • Open one joint brokerage account	• Leave all current accounts as is • Use the joint checking account to pay joint expenses and deposit gifts • Calculate and send joint expenses to the joint checking, via direct deposit, ACH or QuickPay • Start using the joint credit card to pay joint expenses • Pay personal expenses separately • Decide how much (if any) should go toward personal savings
FULL COMBINATION	• Rename all/most accounts to be joint accounts • Improve credit score by keeping personal credit cards • Open one joint checking and joint credit card • Open one joint savings account	• Change accounts to become Joint tenancy with rights of survivorship (JTWROS) • All family income goes into the joint account • All expenses, family or personal, get paid from the joint account • All savings and investments are jointly held

GRAPHIC

fig. 41

Raising Financially Successful Kids

What kind of adult do you want your child to grow up to be? When I think about what I'd wish for my kids, the following attributes come to mind:

- » Determination
- » Creativity
- » Strength
- » Capability
- » Independence
- » Lovingness
- » Diligence
- » Respectfulness
- » Kindness
- » Compassion

Honestly, the list goes on. I could think of many more attributes to describe my hopes for my children.

What do I need to teach my son now and in the years to come to ensure he becomes the determined, creative, strong, capable, independent, loving, diligent, respectful, kind, and compassionate person that I know he can be?

I bring this up because it's important to think about who you want your children to be at their core before focusing on financial characteristics. By thinking about the results we want for our children, we can more easily see how to guide them. When it comes to money, I'd love for my children to exhibit the following traits:

- » Responsibility
- » Introspectiveness
- » Capability
- » Determination
- » Independence

How do I help my children obtain these traits? It's more than just spitting out a bunch of financial concepts. The process involves giving them the space to learn from successes and mistakes. Trusting your children, even when they don't do exactly what you would do, fosters skill and independence.

Finally, what kind of parent do you want to be? Do you want to be giving "economic outpatient care" to your kids throughout your life? This is a term coined by Thomas Stanley and William Danko, authors of *The Millionaire Next Door*. You're raising your children to one day be responsible adults. Giving them lots of money along the way doesn't teach them to be responsible with money. They must learn to make it and spend it responsibly on their own. This doesn't mean throw your children to the wolves; however, it is important to think about the results you want for them when you're giving them money.

Schools do not make the subject of money a priority. Improvements have been made over the years, but a good percentage of our youth today graduate high school not knowing the difference between a stock and a bond.

Teaching financial concepts and how to be smart with money falls on the parents' shoulders. Good financial tutelage can begin at an early age, when kids can put money in a piggy bank and understand why they are doing it. It can and should continue through their high school years when it is vital that they learn about the pitfalls of using credit cards and taking on excessive student loans (figure 42).

fig. 42

WHAT IS AGE APPROPRIATE?		
KIDS AGED 3–5 CAN:	• Learn to wait for things they want • Understand we need money to buy things • Grasp that one or both parents work to earn a living • Learn the difference between wants (candy) and needs (water) • Associate "no" with spending	**PARENTS OF KIDS AGED 3–10 CAN:** • Have honest discussions about money with your children • Set guidelines on how to receive the allowance • Set goals with your kids • Introduce budgeting and saving for something in the future • Teach responsibility regarding money • Help your kids to understand their why–help them believe in what they're doing or why they are saving • Praise your kids when they accomplish their goals • Trust your kids to manage their money; let them lose it, spend it, and give it away—all good lessons! (And not your problem)
KIDS AGED 6–10 CAN:	• Receive an allowance • Say or draw what they want to be when they grow up • Talk about money with the family • Have a savings account and piggy bank • Compare prices of items they want • Understand why they shouldn't share certain information online	

WHAT IS AGE APPROPRIATE?		
KIDS AGED 11–13 CAN:	• Save a dime for each dollar they earn • Protect themselves against advertising • Learn about credit vs debit cards • Demonstrate wise purchases • Understand compounding interest • Learn that saving earlier is better for long-term growth • Interact with the stock market (age 13)	**PARENTS OF KIDS AGED 11–18 CAN:** • Demonstrate self-care without spending money • Teach the importance of emergency savings • Explain jobs vs careers • Engage your children in honest discussions about the family's finances • Show your kids your own responsible spending • Teach your kids about credit scores, how they work, why we need them
KIDS AGED 14–18+ CAN:	• Get a job • Open a checking account • Learn that taxes come out of their pay • Compare prices of different colleges • Learn whether they need a degree for their career choices • Save and invest in a Roth IRA • Find balance in their lives	• Explain student loans and credit card debt • Help your kids understand the long-term effects of their choices • Discuss how scams work and how to avoid them • Give your kids space and privacy with respect to money • Stop buying them "stuff"– they will learn to budget for extras

Sports, Clubs, and Other Activities

For parents, having kids can have a huge impact on personal finances and planning. The underlying question is, How do you want to raise your children? There is no one way to approach the raising of children, but there are certainly several important questions.

» Where do you want to raise your family?
» What is the cost of living in that area?
» Will you need to take time off from work to take care of children?
» What does childcare cost?
» Will children be involved in any activities or sports?
» Will you take family vacations and, if so, where?

If you have kids, or plan on having them soon, work your way through this list of questions and write down your answers.

- Where do you want to raise your family?
- What is the cost of living in that area?
- Will you need to take time off from work to take care of children?
- What does childcare cost?
- Will children be involved in any activities or sports?
- Will you take family vacations and, if so, where?

Obviously, as a parent, you are obligated to provide the necessities: food, clothing, shelter. Beyond that, however, your spending will involve a lot of trade-offs. For example, if you spend all your summers in baseball leagues, you will have less time for camping or other types of family vacations.

Whether it's baseball, dance, soccer, music, theater, fencing, the ski team, cheer, football, skating, or unicycle riding, any activity that requires effort and coaching will cost time and money. This time and money comes from somewhere—you. Many families make the mistake of spending for these activities at the expense of saving. Children's activities are important but must be evaluated in concert with the family's overall financial predicaments and priorities.

Providing for children is in large part why those in their thirties have trouble creating savings. Some find it essential to give their kids the moon and the stars, even at the cost of the family's financial security. It is crucial to prioritize your 20 percent savings over your children's extracurriculars. Your family's success as a team depends much more on this than it does on added activities.

Managing Childcare Costs

I do not want you to feel guilty. If you decide to stay home with your children, great! If you decide to work part time, great! If you decide to work full time, that's great too. I am not here to judge how you manage your life and career. I do, however, want you to truly evaluate what is right for you and your family. How much time do you want to spend with your children versus working? How does this family time weave into your most fulfilled life? This is a crucial question to answer, as the average American family pays $1,230 per month, or $14,760 per year, in childcare costs. For a family making $75,000 per year, this is 23 percent of your after-tax budget and costs over $17,000 in pretax dollars.

I know that when you have a results-first conversation with yourself, you will understand how much you want to work and what outcome you want to have regarding time with your children.

Childcare can be a want or a need. For example, is getting a babysitter for date night a want or a need? Maybe it's both or maybe it's neither. Having help with the children and some time alone with your spouse can help solidify your relationship. Using childcare as both a want and a need is not a bad thing if the spending is within your budget and improves your quality of life.

Think back to chapter 3 when we discussed deliberate saving and spending; you simply have to work out how everything fits together. Even if childcare is a need, it is still important for you to save 20 percent. If you find yourself dipping into savings to pay for childcare, then it's time to assess the other aspects of your spending. I want to reiterate how important it is for you to save when you're young. The more you can save when you're young, the less work you will need to do later. Often young couples think they have a lot of time and can put it off while they have young children and the budget is tight. I disagree. Find a way to save something!

Paying for College

In 2017, the US Department of Agriculture released a report stating that the average cost of raising a child from birth to age seventeen was $233,610. Since this report is a few years old, it is now even more expensive! The important thing to note is that this figure does not include the highest cost: sending your child to college.

According to EducationData.org, the average total cost of four years of tuition, fees, and room and board was $122,000 during the 2019–2020 academic year. College increases your overall cost of raising a child by 52 percent!

Paying for college is an important goal for many parents. If this is crucial for you, then you must think about how you want to do it. While I would love for your little Johnny to get a free ride through college due to his immense talents, a scholarship is not something you can count on. You won't have any degree of certainty about the scholarship until the final year or two of high school. By that point, it will be too late for you to catch up on savings. The only assured way to pay for college is through savings or loans.

You have eighteen years to put away the money. This long period of time can be deceiving and lull you into complacency, causing you to put off saving.

However, recall the power of compounding: the earlier you begin to save for school, the less money you will need to put away.

If you want to pay for college, I recommend saving 70 percent of the projected cost. Your savings endeavor is most easily accomplished when spread out over the first seventeen or eighteen years of the child's life. It can be done in monthly, quarterly, or annual installments, whatever works best logistically for you, so long as you do it consistently and with commitment. I say 70 percent because the remaining 30 percent can be paid out of your income at the time your child attends school. If you save 70 percent, then you will likely not feel severe financial impact from paying the remaining 30 percent—it will merely displace the typical child-related expenses you've incurred every year since birth.

As parents, it is easy to prioritize what your family needs now over the distant costs of school in the future. If your most fulfilled life includes gifting your children their higher education, then you must think of your results first in order to produce the energy you need to save for this goal now.

Let's consider an example. Brenda and John want to pay for their child Annie to go to college. Annie is one year old. Brenda and John want to save for a four-year private college so they can shoot for the moon and be pleasantly surprised if their daughter decides on a state school instead. Here's the math:

- » One year of private school tuition: $74,399
- » Cost of a four-year college in 17–21 years (using a 4 percent inflation rate): $627,207

John and Brenda need to save $20,850 per year to cover the cost of school. Figure 43 shows a savings and withdrawal table for little Annie.

John and Brenda look at that $20,000 number and are *shocked*. How can it possibly cost this much to send Annie to school? I agree, it is quite expensive! There are several things to consider in regard to paying for your child's education:

1. Your child does not have to go to an expensive four-year college. You are the parent; you decide what is financially appropriate for you and your family, not your seventeen-year-old. They don't know any better unless you help them. It is your responsibility to help them understand the consequences of their decisions. Besides attending a state school, another way to significantly save money is to have your child attend a two-year college for the first two years and transfer to a private four-year college for the remaining two years. Your child graduates with the fancy degree at half the cost.

COLLEGE SAVINGS AND WITHDRAWAL TABLE

YEAR	DEDICATED ASSETS (Beg. of Year)	GROWTH	DEDICATED SAVINGS	DEDICATED WITHDRAWALS	DEDICATED ASSETS (End of Year)
2020	$0	$0	$20,850	$0	$20,850
2021	$20,850	$1,195	$20,850	$0	$42,895
2022	$42,895	$2,458	$20,850	$0	$66,203
2023	$66,203	$3,793	$20,850	$0	$90,846
2024	$90,846	$5,205	$20,850	$0	$116,901
2025	$116,901	$6,698	$20,850	$0	$144,450
2026	$144,450	$8,277	$20,850	$0	$173,577
2027	$173,577	$9,946	$20,850	$0	$204,373
2028	$204,373	$11,711	$20,850	$0	$236,933
2029	$236,933	$13,576	$20,850	$0	$271,360
2030	$271,360	$15,549	$20,850	$0	$307,759
2031	$307,759	$14,465	$20,850	$0	$343,073
2032	$343,073	$16,124	$20,850	$0	$380,048
2033	$380,048	$17,862	$20,850	$0	$418,760
2034	$418,760	$19,682	$20,850	$0	$459,292
2035	$459,000	$21,587	$20,850	$0	$501,728
2036	$501,728	$23,581	$20,850	$0	$546,160
2037	$546,160	$25,670	$0	$72,402	$499,427
2038	$499,427	$23,473	$0	$150,597	$372,302
2039	$372,302	$17,498	$0	$156,621	$233,180
2040	$233,180	$10,959	$0	$162,886	$81,253
2041	$81,253	$3,819	$0	$84,701	$371

GRAPHIC

fig. 43

2. Your child may not want to go to school at all. They may want to start a business or be a plumber. You have no way to know this when your child is young. I wanted to be a famous singer when I was three!

3. You do not have to fully fund your child's education. It may even be in their best interests to have some skin in the game—they will be less likely to cut classes and slack off.

4. Education is changing. More and more courses and schools are going online. There are new programs available for those who want to study specific topics. The world may be an entirely different place by the time your child is ready for college.

Finally, if your child's education is truly a priority for you, then you must make it happen. I often hear parents say they want to pay for school and that it is important to them, but their actions dictate otherwise. If this is your dream, I say go for it! Muster the energy and start saving. However, if it feels more like an "ought to" than a "want to," you may want to rethink the idea and plan the conversations you will have with your child later on to ensure a financially responsible higher education decision.

529 Plans and UTMAs

When saving for college, you have the option to save in a trust for the benefit of your child. You can contribute up to the ***annual gift tax exclusion*** amount in these accounts without any tax consequences. In 2020, the annual gift tax exclusion was $15,000. Anything you give in excess of $15,000 is generally taxable.

The 529 plan, which gets its name from Section 529 of the Internal Revenue Code (IRC), allows you to save and invest specifically for higher education. If the funds are used for higher education, then you can typically take a tax deduction on the way in, have the funds grow tax-free, and then use them to pay for school. Some states allow tax deductions for contributions to the account. Additionally, some states allow you to use the plan for private primary and secondary school in addition to college and graduate school.

Another benefit of 529s is that you can gift $75,000 in one year as long as you do not make another contribution to the same beneficiary within the next five years. Assuming you have the money to contribute, placing it in the trust early is preferable, because it will have more time to grow through the power of compounding. You can put $75,000 into an account for your six-month-old and have $277,000 for their education in seventeen years, assuming the funds grow at 8 percent.

The beneficiary of the 529 can be changed to anyone else in the family. Fortunately, the IRS's definition of a family member is quite liberal. It even includes aunts, uncles, and in-laws!

A 529 plan cannot be used for anything other than education. If your child goes to a less expensive school or ends up not going to college at all, or you decide not to save for Uncle Thomas's dream of going back to school at age 70 to finish his masters, then you may find that you have overcontributed to the 529 account. Taking funds out of a 529 and not using them for college comes with a hefty 10 percent penalty. Therefore, I never recommend that clients use 529 plans to save all the funds they earmark for school. This is because a 529 plan cannot be used for anything other than school. If your child wants to start a business instead of going to college, and you want to help, you will owe penalties on the funds.

An UTMA trust is another option for saving money for school. UTMA stands for Uniform Transfer to Minors Act. Most states have UTMA legislation in place, whereby you can easily set up a trust for your child without the help of an attorney. When you put money into the trust, that money is no longer yours. It is irrevocable. Like the 529, you can put up to the annual gift exclusion amount into the account. There are no deductions allowed for gifting assets to your child. Income earned in the trust will be taxed at your tax rate. The funds can be used for anything, with no penalty, unlike 529s, which will incur penalties if funds are used for purposes other than education. The lack of strings attached to UTMA funds can be as much of a disadvantage as an advantage: because you can use the funds for anything, your child can also use the funds for anything. Most transfers of these trust accounts happen when the child is between age 21 and 25. Hopefully, you will have taught your child the value of money before then; however, most lack the experience and knowledge to make practical decisions with the funds.

NOTE

You can also pay an attorney to set up a stricter trust with more rules about when your child will have access to the funds. This costs money up front, and a tax return will need to be filed on behalf of the trust, but the ability to condition distributions from the trust will help navigate around your child's stupidity in their twenties. (Weren't we all stupid in our twenties? Who could blame us—our prefrontal cortex wasn't fully formed yet!)

FAFSA

The Free Application for Federal Student Aid (FAFSA) is the form completed by prospective college students to determine their eligibility for financial aid from the federal government, states, colleges, and other organizations. FAFSA filing season opens October 1, and students and parents have until June 30 to file. The amounts held in an incoming student's 529 and UTMA accounts can affect how much aid is given.

The information reported on the student's FAFSA is used to calculate their Expected Family Contribution (EFC), an important figure for students applying for need-based financial aid. Ideally, since you are charting a course toward wealth and financial superstardom, you won't even need to submit a FAFSA application. But in case you do, you should know how your 529 and UTMA accounts will come into play. For 529s, if the parent is the grantor of the account, then 5.64 percent of the account's funds count toward the EFC. If a grandparent is the grantor, then 20 percent counts toward the EFC. This is one of two reasons why I always advise that parents, not grandparents, be the grantors of 529 plans and also UTMA accounts.

The other reason grandparents should not be grantors is that it can be a pain in the neck to change grantors once they've been established. The process typically requires a medallion signature guarantee, and you don't want to put Grandma in a bad place when she's the grantor and also in an assisted living facility.

UTMAs are considered a "student asset" and are therefore assessed at 20 percent rather than 5.64 percent in terms of EFC.

The Cost of Attendance (COA) minus the EFC equals the student's Financial Need. An entity that uses the FAFSA to award need-based aid will not award an amount higher than the student's calculated Financial Need. For example, if the COA is $25,000 and the EFC is $20,000, a student will not receive more than $5,000 in need-based aid.

Your convictions, behaviors, and results regarding money will impact how you make every financial decision. Your children will learn by example. The best education you can give them is one of a balanced household where both you and your spouse understand the value of money and how you can use it to improve quality of life. If your children see you acting irresponsibly, they will notice this and develop money scripts of their own. Envision the foundation you wish you'd had with money and your relationship to it. You now have an opportunity to create something similar for your children in your own style.

You can generate creative energy by thinking, What kind of role model do I want to be for my kids? Do I want to be helplessly absorbed with my smartphone while my child is playing, showing him that my phone is more important than he is? Do I want to be shoving chocolate in my face, or demonstrating health by eating healthy meals with my kids and being active with them outside? Do I want to model healthy financial behaviors and teach them how I think about, invest, and use money so they can form their own convictions? Your children will appreciate learning good habits from you.

Chapter Recap

» Paying for a wedding need not be a major financial hurdle, so long as you are able to zero in on what's most important to you and cut back on the nonessentials.

» Communication is the key to successful financial planning as a couple, even if one person is largely responsible for implementing the major aspects of the plan.

» Raising a child is expensive. While it is great to enthusiastically support your children's passions and aspirations, it is also important to teach them how to pick and choose, sacrifice when necessary, and be a team player.

» Taking advantage of trust accounts to prepare for college can lead to more financial flexibility come graduation day.

| 14 |
Making Your Own Living

If you had to identify, in one word, the reason why the human race has not achieved, and never will achieve, its full potential, that word would be 'meetings.'

— DAVE BARRY

We are so lucky to live in a world where we can choose how we generate income. Many people like the idea of a steady nine-to-five job with W-2 wages and benefits. Others prefer to work independently as a freelancer or a business owner.

Anything is possible with some planning. Even if you have no savings and a job that doesn't bring you the most satisfaction, there are ways to fix almost any employment situation with time, persistence, and a clear game plan.

If you are one of those who really wants to freelance or start a business, there are many advantages and disadvantages to consider before jumping in. That's what we're talking about in this chapter, as well as how today's entrepreneurs can adequately prepare for the future, however uncertain.

Sudden Job Loss

Time is our most precious commodity, and spending hours, days, months, and years at a job that you dislike can lead to frustration, anxiety, and even depression. Yet, every day many people are forced to go through the unpleasant cycle of working at a job they do not really love, just to earn a paycheck.

The key to ending the seemingly endless cycle is having a good emergency fund and increasing savings in general so that you are in a position to invest in yourself—that is, you can use the funds you've saved to figure out what you really want to do in this life and get the necessary training to do it.

The first step in insulating yourself from either sudden job loss or mounting job dissatisfaction is to stop living paycheck to paycheck. The key to stop living paycheck to paycheck is to manage your income and expenses so you can build a reserve.

If your job is at risk of automation, it is even more important for you to save and think about what is next for you. While it may not be at risk today, there is a higher risk in the future that you will be out of work. If you are saving at least 20 percent of your after-tax income and investing, you will be in a much better position to fuel your dreams of a different career.

Sudden job loss is a time to figure out what you want to do next. It's an opportunity, provided that you've saved accordingly. For example, a client of mine had saved two years' worth of expenses before she was unexpectedly laid off. She traveled for six months while she interviewed for jobs and eventually found the next thing she wanted to do. She deeply enjoyed her time off and was able to spend that time actively looking for a dream position because she had the savings. Wouldn't you like to be in that position, rather than scrambling to take the first job that comes along because you're out of money?

At the end of the day, there is no way around it: the best way to prepare for joblessness is to stop living paycheck to paycheck. Build savings and develop good habits. That will give you the flexibility you need if you get laid off or if you simply decide to quit because you have had enough.

Starting a Business

People often leave their careers to begin consulting or start a business. For example, an engineer might leave a company to become a software consultant for many companies. A doctor might shed the scrubs to become a freelance editor of medical journals. A truck driver might permanently park the big rig and open a tap dance studio in Tuscaloosa. Anything is possible! Others, like Uber drivers, landscapers, and dog sitters, rarely work as regular employees but are almost always independent contractors (freelancers working for "gigs"). There are a unique set of financial planning challenges for all these business owners and freelancers—issues that were not so pervasive two decades ago.

Tapping into Your True Value

A common misconception is that being a business owner is risky (or riskier than being a W-2 employee). People tend to think that because a business can go broke or because so many startups fail, the probability of finding success on their own is not great. Many new businesses *do* fail, but a lot depends on the type of business and how the owner runs it.

A consulting business can lose a client, and that represents a setback, but if the firm has many clients, then the loss of just one likely represents a relatively small percentage of income. On the other hand, a salaried employee is binary—if you lose your job, then you've lost 100 percent of your income. It happened to us when my husband lost his job and we immediately lost half of our household income. It is not a good feeling!

Often our preconceived notions about ourselves hold us back from starting a business. Additionally, running a successful business takes hard work, persistence, and dedication. It requires resilience when rejection or failure hits. It demands an understanding of both business and personal finance. Over the long term, owning a business can offer better financial security if you create a diversity in your revenue, meaning you don't receive all your income from the same customer.

There are some levers you can pull to make sure you are successful. You have your time and the price you charge for your goods and/or services. Generally, at the beginning, your business will require much of your time and you may feel pressure to charge less than you are worth. Over the years, your business will gain efficiency and you will be able to raise your prices.

A new business typically takes three years to become successful. In the meantime, the aspiring entrepreneur is generally burning through savings. Therefore, the most important thing for a new business owner to do is manage their personal finances as well as their business finances. Often, the biggest risk a business owner faces is running out of money, and by that I don't mean the business's money but the owner's personal money.

There is generally more security in a service business than in a product business. This is because you build relationships in a service business and you generally have less overhead. However, in an economy where people are making less money, they buy fewer goods and services overall. Therefore, it depends on the stickiness of the service.

Let's consider an example. I have a client, Beverly, who is married with two kids and works for a large company as a seamstress. Her husband often badgers her to go out on her own and start a tailoring company. He says things like, "Beverly is amazing and so talented. People already want her tailoring services, but she's too busy with her job. She's always working on something or other for a side client at night. I'd love for her to be able to do it full time. She just needs to quit and start it already!"

However, Beverly sees it in a different way. She said:

» *I don't like the finances.*
» *I can't run a business because the finance part is too hard and overwhelming.*
» *I'll probably go out of business quickly, because I don't know what I'm doing.*
» *I'm an artist, not a business owner.*
» *How would I get people to buy my services?*

Here's what Beverly wasn't saying, but what I could feel from talking with her:

» *I'm terrified of starting a business.*
» *I'm afraid no one will buy my services.*
» *I'm overwhelmed by the finances.*
» *I'm not confident in myself.*

Wouldn't it be great if Beverly were to say this to herself instead:

» *I'm terrified of starting a business, and that's okay.*
» *I'm afraid no one will buy my services at first.*
» *I'm overwhelmed by the finances, but I can ask for help.*
» *I'm not confident in myself yet, but I am working on it.*

I realize these aren't exceedingly positive, but if we're going to pick a new thought to think, it ought to be something we can actually believe, not something completely crazy like "I'm confident my new business will be raining money."

Often what holds us back from starting a business is *us*. We get in our own heads. We do not think we are worth it or that the world will pay us for our good or service. I invite you to challenge that thinking.

Look at it this way: if your employer pays you to do a job, then you are adding enough value to justify your compensation. The company is making a profit in addition to paying you. Becoming a business owner is a way to fully capture the value you add, plus profits that would otherwise go to an employer.

For example, a nurse practitioner (NP) can make anywhere from $90,000 to $125,000 per year working in a family clinic, depending on the location. NPs are highly paid because they help the clinic operate smoothly, take care of patients, and chart patient histories. All of the work an NP does helps bring in more patients. The revenues from those patients must earn more than the $90,000 to $125,000 in annual salary. If not, it would be difficult for the family clinic to justify the NP's salary.

 Businesses pay roughly 22 percent above and beyond the salaries of their employees, for payroll taxes owed to the IRS and benefits paid to the employee. Someone making $100,000 will cost the company about $122,000.

Some nurse practitioners open their own clinics. Why? Because the net cash flow from owning a clinic (in states that allow NPs to operate independently) is generally greater than the salary an NP would make.

Starting a business is sometimes the best way to extract and monetize the true value that you offer. And you should be compensated for taking a risk.

It is not easy. You cannot control the outcome of any sale, or a last-minute cancellation, or whether a client drops you for a competitor. But you can govern how you think about your business, what work you put into growing and maintaining your practice, what controls you put in place to manage business and personal cash flow, and your general offering to the world. At end of the day, doing business is about two parties coming together: one who has a problem and one who has a solution. The value you add is your solution. When thought of in that way, business is beautiful.

Self-Employed vs. Employee

If you work for a company as an employee, each new year you receive a W-2 outlining all the taxes you paid and benefits you accrued. As a business owner or freelancer, you are responsible for tracking your own income. You may receive 1099 forms in January from clients for whom you worked. Only business owners who pay more than $600 in income must issue a 1099, so be sure to track all income as it arrives, since you may not receive a 1099 from all your clients.

The biggest difference between a business owner and a W-2 employee is how they pay taxes. Employees have their taxes deducted from their paycheck directly. They have the option to withhold more or less, depending on how they complete form W-4. As a self-employed individual, no income taxes are withheld from any income you receive. You are responsible for your tax filings and for paying estimated taxes throughout the year.

The IRS says all self-employed must pay at least 90 percent of what is owed over the course of the year to avoid penalties. If you wait until April 15 to pay 100 percent of your taxes, you will be penalized. If you are unsure what you'll owe, you can pay 110 percent of last year's taxes. Or you can do some planning, estimate revenue and expenses, and then decide what to pay this year.

Although the tax situation may seem like a hassle, being self-employed has distinct advantages. You have the freedom to make decisions: you choose your work hours, how many companies or clients you work for, and which health care and retirement options are right for you. When envisioning a most fulfilled life, the freedom to decide is ranked highly on many lists. It is worth considering if you find yourself wanting to make your own schedule, take a vacation whenever you like, or spend more time with family or engaged in important hobbies.

While health insurance plan options are limited today, some of the small business owners I work with find their best health insurance option is to pool with other small businesses and participate in a group plan. Another good option is health care ministries that pool expenses with other Americans without standard health insurance plans.

There are many advantages to being self-employed, but there are also some distinct disadvantages. For one, being self-employed takes discipline. No one automatically sends money to the IRS, into a retirement plan, or to pay health insurance premiums on time. Furthermore, health insurance options can be limited when you're self-employed.

Self-employed people who take contract gigs must exert sound judgment when negotiating the terms for each job they take. Many employers prefer to hire 1099 contractors rather than W-2 employees because doing so relieves them of the burden of paying payroll taxes and offering benefits like retirement plans and health care options, all of which are costly.

MY TAKE

Just like other skills, negotiation is a skill that can be learned and improved over time. If you have never been self-employed before, then it may seem like a tough row to hoe, but it gets easier. Stay focused, persistent, and determined, and you'll find the pros outweighing the cons in no time.

The choice is ultimately yours. Both have advantages and trade-offs. Think about what results you want to have from your work situation before making a major decision like starting a business. What do you hope to accomplish? Are the elements you want in your life achievable with what you have now or do you need to make significant career changes? My hope is that in answering these questions you will find a career path that gives you satisfaction, meaning, and purpose.

What Is QBI?

In 2017, Congress passed the Tax Cuts and Jobs Act. This act allowed for a significant reduction in corporate taxes. In order for small businesses to be competitive in the new tax environment, the bill introduced the qualified business income deduction (QBI), allowing eligible small business owners to deduct up to 20 percent of their qualified taxable income.

Specifically, owners of partnerships, S corporations, limited liability companies (LLCs), and even sole proprietorships can deduct the lesser of 20 percent times "the combined qualified business income" or 20 percent times taxable income minus net capital gain. Combined qualified business income is net profit (your business income) plus any qualified REIT dividend income (any public real estate investments) and publicly traded partnership income (any K-1 income).

NOTE

If you're feeling your head start to spin, don't panic. Any good-quality accounting software will calculate your QBI deduction for you.

As usual, the IRS loves its phaseouts. Once you reach total taxable income of $163,300 if you're single or $326,600 if you're married filing jointly in 2020, then you may no longer be eligible for the QBI deduction. There are ways to "save" the deduction that are beyond the scope of this book.

NOTE

The phaseouts at $163,300 and $326,600 only apply if you operate a "specified service trade or business" (SSTB). If you own an SSTB and want to "save" your deduction, then I highly recommend consulting with a CPA. They may be able to help you legally take full advantage of the deduction.

Personal Finance for Business Owners

A successful career as a freelancer often leads to a small business opportunity. If you are an accountant preparing taxes for just a few friends and family members, then you do not need a complicated business structure or to make significant changes to your financial plan. At some point, however, you might want to start a small business and separate your business assets, liabilities, income, and spending from your personal stuff. That, in turn, opens the door to a series of important questions:

- » How will you make money?
- » What do you need to do to start a business?
- » How can you reach your financial targets?
- » How many widgets do you need to sell?
- » Or how many clients do you need to service?
- » What are your pretax and after-tax numbers likely to be?
- » What is your offer to the world? What value will you provide to clients and customers in exchange for their money?
- » How much money do you need to have in the bank (liquid) before leaving W-2 income behind?

Cash Flow Needs Example

Bobby wants to start his own plumbing business. He's been working for a company for years and wants to go out on his own.

How will Bobby make money?
- » By fixing the plumbing in homes or installing new plumbing.

What does Bobby need to do to start this business?
- » He needs to incorporate, because people can sue over plumbing issues and incorporating will limit his personal liability. Bobby also needs to buy tools of the trade, and he needs a van to haul his equipment.

How can Bobby meet his financial targets?

» First he needs to know what his financial targets are. Bobby is married with three kids. His wife works as a nanny making $35,000 per year after taxes (roughly $41,000 pretax). Their expenses are $55,000 per year. Bobby needs to make at least $20,000 after tax to cover their expenses (or roughly $23,400 pretax net revenue). Bobby thinks he can make, on average, $525 per job. He figures each job will cost him a minimal amount, maybe $25 per customer, for gas and small parts/tools, since customers will typically pay for parts in addition to Bobby's time. He has about $5,000 in start-up costs. So he needs to make $28,400 in his first year to break even personally.

Bobby needs to take on at least fifty-seven jobs this year to meet his expense needs (28,400 ÷ 500). Otherwise, his family will have to cut expenses and/or dip into savings. Bobby wants to be conservative here so he has a good target to shoot for. It's possible that he'll incur less than $25 in costs per job, but it's better to go ahead and work with the conservative $25 estimate.

Bobby thinks about it and decides to go door-to-door in his neighborhood with brochures about his new business. He also tells all his friends and family that he is open for business and asks for referrals. He starts networking with contractors in order to be someone they think of when they hire for plumbing gigs.

What is Bobby's offer to the world?

» To do the best darn plumbing around! To make sure that his clients always have working appliances, heat running in the winter, well-flushing toilets, and clear pipes and drains.

How much money does Bobby need to start his own business?

» Ideally, he would have $60,000 in the bank to get his business humming. This is to cover three years' worth of after-tax expenses for the family in case his business takes longer than expected to get off the ground. Twenty thousand in the bank is the absolute minimum Bobby would want to have reserved, unless his wife agreed to work extra shifts.

Business owners tend to feel optimistic about their prospects, myself included. If I had thought my business would be unsuccessful from the beginning, then it would have been very difficult for me to find motivation to start it. If you believe you can make money as an entrepreneur, you are much more likely to start. The rosy outlook is not something you should lose, but you still need to be realistic. What kind of money do you need to make? This is an extremely important question that you cannot ignore.

There is a handy way to calculate how much you'll need: your emergency fund! In general, it's a good idea to have at least six months' worth of emergency savings. When you are in the first three years of operating a new business, you should have one to three years' worth of expenses in cash and short-term bonds. Instead of thinking of it as an emergency fund, you can think of it as your burn rate. This is the amount of money you can expect to spend in the first six months to three years, depending on how well your business does. Here's how to determine it:

1. Divide your one-year emergency fund by 1 minus your tax rate to calculate your necessary net income. This is the amount your business needs to make pretax and *after* expenses.

2. Add up all your estimated business expenses and add that number to your necessary net income to get the revenue you'll need to make (net income + expenses = gross income).

3. Divide your revenue by the amount you will charge for your goods or services. That is how many sales you need to make.

4. Create your business plan.

A business plan is a formal document that outlines all business goals and how and when they can be accomplished. The business plan should focus on answering the question, How will you make money? It will also include details such as the business's legal name, the tax ID number, the legal structure (see below), and what kind of insurance (if any) you potentially need to run your business.

Often these plans include projections for how much the business can make. I don't want you to waste your time doing that. The plan is there for you to flesh out exactly what you intend to do and when you intend to do it. It should include revenue goals, but not revenue projections. The difference is that goals are things to strive for, while projections are suppositions about what the business can do. You should absolutely set goals and a practice by which you can achieve them. Worry less about fictitious revenue projections.

Don't spend one hundred years thinking of a business name, getting a logo, and creating a website. Get a minimum viable product out the door and refine as you go. I have a client who's been working on his business's name for three years, and he's still working in the corporate world. The name doesn't matter—just get cracking! Pick a name, throw up a website, and start making calls. You can always add a "doing business as" (DBA) later and call your business something else. For a comprehensive resource for entrepreneurs, check out *Starting a Business QuickStart Guide* from ClydeBank Media.

#22

This on your own assignment is for aspiring entrepreneurs. I suggest creating a business plan that answers the question, How will I make money? Write everything down. Decide on a business name, legal structure, products or services sold (and rates), revenue goals, and cash flow needs. Clearly define your offer to the world. This is not a full-blown business plan, which can be a relatively massive undertaking. It is more of an outline with key bullet points. If you get stuck on one of the steps, just skip it and keep going; it may come to you later!

Separating Business from Personal Expenses

An essential part of operating a business is separating your business from your personal expenses. This might seem obvious, but sometimes spending that appears to be purely for personal reasons might in fact be a business expense, such as paper for the printer in your home office, fees to your accountant for preparing business taxes, or a plane ticket to see Aunt Mildred, who also happens to be your biggest client.

If you are not entirely sure, your accountant can help you determine which expenses are legitimate business deductions, because sometimes the rules are not obvious (such as the 50 percent rule for deducting spending on meals).

Don't mix personal and business expenses, and follow IRS guidelines on what qualifies as legitimate business spending. If you are not sure, talk to an accountant. The last thing you want is an audit, because dealing with IRS officials will take time away from your business and, even worse, can result in penalties and fines. And don't spend an inordinate amount of time focusing on deductions. Focus on what matters most: top-line revenue growth. No one ever got rich on deductions. You get rich by generating income and managing expenses.

Cash Flow Needs

You also want a plan for covering your business's expenses and a crystal-clear picture of what your cash flow needs are:

» Calculate your average monthly business expenses.

» Create a business budget and a personal household budget, and honor them both.

» Understand when you get paid. For example, some business owners only get paid at the time of sale, some are paid through monthly subscriptions to their services, some are paid quarterly, and some have contracts that stipulate when they get paid.

» Know what your operating expenses will be. I suggest adding a miscellaneous line for random expenses that come up. You'll want this line item to be about 5 percent of total business expenses; that way you have a good buffer.

» Make sure your cash reserve exceeds your operating expenses and your personal expenses by at least three months.

» Be mindful of your personality, as it plays a big role in business decision making. Are you a risk-taker who will want to make big investments in your business with potentially large payoffs? Are you the kind of person who slowly chips away at tasks until they are complete? Are you someone who needs external forces to motivate you to action? These will influence how much cash you should keep on hand.

» Track successes and failures. It is important to know why you were successful, but also to learn from your failures. What better way to evolve and learn as a human than to do something stupid in your business and never repeat it again!

» Manage your business and personal finances with rigor, especially in the early years. It is important to run a lean operation both personally and professionally to give yourself the greatest chance of success.

After setting money aside and building up enough liquid savings to get things rolling, tally up all the business expenses you expect in the first year or two. In addition, budget for the unexpected in case emergencies come up.

Business Mindset

Deciding to start a business sometimes requires a dramatic change in thinking and a truly entrepreneurial mindset. What kind of business owner do you need to be right now? Will you keep going when the going gets tough? How can you make yourself more resilient? Only you know the answers. There are some things you can do right away, even if you've yet to fully cultivate your business mindset: compute your business and personal expenses, find motivators that remind you why you are working for yourself, and keep enough cash around to cover periods when revenue falls short of your goals.

Once you are up and rolling, track key performance indicators that are relevant to your profession. My performance indicators are in the world of financial planning; you might need to run a Google search or talk to people in your industry to find yours. Some metrics will be similar across many types of businesses, like how many people you reach through marketing compared to how many buy your product or service. These metrics will help you tailor your business message and who you market to, to increase sales. On the other hand, perhaps you consult only with two large companies; in that case, sales rates will not be relevant. Maybe time tracking would be more insightful. In my practice, my favorite metric is keeping track of my personal hourly wage: how much time, how much revenue, and how much cost.

Business Structure and Tax Considerations

The simplest method of self-employment is working as a sole proprietor, but as the business grows, it can make more sense to operate as a corporation or a limited liability company (LLC). A tax professional can help you decide which "vehicle" is most appropriate. Here is an overview of the viable options for most business owners and how the decision affects taxes, compliance, and personal liability:

Sole Proprietorship

The simplest structure for operating a business is the sole proprietorship. In fact, anyone doing business activity—with or without a trade name—and who is not registered as a business is automatically considered a sole proprietor. Income from any business activity is reported on personal income tax returns.

Because sole proprietorships do not produce a separate business entity, business assets and liabilities are not separate from personal assets and liabilities. Therefore, the sole proprietor can be held personally liable for debts and obligations of the business.

Sole proprietorships are good options for businesses with low risk of legal problems and for people who want to test the waters of an idea before creating a formal business.

Partnership

Partnerships are created when two or more people want to own a business together. There are two types: limited partnerships (LPs) and limited liability partnerships (LLPs).

Limited partnerships have one general partner with unlimited liability, and all other partners have limited liability and limited control of the company. As you might have guessed, the main difference between this and the limited liability partnership is that in an LLP every owner has limited liability.

Businesses with multiple owners, and professional groups such as attorneys, often operate as partnerships. Like sole proprietorships, partnerships can be a good first option before forming a more complicated and formal business arrangement.

Corporation

When you think of corporations, maybe you think of Microsoft, Tesla, or Enron. But incorporating a business is not as difficult as it might sound, and sometimes is the best option for small business owners. There are three different types: Subchapter B, Subchapter C, and Subchapter S, or S corp.

The S corp is often the most sensible option. The structure allows the profits, and some losses, of the business to be passed to the owners' personal incomes without being subject to corporate taxes. There are some limits; for instance, S corps cannot have more than one hundred shareholders, and all shareholders must be US citizens. The business operates separately from the individual and, if a shareholder leaves the company or sells their shares, the S corp can remain in business.

Under rules enacted in the Tax Cuts and Jobs Act of 2017, for an S corp to make sense you must answer yes to the following three questions:

1. Is your business an LLC, partnership, or sole proprietorship that restricts you from paying yourself a salary?

2. Is your business *not* a specialized trade or service business (that is, any business in which the principal asset of the business is based on the skill or reputation of one or more of its employees, for example, doctors, lawyers, CPAs, financial advisors, athletes, musicians, etc.)?

3. Do you have taxable income over the QBI threshold amount of $210,700 if single or $421,400 if married filing jointly?

If the answer to all three of these questions is yes, then the business owner is a prime candidate for considering a change in entity to an S corporation. This is because you can "save" your QBI deduction by paying salaries to the S corp owners, thereby decreasing business income below the threshold amounts. Moving to an S corp generally makes sense for businesses with earnings much higher than the threshold amounts and whose owners want to take advantage of the deduction.

MY TAKE

If all this seems daunting, don't worry. You are not alone. Tax law changes are very complicated, and if you're a business owner generating high profits, it will be profitable for you to consult a financial planner and/or a CPA.

The key point is that the S corp is often best for those in relatively high-risk businesses that want to separate their business and personal taxes, while looking to save money through deductions or payroll taxes. There are trade-offs, as S corps have added costs associated with registering, filing, and keeping records. However, the key advantages to this corporate structure are that you can pay yourself a wage, you can run a monthly payroll, and you do not have to pay quarterly estimated tax payments.

NOTE

If you have a small business such as an S corp, then you must file federal and state business tax returns (by March 15 rather than April

15) in addition to your personal tax returns. The business will also file both federal and state quarterly tax filings.

The S corporation is not ideal for building a large company because of the limit on the number of shareholders. If the long-term goal is to raise money through an initial public offering, then a C corporation is probably the better option. An important distinction is that owners of C corps face the issue of double taxation—profits are taxed once on the corporate level and again on personal income taxes.

The B corporation entity is reserved for "benefit corporations," where shareholders hold the owner accountable to produce a public benefit in addition to a financial profit.

Limited Liability Company

The limited liability company has some of the features of both corporations and partnerships. The owner's assets are typically shielded from any bankruptcy or legal action if the LLC runs into trouble. Meanwhile, the profits and losses are passed through to the individual without facing corporate taxes. However, members of an LLC pay the hefty self-employment tax contributions toward Medicare and Social Security, because they are considered self-employed.

Owners with substantial personal assets and those who want to pay a lower tax rate than they would with a corporation might consider the LLC structure an attractive option. When considering your business structure, it is important to determine which entity offers you the best combination of protection and tax benefits.

Business Loans

In chapter 8, we talked about loans and when it makes sense to leverage borrowed funds to help finance a business. The business should be viable enough to generate enough revenue to still make a profit after covering all required payments plus the interest on the loan as the balance is paid off.

How does one go about getting a business loan? Credit cards are available to qualified business owners, and you can ask your bank to extend a line of credit. When using credit cards in your business, the same rules apply as with personal use: you should pay off your balance at the end of each month, as much as possible, and you should not carry large balances, because business credit cards have very high interest rates. If you find yourself needing access to credit, your credit card should be a last resort. A line of credit is a much better option.

For larger loans, banks and lenders typically look at the business's credit score using the three main rating agencies:

» Dun & Bradstreet
» Equifax
» Experian

Credit reports are used to identify any potential disqualifiers to financing, such as past judgments, liens, or bankruptcies. It can get a bit murky here because not every credit account is reported to the credit agencies equally. For instance, a credit account that is reported to Experian might not be reported to Equifax. It is important to review your credit report for accuracy.

Aspiring entrepreneurs and business owners are sometimes left in the dark regarding credit decisions, because there are no requirements stipulating that a lender must disclose things like why they're using a business credit report to make a decision or why your business has been turned down for financing based on a credit report. Any negative information can have important implications. For example, it is a bad time to find out about dings on your credit report just as you are trying to sell the business, because it could potentially thwart the deal.

EXAMPLE

Bob is a business owner selling farm equipment and is trying to win over a large potential client. Bob knows that he will need to increase production immediately after signing this new client, due to the scope of their needs. Increasing production requires financing through a loan. Bob applies for several loans from different lenders but is rejected each time. With no way to fill the orders, Bob's business abandons efforts to deal with the new large client, and the business goes to his competitor. Bob is furious. His credit is strong, and the new client would have tripled his business. Digging for answers, he finds a copy of his credit report and sees that there are several dings from events four years earlier. However, Bob bought the business only three years ago. The negative information on his credit report had to do with the previous owner, and Bob did not know it existed. Lenders are not required to tell you. Bob should have made an inquiry at the time of the sale.

Not all business lending decisions are based on credit reports. Instead, commercial financing companies use the FICO Small Business Scoring Service (SBSS), a rating system that looks at any credit history of the business as well as the personal credit profile of the business owner. Using SBSS is most common with loans from the Small Business Administration (SBA), the body that sets the standards for commercial lending. On a scale of 0 to 300, lenders look for an SBSS score of at least 140 for most business financing, but many want to see 160 or better. Roughly seven thousand non-SBA lenders also use SBSS scores, according to FICO.

If you want a loan to help you achieve your business dreams, then you need to keep your personal credit score in good shape. In addition, most lenders want to see an established business credit report with the major agencies, and that will require some reference accounts, such as a business credit card or line of credit. To boost credit scores, all your accounts should be paid in full and on time.

It makes sense to monitor credit reports for potential disqualifiers or new accounts being opened and to keep an eye on the business's credit standing over time. Keeping an eye out for updates is a smart practice for monitoring your personal credit as well.

Retirement Plan Options

If you are a business owner or self-employed, then you have a unique set of retirement planning needs, because you do not have an employer offering you a retirement plan. Therefore, it is up to you to decide how best to invest in your retirement with the aid of a tax-deferred savings plan.

Like nearly every chapter of this book mentions, savings will provide you with freedom and flexibility. This is especially so for business owners. Some of the best deductions are available through retirement planning. If you do not manage your personal cash flow well enough, you will not have the money to take advantage of these plans and will therefore pay more in taxes.

It is important to balance the money put into a business retirement plan with the new tax law, which allows for a 20 percent small business QBI deduction. Because retirement plan contributions reduce your business's income, they will necessarily reduce the amount deducted through the QBI. Please don't think I'm saying not to fund your retirement accounts. I can't emphasize this enough: you should always, absolutely put money away for retirement. You just need to balance the advantages of the QBI deduction with appropriate savings for retirement.

The simplest way to start building retirement savings is to contribute to an IRA or a Roth IRA, which we covered in detail in chapter 12. These plans are not just for business owners but for anyone who has the disposable income and wants to set money aside. Some retirement plans are specifically designed for the self-employed and for operators of small businesses. There are pros and cons associated with each one.

SEP IRAs

The simplified employee pension (SEP) is a retirement plan that any employer can establish. The employer is allowed a tax deduction for contributions made to the SEP plan, and the contributions to an employee's SEP IRA are made on a discretionary basis. The employer decides when and how much to contribute.

SEP IRAs are like traditional IRAs but with the ability to receive contributions from an employer. Also, SEP IRAs often have higher annual contribution limits than standard IRAs, depending on the income of the business owner or employee participant.

Contributions to SEP IRAs by employers cannot exceed the lesser of 25 percent of an employee's compensation or $57,000 (for 2020). Like traditional IRAs, withdrawals in retirement are taxed as ordinary income.

The SEP is generally favored by self-employed business owners who like the ability to contribute as late as possible. Contributions can be made as late as October 15 for the prior year, as long as the individual files an extension on his or her taxes. In addition, the plans are incredibly simple to set up and maintain.

However, for business owners with many employees, these plans can get expensive. Anyone earning $600 or more is entitled to a contribution. The business owner chooses what percentage to contribute, but they must contribute the same amount to all employee accounts. As an example, if a business owner decides to put 25 percent of income into their own SEP IRA, they would need to contribute $25,000 to an employee's SEP IRA account who made $100,000 that year.

Solo 401(k)

The solo 401(k) is available to self-employed individuals with no employees other than a spouse. These plans are quickly becoming more popular than the SEP IRA, because any participant can contribute the maximum 401(k) limit of $19,500 (in 2020) if income is equal to or greater than the overall contribution. If using a SEP IRA, the business owner would need to net $78,000 in order to be eligible for a $19,500 contribution ($78,000 x 0.25).

The total solo 401(k) contribution limit is $57,000 in 2020, with an extra $6,500 catch-up contribution available for those fifty or older. The overall $57,000 contribution is a combination of an employee contribution and a profit-sharing in the business:

» The employee can contribute up to $19,500 in 2020, or 100 percent of compensation, whichever is less. Those fifty years of age or older can contribute an additional $6,500.

» The employer can add another profit-sharing contribution of up to 25 percent of the employee's income.

Jenny and Christian are a married couple. Jenny works as a W-2 employee and Christian runs his own business. Christian's business is young, and the couple lives predominantly on Jenny's income. Christian nets $35,000 in his business before taxes. With a SEP, Christian would only be able to put in $8,750. With a solo 401(k), he could make the $19,500 contribution plus $8,750 in profit-sharing.

With the solo 401(k) plan, the business owner must file form 5500-EZ if assets are above $250,000.

401(k) PSP

A 401(k) with a profit sharing plan (PSP) is a pretax retirement plan whereby employers contribute to employee accounts at year-end. The 401(k) portion works like any other plan: employees make contributions based on their salary through payroll. Employers prefer profit-sharing plans over matching plans because they can assess their overall profits at the end of the year and decide how much to contribute on behalf of employees. Some other reasons you may want to consider a 401(k) PSP:

» You can take care of your highly compensated employees. PSP plans allow you to contribute more to the employees that drive revenue in your business, without failing any discrimination tests or IRS compliance limits.

» It is a great way to offer employees a bonus without having to pay payroll taxes. It also does not increase the employee's taxable income.

» You can create a vesting schedule to incentivize employees to stick around a little longer.

Defined Benefit Plans

While defined benefit plans can be costly for large employers, as a self-employed person or small business owner you may find that this plan will best suit your needs. You decide how aggressively to save for retirement by targeting a desired level of retirement income. Your contributions are adjusted based on this target and your age at the time of contributions.

I like these plans most for business owners in their fifties and sixties who are generating high profits and also have their personal cash flow needs met. Since contributions are age-based, as you get older you can put away more funds into a defined benefit plan than into a 401(k) PSP plan. The assumption is that as you get older you need more for retirement, since it has less time to grow. Contribution limits for 2020 cannot exceed the lesser of 100 percent of average compensation over the last three years or $230,000.

The main thing to keep in mind is what your goals are. If you're looking to have money saved outside of a retirement account for flexibility or to fund a goal preceding retirement, then a defined benefit plan may not be right for you, despite the large tax deduction. However, if you already have substantial assets outside of retirement accounts, then you'll be in the best position to use this plan to lower your taxes.

Five-Step Plan for Handling Irregular Income

Sometimes people ask me how to plan for retirement and other business expenses when their income is sporadic or irregular. For example, a couple might have one person making standard W-2 wages with a predictable income stream every two weeks, but the other is a freelancer and receives the bulk of their payments in six-month intervals.

This scenario is not as uncommon as it might seem. One of my clients, Chuck, was two years into a new business. His wife, Suzy, is a data scientist, making roughly $100,000 per year as a W-2 employee. Chuck is an artist who sells commissioned paintings inconsistently and is paid royalties for other works on a more consistent basis. Every year in June, he receives about $50,000 for participating in an art show where his work is in high demand. The amount is not always $50,000, but close enough that Suzy and Chuck can plan around it. This is a perfect scenario for the five-step plan for dealing with irregular income:

» **Step 1**: Estimate business expenses.

» **Step 2**: Focus on the most regular income.

» **Step 3**: Plan your taxes around the most regular income. This means you either run payroll or send estimated payments when income arrives.

» **Step 4**: Control spending during dry spells.

» **Step 5**: Plan better when income arrives by setting aside both savings and the funds you need to pay regular expenses.

The first step is to estimate business expenses for Chuck. If he makes $50,000 per year in June but also spends $50,000 throughout the year on business expenses, then Chuck's business does not actually make any money, in which case it doesn't really matter when he receives the income, as long as he does receive it. Actually, Chuck's business expenses typically run $15,000 per year. Therefore, his net income is $35,000, not including any commissioned artwork he may sell.

Step 2 is to plan around the most regular income. In our example, Chuck nets $35,000 and Suzy makes $100,000 per year, for a combined annual total of $135,000. When doing any financial planning, like setting aside 5 percent for a car loan, 10 percent for retirement plans, 20 percent for housing expenses, etc., we can only focus on $135,000 as reliable total income. We would not take into account any additional income Chuck may bring in through other endeavors. He may make other money, but we don't know when he will make it and therefore should not count on it for regular expenses and savings.

Step 3, taxes! If your business is an S corporation, then you can run payroll to include the required federal tax, state tax, Medicare, and Social Security payments. I typically advise S corp clients with irregular income to run payroll for shareholders only in "good" months when it's easier to plan. As long as you pay in 90 percent of your tax burden throughout the year, the IRS will not impose any penalties. Chuck currently operates as an LLC and must send quarterly estimated tax payments. Given that he makes his most reliable income in June, he should consider overpaying his quarterly estimated taxes once he receives the $50,000 payment.

Owners can choose when to pay taxes, and that flexibility is one benefit of starting your own business. Yes, the IRS expects you to make quarterly payments and you can get hit with penalties, but those are typically less than interest rates charged on credit cards. In Chuck and Suzy's situation, it would be best for Chuck to wait to pay his taxes until after he receives his $50,000 in compensation. Even if he receives small payments along the way for commissioned artwork, he should set that money aside for savings and expenses, rather than taxes.

Step 4 is controlling your spending during dry spells. This step is most appropriate for business owners who do not yet have a handle on their cash flow. If you are in year six of your business and you have your personal and business expenses down to a science, then you already have a plan in place, even if it is less formal than what I propose. Still, no matter where you are in your business cycle, it's always a good practice to check personal and business expenses to ensure you are spending and saving appropriately. If you are behind on taxes or feel like you are living "business income distribution to business income distribution," then it's time for you to tighten your belt and see how you can create a cash reserve. Controlling spending during dry spells is the best way to ensure this can happen.

The final step is about planning. Plan when there is ample cash flow. For Chuck and Suzy, an ideal time to review their budget is in the middle of the year when Chuck's lump sum $50,000 royalty check comes in.

MY TAKE

If the idea of running payrolls and paying quarterly estimated taxes makes your head spin until you feel like puking all over your 1040, work with an accountant. Find someone with experience in dealing with your business structure (sole proprietorship, S corp, or LLC).

If you are considering starting a business or you are already out on your own, then you have the entrepreneurial spirit. I encourage you to tap into that spirit when times are tough. Your business will not always get the results you want. There will be hiccups. There will be pain and suffering. There will be months without any revenue. That is the nature of being a business owner. Self-employment comes with so many benefits, but they come at a cost. You, as the business owner, must not only provide the service or goods you intend to provide, but you must also run the business itself and manage your personal cash flow. While this may seem overwhelming, like anything, it simply takes practice and the energy.

If you are like me, it is a calling and one for which are you willing to make many sacrifices. When I struggle, I remind myself of all the reasons I run my own business, and it gives me great pleasure and motivation to continue.

Chapter Recap

» Income from W-2 earnings is typically viewed as more stable and predictable than that which comes from freelance work or small business ownership, but in reality this is not always the case.

» The entrepreneurial personality and mindset don't come easily to everyone, but small adjustments to your thinking and a focus on the benefits can initiate a personally transformative process.

» Establishing cash flow needs and deciding on a legal business structure are essential steps when starting a new business.

» When owning and operating a business, you become even more responsible for your tax liabilities, your cash flow management, and your retirement planning, which can include the use of accounts such as SEP IRAs and solo 401(k)s.

» The best way to ensure that a business is successful is to maintain a healthy amount of cash to support business and personal spending.

| 15 |
Estates, Windfalls, and Charities

Only put off until tomorrow what you are willing to die having left undone.
— PABLO PICASSO

For many, giving provides deep personal meaning. There is something beautiful about passing a blessing, monetary or otherwise, from one person to another. When we have generosity in our hearts, we feel tingles and warmth within. My hope is that with all your efforts at financial planning, you will find it in your heart to give in some way. You will receive great benefit from doing so.

From a personal finance perspective, there are many ways to give. We typically think of charities; however, estate planning is a form of giving by which we outline what will happen to our assets after we die, perhaps leaving them to family, a loved one, or a charitable cause. We can also give gifts in our lifetime; we don't have to wait to die! I like this type of giving, as you get to see the blessing of your gift on the recipient and feel the benefits of giving in your own heart.

We can also give our time. As with money, it does not have to be given to a charity. We can give of our time by helping anyone, in any way we can, which in turn helps us feel connected to those around us.

If you do give financially to charity, the best gifts are donations that matter to you, that can lower your tax bill, and that do not take away from the necessary saving and investing you're doing to reach your financial goals.

On the other side of giving is receiving. Inheriting money is not always as easy as it sounds. While receiving a windfall can solve financial problems, many people feel negative emotions about receiving a large sum of money. What may seem like a blessing to one can feel unearned or even oppressive to another. Additionally, those receiving windfalls after someone dies would often rather have the loved one than the money.

Therefore, estate planning needs to be done thoughtfully and fairly to achieve your desired outcomes. It always helps to think of results first; this will help you create the best path for your money to pass to the next generation.

Estate Planning

Estate plans ensure that final wishes are honored and that loved ones are provided for after a person dies. The estate plan determines what becomes of their personal property and the financial assets they owned. The process involves a will and sometimes a *trust* and answers important questions like who gets what, how much tax will be paid, and who will have custody of minor children. While insurance policies and retirement accounts are included in your estate for estate tax purposes, the beneficiaries of these plans and accounts must be named outside of your will. Therefore, you will want to ensure that your beneficiaries are up to date, since whoever is named "beneficiary" on these accounts or policies will receive your assets when you die.

Who needs an estate plan? Anyone with a spouse or domestic partner, minor children, or dependents who are not children, such as elderly parents or special-needs family members who cannot handle money. You'll need a plan for your estate if you have substantial assets and specific items that you want to go to specific people, or if you have charitable objectives or issues that need to be dealt with after your death. These "issues" can be unrelated people you want to provide for like a life partner, pets, business interests, or problem family members who may contest your will.

If all you own is a checking account and a retirement account with a named beneficiary, then save your money for the day when you have more complicated planning needs.

Children, especially minor children, present another set of estate planning needs. If you and your spouse die in a car accident together, who will take care of your children? Without a will and a listed guardian, the court will appoint one on your behalf. This may be fine if you have one sibling and had already intended for them to be the guardian. It can be problematic when all siblings on both sides of the family start fighting over your children. In addition, you likely have life insurance if you have young kids. That life insurance needs to be put into a trust for the benefit of your minor children. A trustee can then dole out funds for whatever they need throughout their childhood and adolescence.

Unfortunately, I have seen it get ugly after loved ones pass. People can be very funny about money. The best way to avoid this ugliness after your own demise is to create a detailed estate plan. The more specific you can be about who gets what, the less fighting there will be. I wish it were not like this; however, planning can help avoid the unfortunate realities of property disputes.

When creating an estate plan, what is the result you want to achieve? What is the feeling you want to have now about your estate after your death? Here are some key considerations:

- » Do I have substantial assets and need to minimize gift and estate taxes?
- » Do I need to avoid probate for some reason?
- » Do I want to make gifts in my lifetime or only after death? (Most like to give during their lives.)
- » Do my kids need a guardian?
- » How will my kids get access to money?
- » What will happen if I become incapacitated?
- » What will happen to my spouse or partner if I die?
- » Have I given to charity in an amount that feels good to me? Should I give more?
- » What will happen to my business if I die?
- » What will happen to my other family members if I die?
- » What happens to my dog if I die?

People often drag their feet in regard to estate planning because it is hard to get excited about a topic that has to do with our own death. I encourage you to think about the results rather than the process. Wouldn't it feel great to know you had a plan in place to protect your children and spouse if something happened to you?

Acting now is better than the alternative, which is leaving your family to pick up the pieces after you die or become incapacitated. It is easy to modify an estate plan should your circumstances change, and therefore it is better to create one now even if you don't have all the answers. An important but less obvious reason to plan is that an estate plan is not just about the people you love and care about, it's also about *you*. It is your legacy and gives you control over what happens after your death. For that reason, it's very powerful.

How Estates Work

If an estate consists of all of an individual's financial assets, *probate* is the process that determines how those assets are transferred to beneficiaries upon death. Probate will confirm whether any **will and testament** is legal and ensure that the deceased person's intentions are carried out. Probate can also happen when there is no will; a probate court decides how to distribute the items in the estate.

Probates can take just a few weeks for small estates or several years for large complicated estates with poorly made plans of succession. Anyone with a valid claim to any assets can drag the process out by contesting the will or filing a petition with probate court.

The length of probate is also very contingent on the state in which you live/die.

A will can help guide probate, but it does not preclude the process from happening. However, there are some assets that do not go through probate. For instance, retirement funds and life insurance policies with payable-on-death beneficiaries are transferred upon the owner's death. Assets in a trust are governed by the terms of the trust and are not subject to the verdicts of a probate court. For that reason, many financial planners and estate attorneys like to recommend that everyone have a revocable trust. My opinion is that trusts need to be considered on a case-by-case basis.

Estate Planning Tips

Some aspects of estate planning are straightforward. You want to name the family members and loved ones that will receive your assets and personal property after your death. This can be done through a will, but if the estate is considerable, there might be legal hurdles, which can be minimized by forming a trust.

Not all trusts are created equal. Some are irrevocable, meaning that once the trust is established it cannot be modified by the grantor. Other trust types include revocable ones, UTMAs, testamentary trusts, and special needs trusts:

1. **Revocable Trusts:** These trusts are created to avoid probate or to make handling financial affairs situationally easier. In a state where probate takes a long time, a **revocable trust** can make sense, because the assets will pass more quickly to your loved ones. Another reason to create a revocable trust is that as you age you may want to deal less and less with your personal finances. You can add a trusted adult child as a trustee on the account and have a rule that each of

you can act independently of the other. This is nice if, for instance, you want to travel around the world while your doting child takes care of your financial matters, or if you start to lose mental capacity but no doctor would actually declare you incapacitated. I typically use these in my practice when a client is single and therefore needs backup help or when it's clear that a couple will need help down the road, due to a history of family illness. These typically turn into *irrevocable trusts* upon death, depending on the language of the trust when written.

2. **UTMAs:** The Uniform Transfer to Minors Act is a type of trust designed expressly for leaving money to children (and was covered in greater detail in chapter 13).

3. **Testamentary Trusts:** These are trusts created in wills. They can be used to appoint trustees to oversee assets until minor inheritors are of an age to assume responsibility. *Testamentary trusts* can also be used to set up special-needs trusts for those unable to hold money on their own, such as disabled family members. Essentially, a testamentary trust can be defined as any trust created in your will with stipulations as to how the trust will operate after you die.

4. **Asset Protection Trusts:** These are trusts created for the purpose of shielding assets from creditors. A common example is when someone puts assets in a trust at least five years before having any kind of health event that might require a nursing home. This is done because Medicaid has a five-year "look-back period," and they will not pay for nursing care if you have assets available to pay for it yourself. This is useful for folks that don't have long-term care insurance or would not otherwise be able to afford the cost of private nursing care. I am not an expert in elder planning; therefore, I suggest you do more reading and consulting on this subject prior to any trust creation.

5. **Special-needs Trusts:** These trusts are created to set aside money for the physically or mentally disabled or the chronically ill without affecting any government assistance they may receive from Social Security disability benefits. You can establish this trust during your lifetime or as a testamentary trust. As with Medicaid planning, I am not an expert and highly recommend additional reading or consulting.

You'll also want to consider the taxes that need to be paid when the estate passes to others after your death. Using estate planning devices like trusts can help to minimize estate taxes and other costs for beneficiaries.

The federal estate tax is a tax on the transfer of property when someone dies. It applies when an individual's assets are worth more than $11.58 million at the time of their death, so very few estates are subject to this tax. Your state may have much lower limits, in which case you will want to review them and decide whether a trust makes sense for state estate tax purposes. The lifetime annual gift exclusion is currently $15,000, meaning you can give gifts in your lifetime of up to $15,000 without tax consequences.

If you are single and your life is simple, then you probably do not need elaborate estate planning. Likewise, if you are young and have not yet accumulated a significant net worth, there is probably no need to spend the money on a plan—yet. If you have assets in a taxable account or a bank account and don't need estate planning, you can add a "transfer on death" clause to your account. This will immediately transfer assets to a designated beneficiary if you die without the need for probate.

I typically suggest that when a person gets married and is hoping to start a family *or* has substantial assets, then it is time to meet with an estate planner to learn the basic structure of planning an estate and to discuss what laws apply where they live.

You might not have thought about it in these terms, but meeting with an estate attorney can be a beautiful experience. It gives you a safe space to discuss what life would look like after you've gone, a subject not often discussed in everyday conversation. You have a chance to create your legacy and feel what it would be like after you die. What do you want for everything you've worked so hard to create? When my husband and I met with our attorney, it was the best. We asked so many questions. We shared the dark thoughts that were on our minds. We collaborated to create a vision of what it would be like after we died. We listened to our attorney tell us about standard practices and other couples he had seen just like us. And then we made the best decisions we could with the information we had. I remember feeling exhilarated after signing our documents, knowing we had developed the best possible plan for our family. And then I remember being much more careful as I walked down the streets of New York City. You become more aware of your mortality for a short while afterward!

If you own real estate or a business, then the time is right to sit down with an attorney who can talk you through everything that's on your mind. If you're married to someone who does not have citizenship, talk to an attorney. If you have kids, talk to an attorney. You get the idea.

Choose your beneficiaries and designate them on any retirement accounts or insurance policies you have. Generally, people pick their spouse as their primary beneficiary, and if they don't have children, they have a difficult time picking the secondary beneficiary. If you have young children, you will want to consider an adult as your secondary person to take care of other parts of your estate plan, like being executor, guardian, power of attorney, or health care proxy on your behalf. Minor children cannot be any of these if you and your spouse die at the same time.

Ask yourself key questions:

ON YOUR OWN
#23

- Who would you pick as an executor? This person needs to be organized, willing, etc.

- Who would you pick as a guardian of your kids? This person should love your kids as if they were their own and raise them similarly to how you would.

- Who would you pick as a health care proxy? Choose someone in the family or a close friend who works in the medical field or has the ability to make decisions under lots of pressure.

- Who would you pick as a power of attorney? This is usually the most financially responsible person you know and trust.

- Who would you pick as a trustee if you created a trust in your will? This is usually the same person you select to hold the power of attorney, but not always.

- What kind of legacy do you want to leave?

You can choose anyone you like for any of these roles. I highly recommend considering all these questions prior to creating an estate plan with an attorney.

Experienced estate planners and attorneys have seen (or have learned how to handle) most scenarios, from the simple to the complex. In highly complicated situations, with disagreements among family members and anger boiling over, a professional can serve as an objective observer who offers insights into the legal considerations surrounding the future of the estate. That person can be a voice of reason in chaotic times.

Health Care Proxy and Power of Attorney

An estate plan will also address the issue of life-prolonging medical care if you become ill and are unable to make your wishes known when the time comes. Funeral planning is part of the process as well. I recommend you have a will (including guardianships for children), a health care proxy, and a power of attorney as part of a complete estate plan.

» **HCP**: A health care proxy is a straightforward document that allows an individual to decide who will make health care decisions for them if they can no longer communicate their wishes.

» **POA**: A power of attorney is a legal document that gives a person the legal authority to make financial decisions on your behalf. A POA can apply not only to financial and business matters, but also to health care and end-of-life decisions.

Beneficiaries

Certain account types, like retirement accounts or life insurance policies, allow you to name beneficiaries directly without listing them in your will. These assets will pass directly to the named beneficiary. It is incredibly important to name beneficiaries, because if you do not name a beneficiary, then your estate becomes the beneficiary. That means that your assets, which otherwise would have easily passed to whomever you named, will be subject to probate. Probate can take time and be quite costly. Therefore, it is incredibly important to name both a primary beneficiary and a contingent beneficiary who would receive the assets if both you and your primary beneficiary died.

You must also regularly check your beneficiaries to ensure that the person you chose is still the one you want to receive your assets. A common example of this is choosing your sister to be your 401(k) beneficiary and then changing it to your spouse after getting married. If you do not change the beneficiary to be your spouse and you die, your sister will get the money, even if you have been married for 30 years and have adult children. Therefore, always check beneficiaries after major life events such as marriage, birth of a child, death of parents, etc.

There are two possible distribution methods for beneficiaries, *per stirpes* and per capita. The best way to explain these terms is through an example: You name your spouse as primary beneficiary and your three kids, Marty, Julie, and Chris, as contingent beneficiaries on your IRA. You, your spouse, and Marty all die in a car accident. If you chose the per capita method for distributing assets, Julie and Chris will each receive 50 percent of the assets. If you chose per stirpes, Julie and Chris will each receive 33.3 percent of the assets and any children of Marty's will receive 33.3 percent of the assets divided among them. I happen to like per stirpes, because it allows you to direct assets to future generations without any adjustments to your will. However, if you despise Marty's kids, maybe you'll want to choose per capita!

The most important thing is to choose (and remember to update) your beneficiaries. Though you will not be around to witness the aftermath, your loved ones will greatly appreciate your meticulousness during your lifetime.

Windfalls

A windfall is a sudden lump sum of cash paid to a person or family. The money can come from an inheritance, a life insurance policy, or even the lottery. Unique emotional and financial challenges can arise from the newfound wealth.

Inheriting Money

An inheritance is a type of financial windfall that can be difficult to deal with emotionally. If you have inherited a substantial amount of money, chances are you lost a loved one and are dealing with a significant amount of grief.

Someone receiving a windfall may also feel guilty, with a sense that they do not deserve it. Negative thoughts like these make it difficult to move forward and make financial decisions after inheriting money or a windfall.

If you find yourself in this situation, you will want to acknowledge and freely experience your feelings first, and then decide how you want to proceed. The last thing you want to do is make an impulsive emotional decision before dealing with the emotions themselves. This process can take some time, especially if you are grieving.

The important thing to bear in mind when you receive a windfall is that it is only money, and money does not change who we are. I have seen clients receive large settlements, and in all cases, the money made them more of who they already were. A big spender before a windfall will continue to spend. A prudent spender may upgrade a car or a home, but he or she will continue to save. Money does not dramatically change lives from one day to the next. Only we can do that from within.

Lump Sum or Annuity?

Sometimes a windfall can be disbursed to you either as a lump sum or in a series of annuity payments. Examples include pension plans and legal settlements for accident or injury. A lump sum is just as it sounds—you receive the entirety of what is owed to you in one payment. An annuity provides a series of payments over time. The number and amount of payments depends on the contract, pension, or settlement terms.

It is tempting to choose the lump sum; the neon blinking dollar signs of the largest amount of money you have ever seen can be dazzling. But before deciding between lump sum and annuity, numerous factors must be considered.

Lump sum payments offer much more flexibility than annuities. Whether you receive the money from a legal proceeding or a pension, you will be drawing from that pool of funds for a long time, and a lot of unexpected events could come your way. If your wife becomes seriously ill and your medical expenses skyrocket, then you will be better positioned to access the cash necessary from your lump sum rather than having to wait for your stream of annuity payments.

A lump sum must be invested properly. If you expect it to provide lifetime income, then you must invest the funds with a diversified asset allocation according to your risk tolerance. Beware that if you have a very low risk tolerance, then you risk outliving your money by being too conservative with the asset allocation. The advantage of an annuity over a lump sum is that a professional manager will ensure that the assets are invested for you, while you continually receive income. If you have no idea how to manage your money, then I highly recommend taking the annuity.

An annuity will provide you with income for life, and, depending on the options you choose or the kind of contract, it may also provide income for the life of your spouse. It is possible that you'll outlive your money by taking a lump sum. On the other hand, if a pension administrator or insurance company goes bankrupt, your annuity payments are at risk.

Annuity payments are typically taxable, with the exception of structured settlements, discussed in the next section. An option for retirees with pensions is to roll their lump sum into an IRA and avoid the tax consequences of the lump sum. The retiree must start taking required minimum distributions (RMDs) at age seventy-two. Depending on how much income the retiree needs, RMDs are often much lower income distributions than pension payments and can be a source of tax savings in retirement. Other settlements do not have the same luxury. Depending on how you received your windfall, it may be taxable.

As always, you have to do the math. What amount will they give you in a lump sum compared to lifetime income payments? How long do you have to live before you break even? Does the math work out better if you invest it and take distributions in the same amount or more than you would have gotten in annuity payments? If you'll have to live to be 104 before you get enough annuity payments to equal the amount of the lump sum, then it likely makes sense to take the lump sum and figure out how to invest it.

Here is an example: Howard is sixty-five years old and is retiring. He has the option to take a lump sum payment of $450,000 on his pension or a lifetime annuity of $2,587 per month. In this case, Howard will need to live to be at least seventy-nine and a half to break even (when the total annuity payments would equal the lump sum). If he took the lump sum now, he could invest the $450,000 and take his own distributions. If he got a 6 percent return on his investment and took out $2,587 per month (same as the annuity payment), he would run out of money in twenty-nine years, or at age ninety-four. If Howard thinks he will live longer than ninety-four years, then the annuity is a better option.

You must also consider your legacy. If you want to leave assets to family, loved ones, or a charity, an annuity payment will not enable you to do so. The annuity stops paying when you die. A lump sum, if managed properly, can last in perpetuity if left in competent hands.

It always comes back to the results you want to have. If lifetime income is important to you and the math supports it, then I'm all for the annuity. If you want more flexibility and you will either manage the money well yourself or hire help to ensure that the funds last, then I'm all for the lump sum! I highly recommend including the math in your decision, because often it makes the decision for you.

Structured Settlements

A *structured settlement* is a special annuity contract that is offered only to victims of an accident after the settlement of a lawsuit. It is special because the income from this annuity is tax-free, rather than partially taxable. Except for taxes, all the same principles of a regular annuity contract apply, typically making these a bad deal.

The insurance company offering the contract is usually the same insurance company that would have paid you the lump sum after the decision on your case. Therefore, there is an inherent conflict of interest when they offer you the annuity. Instead of making a lump sum payment, they can pay out income to you over time, thereby reducing their immediate liability. This is beneficial to them because of the time value of money: money now is worth more than money later, due to its ability to earn money. Conversely, if it is more beneficial to them, it is less beneficial to you, also because of the time value of money: money now is worth more than money later.

Generally, the insurance company shows recipients an inflated rate of return on medical settlements (and on all annuities—they're not discriminating). The return is inflated because it includes return of capital in this calculation, which is an assumption that you will inevitably receive back the full value of your settlement. However, unless the contract stipulates that you will receive your capital back, there is no return of capital.

Let's use the following settlement offer as an example:

Aldo is a twenty-nine-year-old man who had an unfortunate accident. He was awarded a $2 million medical settlement. If Aldo agrees to take the structured settlement, the insurance company will pay him $72,000 per year for fifty-eight years (his actuarial estimated lifespan), or $4.176 million. The paperwork has a stated internal rate of return of 2.92 percent.

If Aldo decides to take the structured settlement contract, his only way out is to surrender the contract with penalties or sell his future payments to an interested party at a discount. Assuming he does neither, he would make $2.176 million (net) over fifty-eight years. This is 109 percent over fifty-eight years, or 1.88 percent per year.

Now, let's say Aldo decides to take the lump sum of $2 million and invest it in a bond with the same terms as the contract:

» He buys a fifty-eight-year bond with a 2.92 percent coupon. (I know, there's no such thing as a 58-year bond, but indulge me.)
» Aldo gives the issuing company $2 million.
» The bond pays $58,400 per year for fifty-eight years, or $3,387,200.
» The company returns $2 million at the end of fifty-eight years.
» Aldo makes a true 2.92 percent internal rate of return over the life of the investment.

NOTE

If you invested a $2 million settlement in a 50 percent stock, 50 percent bond portfolio, you could withdraw 4 percent per year without risking asset depletion. This would give you $80,000 per year in income. While it would be taxable, you would not give up any principal.

The structured settlement is tax-free, so we must consider taxes. Unless Aldo is earning money elsewhere, he will have a fairly low tax rate on the income from the bond:

» He will get a standard deduction of $12,400 on $58,400 per year, leaving him with $46,000 in taxable income.
» He will pay 10.3 percent in federal taxes.
» This reduces his return to 2.68 percent per year, still higher than the 1.88 percent offered by the annuity.

What if Aldo has a lot of other income and is in the highest 37 percent tax bracket? Great question! This means the annuity and the lump sum will have an equal rate of return.

My suggestion is always to consult the math before making any permanent decisions about annuities. It is much easier to crunch some numbers beforehand than to figure a way out of the contract after you have accepted it.

Charities

Winston Churchill once said, "We make a living by what we get, but we make a life by what we give." Generosity is part of the human experience. It gives our lives purpose and helps us feel a sense of where we fit into this world.

The University of California, Berkeley, did a study on how spending money on ourselves and on others affects our psychology. What they found was that those who spent money on themselves had no noticeable difference in affect throughout the day, and those who spent on others were noticeably happier.

We like to give to good causes. We like to see the impact of our gift, as it makes us feel we have truly helped or accomplished something. We like to give to people or organizations we trust. We like to give when we know our donations directly benefit someone we care about, such as helping with a friend's medical expenses or donating to a society researching an illness affecting someone we love. Oh, and there is also a nice tax benefit.

There are also reasons why people don't donate: they don't feel they have the money to do so, or they're unsure of how the gift will be used. Not knowing how the gift will be used makes it difficult to feel good about the donation.

Charities try to focus our giving attention on specific causes. But charitable donations are not the only way to give. Helping a family member or friend in need can be just as satisfying. Donating clothing or other items to someone who can use them, or to the Salvation Army, has the same satisfying effect. There are many ways to donate that do not involve money:

» Donate time.

» Donate skills. I take on a pro bono financial planning case every year that has monetary value; plus, I get to see how much I'm helping!

» Donate your things. You accomplish decluttering, and someone else benefits from items that are no longer loved!

»   Give blood.

»   Help out a stranger. One of my clients paid for the person behind her at Starbucks and she felt good all day. You can also help someone in a non-monetary way.

»   Teach your kids about generosity. Help the next generation learn what is important to you.

»   Take part in a charity run, or another race of your choice.

If you decide to donate money to your favorite charity, keep in mind that there are several ways to do it.

»   You can donate a reasonable percentage of income every year.

»   You can donate to a donor-advised fund in a year when you have a lot of income, to reduce your tax liability.

»   You can wait until you've amassed wealth and leave it to charity later in life.

MY TAKE

Decide how you much you want to "budget" for giving, whether it's to a cause, politics, or helping a friend in need. Always come back to the result you want to have. Where does charitable giving fit for you? If it's just a tax deduction you're looking for, then I encourage you to find a cause that gives you energy. Additionally, always choose where you donate. No one likes to be cornered into giving, even if they would have otherwise given to the same place if they had chosen it themselves.

Charities like it when donors set a recurring automatic donation, but this can remove some of the benefit we receive when we give something. Dopamine, the "feel-good neurotransmitter," is released in our brains when we donate, so if we're unconsciously auto-donating, we will not experience this, without checking our bank statements. Giving deliberately and consciously brings more satisfaction and also ensures that we donate within our budgets.

Regarding donating a percentage every year: the best way to feel good about spending money generously is to know exactly how much money you can spend. I have many conversations with clients about what is an appropriate budget. I do the calculations we have discussed in this book, such as calculating a healthy 20 percent savings rate. Then we evaluate what is left over. If there is no room for charity in the budget after savings, then we have a conversation about where spending, not savings, can change to enable charitable giving. If you become a charitable case yourself, then you cannot continue to help others.

Donor-advised funds (DAFs) are dedicated accounts for giving to charities. These are great for anyone with a stellar year of income who regularly donates or wants to start donating to charities. You take a deduction in the year you create the fund and can spend the money on charities in subsequent years, rather than donating out of your regular cash flow. One caveat: you can only use the money in a DAF to give to 501(c)(3) organizations. If Aunt Mary needs help with her medical bills, you'll need to take it out of personal savings.

Another way to give is through donating appreciated stock. This is one of my favorite tactics. You give your charity of choice a portion of a stock, a mutual fund, or an ETF when you have a large gain in the position. Then you take the cash that you would have given to the charity and purchase more shares of the position you donated. This is smart for three reasons: You take a deduction for donating the investment. You raise your cost basis, by purchasing new shares at a higher price. And the charity can sell your investment without tax consequences. Win–win–win. Note: you can also create a DAF using an appreciated investment. Here are the tax implications for different giving strategies:

» Giving long-term appreciated assets like stocks, bonds, or real estate removes capital gains taxes, and you can take an income tax deduction for the full value of the asset, up to 30 percent of adjusted gross income.

» Due to the increase in the standard deduction to $12,400 for single filers and $24,800 for joint filers, many Americans are no longer itemizing. Therefore, it may make sense to save multiple years' worth of charitable contributions in a savings account and then donate them all at once to take the deduction. If you itemize and donate cash, you can deduct the full value of the donation up to 50 percent of adjusted gross income. The CARES Act of 2020 made it allowable to deduct up to three hundred dollars in charitable contributions without needing to itemize. Any donations in excess of three hundred dollars will be deductible only if you itemize.

» A donor-advised fund is a dedicated account for charitable giving, and any donations are immediately eligible for a tax deduction. If cash is contributed, then you can take an income tax deduction for the full value up to 50 percent of adjusted gross income. If an appreciated asset is contributed, the deduction is the full value up to 30 percent of adjusted gross income.

» Sometimes employers have gift matching programs. If you give, they match one-to-one. This is an excellent way to get more money to a charity of your choice. You'll need to check your employer's handbook for details on participation. Tax deductions are available only if you itemize.

» A qualified charitable distribution (QCD) is a direct transfer of funds from your IRA custodian, payable to a qualified charity. IRA owners and IRA beneficiaries who are at least seventy and a half years old can give up to $100,000 of their IRA money directly to the charity. The amount you give through a QCD is not limited by your required minimum distribution (RMD) and can be used to satisfy all or part of your RMD. You do not get a charitable deduction, but you also do not get your RMD added to adjusted gross income. Note that you actually have to be seventy and a half to do a QCD, meaning that if you turn 70 on June 30, you only have two days (December 30 and 31) to make your QCD distribution to qualify in the tax year. Additionally, there is no special reporting for a QCD. You must let your CPA know; otherwise, this will be considered a taxable distribution.

» A charitable remainder trust is when you, the grantor, transfer appreciated assets into an irrevocable trust, thereby removing the assets from your estate. The trustee sells these assets, paying no capital gains because it is a charitable contribution. The trustee then purchases income-producing assets, like bonds, to be held in the trust. The trustee pays you the income from the assets, and when you die the assets themselves go to charity. This would normally be an effective strategy, except bonds are yielding very little.

Potentially, you could have cash flow issues if you were to grant too much to the trust. Charitable reminder trusts typically only apply to high-net-worth individuals.

There is a human element to estate planning. Sometimes the right thing to do financially is not always the right thing to do emotionally. That is okay. I give you permission! The emotions and thoughts you have are there for a reason. Questions of legacy often strike at the heart of who we are. In essence, what are your best hopes for your family, your loved ones, your community, and for life beyond you?

Chapter Recap

» Receiving a windfall, such as an inheritance, can help solve personal financial challenges, but there are often emotional considerations as well.

» When planning an estate or making decisions about a large lump sum payment, an estate planner can help people stay objective and make informed decisions.

» Key documents in the estate-planning process include the health care proxy, the power of attorney, and the will (including guardianship for children).

» Giving to a charity should make you feel that you are doing something valuable; if you cannot give today, consider donating your time, helping friends and family, or giving later in life when you have more disposable income.

» Charitable gifts and donations can be made through a variety of instruments and vehicles, such as donor-advised funds (DAFs), qualified charitable distributions (QCDs), and charitable remainder trusts. Tax advantages abound.

Conclusion

When I set out to write this book, my goal was to create a personal finance guide that not only provides practical financial advice, but also a framework for how it applies to you, specifically. Our personal finances are deeply human, and the human element cannot and should not be ignored. It is what makes you and your situation unique!

In working with clients through the years, I've found that learning financial best practices is the easy part. The challenging part is more behavioral in nature. It is hard to overcome obstacles and actually implement the plans necessary to achieve financial freedom. In addition, maintaining a high level of enthusiasm throughout the process, and being as motivated on day 85, 126, and 364 as you were on day one, is not only difficult but essential for long-term success.

The incremental changes we make and the actions we take each day are what matter in the long run.

Why is it so hard? Why is it that those people who seemingly have everything going right in their lives sometimes make bad decisions that lead to financial setbacks? Why do people put money in savings accounts that pay zero interest when they know that the only way to build wealth over time is by investing? Why do people start self-improvement programs—whether dieting, exercising, or budgeting—only to give up and quit three weeks later?

We are human. We make mistakes. We get immediate satisfaction by taking certain easy, short-term actions. We are not wired to take risks and prefer the comfort and security that comes from being cautious. We focus more on preserving the here and now than looking at the big picture, setting goals, and putting systems in place to accomplish those goals.

Breaking bad habits is always difficult, especially when we do not realize that our habits are detrimental to our financial well-being. But with practice and time, change happens. You can change thoughts, feelings, and the way you act. You can feel good about money and about spending on things you value, and you can accomplish anything you set your mind to. But what is it that you—you, specifically—want to accomplish?

I provided assignments for you throughout the book (if you didn't do them all, don't worry, the full set is in the appendix). While some of the assignments are designed to increase your personal finance knowledge base, others are there to help you confront tough personal questions that you might not have thought of: What is it that you want to accomplish? What do you enjoy spending money on? What kind of legacy do you want to leave?

These types of questions are deeply personal. By discovering your true motivators, you can focus your energy on the elements that truly matter. Every chapter of this book is designed to get you thinking about who you are, what you want, and how you can use the framework of personal finance to create the life you want to live. You will build new habits and take new steps toward the results you want to achieve.

Real, sustainable behavior change requires high levels of motivation and rigorous maintenance. You must not only understand the why of what you are attempting to change, but you must also have a system in place that allows you to evaluate your decisions at the end of each day, week, month, and year. What are you doing purely out of habit, and what should you be doing if you are to be true to yourself, your goals, and all you value?

Once you know what you value and what you want to accomplish, you will be able to develop a road map. You will put a system in place that will take you where you want to be. You will periodically reevaluate your goals and your progress, checking in with yourself, being honest, and making tweaks along the way.

I have also, within these pages, encouraged readers to decide whether it makes sense to hire a professional financial planner, like me. If not, then committing to the ideas in this book alone should provide a solid foundation for building a bright financial future—through saving, investing, planning for key events in life, and giving to family or charities.

If you do feel you need the help of a financial planner, then this book should guide you in making a wise selection and help you better communicate with him or her. Remember, there are a few key considerations when selecting a financial advisor:

» Give preference to CFP® professionals.
» Choose a fee-only advisor over one that receives incentives or commissions for selling products.
» Choose someone who will listen empathetically to you.
» Choose someone who asks the right questions about your goals and risk tolerance.
» Make sure it is someone you trust.

I hope I have earned your trust. Whatever our future holds, thank you for reading, and I hope to hear from you. If you would like more information about financial life planning, or if you'd like to check out my podcast, please visit https://www.moneyowners.com.

REMEMBER TO DOWNLOAD YOUR FREE DIGITAL ASSETS!

 Net Worth Calculator

 Financial Goal Setting Workbook

 Goal Setting Questionnaire

 Ideal Day Week Year Spreadsheet

TWO WAYS TO ACCESS YOUR FREE DIGITAL ASSETS

SCAN ME

Use the camera app on your mobile phone to scan the QR code
or visit the link below and instantly access your digital assets.

or

go.quickstartguides.com/personalfinance

 VISIT URL

On Your Own Assignments

CHAPTER 1

1. Which archetype do you most relate to? Think of a few times when the scripts associated with that archetype have run through your head. How did it make you feel? Now, try to think of the financial result you want to have. Does it challenge your usual script?

2. Ask yourself what it would be like to live your best, most fulfilled life. Write down anything that comes to mind. Keep asking yourself, Anything else? When you're out of answers, rank them from 1 to however many you came up with. This will help you prioritize what is important. Add a time frame for accomplishing your top three to five priorities. Rewrite your top goals clearly and make sure they are things that you really want to accomplish. Draft a list of tasks you can do right now to move yourself closer to your goals. Schedule when you can do them. Write down any motivators that will help reignite your energy along the way.

CHAPTER 2

3. Why do I want to earn more? What do I need this income for? What is the feeling I want? What is the result I wish to create? These questions may lead to more questions, such as, How do I want to spend my time? or, With whom do I want to be spending my time? Go ahead and ask yourself those questions and give yourself the time to think about your answers.

4. What do you think you are worth? Sit down and think to yourself: How much money can I make? What is the limit for me? And why is that the limit for me?

5. What specific things do you believe hold you back from making more money? What steps would you need to take in order to grow your income?

CHAPTER 3

6. Look up the price of your dream home and estimate how much you would pay annually on your mortgage. Be sure to add in the costs of property taxes, homeowners insurance, maintenance, and home security. How much income would you need to spend only 20 percent on your dream home?

7. On what do you most enjoy spending money? Make a list of those items or experiences. Keep it handy. Refer to your list when making purchases. Are other purchases holding you back from having more of what you really love? Are there expenses that brought you joy in the past but, under your honest scrutiny, do not give you satisfaction now?

CHAPTER 4

8. What do you want? Look back to our Venn diagram and consider what you value. Try to be as broad as possible at first. You want to identify your core values now and build from there as you work your way through this book.

CHAPTER 5

9. Calculate your net worth. Using our helpful "net worth calculator," found in your Digital Assets (clydebankmedia.com/personalfinance-assets) add up all your assets and liabilities. I understand it may take a little time to track down all the details, and even longer to remember every asset and every liability you have. But it doesn't have to be perfect your first time through. Just by getting started you will begin to think about your net worth, and in time more items will pop into your head. For example, if you rent an apartment, maybe you provided a rental deposit? It may help to scroll through some of the reports that your personal finance

application or software can produce, as it may help you remember money you put aside (assets) or money you need to pay (liabilities)

When you're finished, put a reminder in your calendar app to update your net worth once a year, perhaps around the time you do your taxes. That way you can get everything updated when you're thinking about your big-picture financial situation.

10. Given the six-step process described on pages 84–85, what do you need to do to raise your net worth? Where could you make some changes?

CHAPTER 6

11. Revisit your most fulfilled life homework from chapter 1. Evaluate the time horizons of your top three to five goals. Note whether they are short (one to five years), medium (five to fifteen years), or long term (fifteen or more years).

CHAPTER 7

12. Set three financial goals and objectives and think about the asset allocation that best matches the time horizon of each goal as well as your tolerance for risk.

CHAPTER 8

13. Add up all your payments to debt each month: car loans, student loans, credit cards, second home loans, Vinnie the bookie in Brooklyn—all of it. To compute your debt-to-income ratio, simply divide your debts by your gross monthly income. For instance, if you have $2,000 in monthly debt payments ($1,400 mortgage, $400 auto loan, and $200 student loan) and a gross monthly income of $6,000, your debt-to-income ratio is $2,000 ÷ $6,000, or 33.3 percent.

14. Revisit the exercise you completed in chapter 3 called Where Does Your Money Go? Did your spending (the things that you purchased) line up with your values? Is your spending helping you live your most fulfilled life?

CHAPTER 9

15. Calculate 20 percent of your pretax income. This is your housing budget. Are you above or below 20 percent right now? Are you currently saving at least 20 percent of your after-tax income? If not, what changes can you make to get to a healthy financial position?

CHAPTER 10

16. Make a list of your most valuable assets. If something happened to any one of them, could you cover the loss?

17. Determine how much insurance you need: 1. What are the assets that you want covered for your loved ones if you die? 2. What income do you need to protect in case of your incapacitation or death? 3. What burial costs need to be covered? 4. What assets do you currently have to offset these costs? (Hint: refer to your net worth homework back in chapter 5.) Given your goals, is there anything else you need to add to this list?

18. Calculate the right amount of life insurance for your situation. If you are single and in your twenties, then you might not need any. A stay-at-home mom or dad will probably need coverage because, if something happens, there will be childcare costs to consider. If you are a breadwinner in the family, use the withdrawal-rate formula.

CHAPTER 11

19.
   » Take out your 1040 from last year.

   » Write down the amount you see on line 7b, "total income." This is the income you accumulated through wages, business income, dividends, capital gains, and interest.

   » Next, write down the amount you have on line 16, "total tax."

   » Calculate your actual tax rate: line 16 divided by line 7b.

> » Finally, gather your net worth from the exercise we did in chapter 5 and calculate your tax rate as a percentage of net worth.

CHAPTER 12

20. Using the three-step process in the "Retirement Math" section starting on page 239, imagine your retirement and what you think is a realistic plan given your income, your spouse's income, and your current rate of retirement savings. Consider how much you would want to spend, how much you need to save to support that spending, and what it would take to accomplish it. If you fall short, identify three key areas that could use improvement.

CHAPTER 13

21. If you have kids, or plan on having them soon, work your way through this list of questions and write down your answers.

> » Where do you want to raise your family?
> » What is the cost of living in that area?
> » Will you need to take time off from work to take care of children?
> » What does childcare cost?
> » Will children be involved in any activities or sports?
> » Will you take family vacations and, if so, where?

CHAPTER 14

22. This homework is for aspiring entrepreneurs. I suggest creating a business plan that answers the question, How will I make money? Write everything down. Decide on a business name, legal structure, products or services sold (and rates), revenue goals, and cash flow needs. Clearly define your offer to the world. This is not a full-blown business plan, which can be a relatively massive undertaking. It is more of an outline with key bullet points. If you get stuck on one of the steps, just skip it and keep going; it may come to you later.

CHAPTER 15

23. Choose your beneficiaries and designate them on any retirement accounts or insurance policies you have. Generally, people pick their spouse as their primary beneficiary, and if they don't have children, they have a difficult time picking the secondary beneficiary. If you have young children, you will want to consider an adult as your secondary person to take care of other parts of your estate plan, like being executor, guardian, power of attorney, or health care proxy on your behalf. Minor children cannot be any of these if you and your spouse die at the same time.

   » Who would you pick as an executor? This person needs to be organized, willing, etc.

   » Who would you pick as a guardian of your kids? This person should love your kids as if they were their own and raise them similarly to how you would.

   » Who would you pick as a health care proxy? Choose someone in the family or a close friend who works in the medical field or has the ability to make decisions under lots of pressure.

   » Who would you pick as a power of attorney? This is usually the most financially responsible person you know and trust.

   » Who would you pick as a trustee if you created a trust in your will? This is usually the same person you select to hold the power of attorney, but not always.

   » What kind of legacy do you want to leave?

You can choose anyone you like for any of these roles. I highly recommend considering all these questions prior to creating an estate plan with an attorney.

About
the Author

MORGEN B. ROCHARD
CFA, CFP®, RLP®

Morgen B. Rochard, CFA, CFP®, RLP®, is a financial advisor, author, podcaster, and founder of Origin Wealth Advisors LLC, a financial advisement firm. At Origin, Morgen focuses on driving personal connections and getting to the root of the financial success of her clients. This is a natural extension of her mission to help others live their most fulfilled, financially stress-free lives.

Morgen's approach is designed to help her clients find peace of mind with all aspects of their situation—financial and beyond. As a Registered Life Planner® her role is to help others truly live their passion. This framework helps clients explore what is most important to them, dive deeper into what they want to prioritize, and remove any obstacles that may get in their way.

Before going out on her own, Morgen worked extensively with such notable financial heavyweights as UBS Financial Services and Merrill Lynch. Connect with Morgen at www.originwa.com and find her insight at the Money Owners podcast on iTunes.

About QuickStart Guides

QuickStart Guides are books for beginners, written by experts.

QuickStart Guides® are comprehensive learning companions tailored for the beginner experience. Our books are written by experts, subject matter authorities, and thought leaders within their respective areas of study.

For nearly a decade more than 850,000 readers have trusted QuickStart Guides® to help them get a handle on their finances, start their own business, invest in the stock market, find a new hobby, get a new job—the list is virtually endless.

The QuickStart Guides® series of books is published by ClydeBank Media, an independent publisher based in Albany, NY.

Connect with QuickStart Guides online at www.quickstartguides.com or follow us on Facebook, Instagram, and LinkedIn.

Follow us @quickstartguides

Glossary

Amortization schedule
The payment schedule for a loan, such as when paying off a mortgage through monthly combined principal and interest payments.

Annual gift tax exclusion
The maximum amount of money one can gift to an individual without paying any gift tax ($15,000 per person in 2020).

Asset allocation
The process of determining the ideal mix of stocks, bonds, and other investments in a portfolio.

Assets
Items owned by an individual that have value, including real estate, vehicles, investment securities, commodities, jewelry, and cash.

Bankruptcy
A court order declaring that an individual or company can no longer pay outstanding debt, generally followed by a liquidation of assets to pay creditors.

Bankruptcy Protection
The process of reorganizing a business's or individual's assets and liabilities in a last attempt to avoid bankruptcy.

Budget
A fixed amount of money available to cover monthly expenses, to complete a specific project, or to run a business.

Capital
Assets of value, such as a business's plants and equipment or an individual's investment securities.

Capital gains
Profits from the sale of investment securities or assets when the price received is greater than the price paid.

Cost-of-living allowance (COLA)
An increase in pay or benefits to keep pace with the increase in prices for food, housing, fuel, clothing, and other common living expenses.

Credit utilization rate
A measurement of how much credit an individual is using compared to how much credit is available to them.

Debt
Money owed to a lender by a borrower.

Derivative
A type of investment security, such as an option or futures contract, whose value is derived from another investment, like a stock, bond, index, or exchange-traded fund.

Diminishing returns
A situation when the rate of profits or benefits does not increase proportionally with added investment, such as when additional equipment added to a production process does not result in a corresponding increase in revenue.

Dividend
Profits from a company or investment security that are paid to shareholders.

Dollar cost averaging
An investment strategy that involves making regular weekly, monthly, or quarterly payments to a mutual fund or other security regardless of the market price of the investment at the time.

Donor-advised funds (DAFs)
A special tax-advantaged fund used by individuals, families, or organizations who want to make donations to charity; the owner of the fund relinquishes ownership of all moneys contributed but may advise the fund on how to distribute money to various charities.

Exercise
When the holder of an option or other derivative requests that the other party fulfill the terms of the contract, as when the holder of an equity put option contractually obligates the other party to take delivery of shares.

Fiduciary
A person, attorney, or organization that manages investments or assets on behalf of another individual, organization, or estate and does so by putting their clients' interests ahead of their own.

Fractional reserve banking
The most common form of banking practiced worldwide, whereby banks are permitted to lend out more money than they have on deposit.

Grant date
The date when ownership is transferred from one party to another, such as when a company stock option is awarded to an employee.

Incentive stock option (ISO)
A type of company option program that gives an employee the right to buy shares of company stock at a discounted price, with special tax advantages because the profit is taxed as capital gains rather than ordinary income.

Inflationary risk
The potential that savings and other low-yielding investments will lose value over time due to general price increases in food, rent, and other living expenses.

Interest
The profit received from savings accounts, certificates of deposit, or bonds; also the amount paid to borrow money; expressed as a percentage.

Irrevocable trust
A type of trust that cannot be changed or modified without permission from the beneficiaries.

Liability
Money that is owed on debt such as mortgages, car loans, credit cards, personal loans, and lines of credit.

Liquid assets
Investment securities, bank accounts, and other assets that can easily be converted into cash.

Market capitalization
A company's share price multiplied by its total number of shares outstanding, used to evaluate the size and total market value of a company.

Margin
A brokerage term referring to trading or investing with borrowed money.

Maturity
The point in time when a bondholder receives a final payment equal to the par, or face value, of the bond.

Mortgage
A type of loan offered to home buyers that requires monthly payments that are applied to both the principal and interest of the loan.

Mutual fund
A pool of funds from a multitude of investors that is used to purchase investable assets.

Net asset value (NAV)
The value of a mutual fund or exchange-traded fund share when total liabilities of the fund are subtracted from assets.

Net investment income tax
A tax imposed on certain investment gains of higher income earners.

Net worth
The total value of an individual's assets after subtracting liabilities.

Non-qualified stock options (NQSOs)
A method of compensating employees, but, in contrast to incentive stock options, with no special tax treatment and fewer restrictions.

Paid time off (PTO)
A company's policy regarding paying wages or salaries when an employee takes time off from work for vacations or to tend to personal matters.

Per stirpes
Latin for "by roots," an option available to estate planners whereby one's assets may be passed to a beneficiary's children in the event that the beneficiary is dead or otherwise incapable of receiving the assets.

Principal
When applied to debt securities, the amount of money that a bond issuer receives from the investor when the bond is issued and the amount the investor receives from the bond issuer when the bond matures.

Principal risk
The risk that a bond's face value may decline in secondary markets due to the issuance of higher-yield bonds backed by the same entity.

Private mortgage insurance (PMI)
A borrower-funded insurance product that protects lenders in the event of defaults on mortgage loans; required for some mortgages when the borrower makes a down payment of less than 20 percent.

Probate
The establishment, in a legal sense, of the validity of a will.

Prospectus
A document from a mutual fund company that must be delivered to prospective investors, outlining the mutual fund's fees, objectives, and performance history.

Required minimum distributions (RMDs)
The amount of money that must be withdrawn from qualified retirement plans when the retiree reaches a certain age.

Restricted stock unit
Employee compensation in the form of company shares.

Revocable trust
A tool used in estate planning that can help beneficiaries avoid probate court and streamline the transfer of assets upon the death of the grantor; so named because provisions may be altered or cancelled by the grantor.

Spread
The difference between the interest rate a bank charges to its borrowers and the interest rate it pays out to its depositors; the spread allows the bank to make money.

Strike price
Also known as the exercise price, the price at which a security changes hands if the holder of an options contract or other derivative requests fulfillment of the contract.

Structured settlement
A type of legal award that consists of regular payments, usually to an injured party or victim of an injustice.

Tax-loss harvesting
The process of selling an investment at a loss to reduce taxes owed.

Testament
The section of a will that focuses on an individual's personal property.

Testamentary trust
A trust created in a will (there may be several testamentary trusts attached to one will) with stipulations for how the trust is to be managed upon the grantor's death.

Trust
A legal vehicle managed by a person or entity, known as the trustee, that holds assets or property for the benefit of one or more beneficiaries.

Vesting period
The amount of time that an employee must work for a company before being entitled to stock ownership or option grants.

Volatility
The statistical measure of the distribution of returns of an investment security or market.

Wash sale rule
A regulation that prohibits investors from selling an investment and repurchasing an identical security within thirty days.

Will and testament
A legally binding document used in estate planning to expresses the wishes of a person who has passed away.

Withdrawal rate
Generally expressed as a percentage, the withdrawal rate is the amount of money taken out of retirement plans, pensions, and other savings accounts on a regular monthly or annual basis.

References

Bustamante, Jaleesa. 2019. "Average Cost of College & Tuition." EducationData.Org. June 7. https://educationdata.org/average-cost-of-college/.

Clear, James. 2018. *Atomic Habits*. New York: Penguin Random House.

Dickler, Jessica. 2020. "Holiday Debt Could Take Years to Pay Off." CNBC. January 2. https://www.cnbc.com/2020/01/02/holiday-debt-could-take-years-to-pay-off.html.

Dimson, Elroy, Paul Marsh, and Mike Staunton. 2018. "Press Releases." Credit-Suisse.com. February. Accessed June 16, 2020. https://www.credit-suisse.com/media/assets/corporate/docs/about-us/media/media-release/2018/02/giry-summary-2018.pdf.

Duffin, Erin. 2019. "Percentage of American parents saving for their college education of their children from 2009 to 2018." Statista. April 29. https://www.statista.com/statistics/260130/college-saving-behaviour-among-parents-of-children-under-18-in-the-united-states/.

Dunn, Elizabeth W., and Michael I. Norton. 2013. "How to Make Giving Feel Good." Greater Good Magazine. June 18. https://greatergood.berkeley.edu/article/item/how_to_make_giving_feel_good.

FinAid. n.d. Tuition Inflation. Accessed May 13, 2020. https://www.finaid.org/savings/tuition-inflation.phtml.

Hobson, Nick. 2018. "The Million-Dollar Link Between Wealth and Happiness." Pyschology Today. February 27. https://www.psychologytoday.com/us/blog/ritual-and-the-brain/201802/the-million-dollar-link-between-wealth-and-happiness.

Hubbard, Carl M., Philip L. Cooley, and Daniel T. Walz. 1998. "Retirement Savings: Choosing a Withdrawal Rate That Is Sustainable." American Association of Individual Investors. February. https://www.aaii.com/files/pdf/6794_retirement-savings-choosing-a-withdrawal-rate-that-is-sustainable.

Kinder, George. 1999. *The Seven Stages of Money Maturity*. New York: Random House.

Klontz, Brad, Sonya L. Britt, Jennifer Mentzer, and Ted Klontz. 2011. "Money Beliefs and Financial Behaviors: Development of the Klontz Money Script Inventory." *The Journal of Financial Therapy 2*, no. 1: 1–22.

Kondo, Marie. 2017. *The Life-Changing Magic of Tidying Up*. Ten Speed Press.

Lino, Mark. 2020. "The Cost of Raising a Child." USDA.gov. February 18. https://www.usda.gov/media/blog/2017/01/13/cost-raising-child.

Malkiel, Burton. 1973. *A Random Walk Down Wall Street*. New York: Norton.

Paul, Kari. 2018. "Here's How Long It Will Take Americans to Pay Off Their Christmas Debt." MarketWatch. January 2. https://www.marketwatch.com/story/heres-how-long-it-will-take-americans-to-pay-off-their-christmas-debt-2017-12-29.

Pfau, Wade. n.d. "Safe Withdrawal Rates for Retirement and the Trinity Study." Retirement Researcher. Accessed June 18, 2020. https://retirementresearcher.com/safe-withdrawal-rates-for-retirement-and-the-trinity-study/.

Rae, David. 2018. "Should You Ditch the SEP-IRA for the Better Solo 401(k)?" Forbes. April 23. https://www.forbes.com/sites/davidrae/2018/04/23/sep-ira-vesrus-solo-401k/

Stanley, Thomas, and William Danko. 2010. *The Millionaire Next Door*. New York: Taylor Trade Publishing; reissue edition.

Szmigirea, M. 2019. "Value of Debt Owned by Consumers in the United States as of September 2019, By Type." Statista. December 19. https://www.statista.com/statistics/500814/debt-owned-by-consumers-usa-by-type/.

TD Bank News. 2018. "One Third of Consumers Live Paycheck to Paycheck, TD Survey Finds." TD Bank. July 6. https://newscenter.td.com/us/en/news/2018/one-third-of-consumers-live-paycheck-to-paycheck-td-survey-finds.

US Inflation Calculator. 2020. "Food Inflation in the United States (1968-2020)." US Inflation Calculator. May 12. https://www.usinflationcalculator.com/inflation/food-inflation-in-the-united-states/.

Yochim, Dayana. 2020. "What's Your Net Worth, and How Do You Compare to Others?" Market Watch. January 23. https://www.marketwatch.com/story/whats-your-net-worth-and-how-do-you-compare-to-others-2018-09-24.

Index

WHAT DID YOU THINK?

We rely on reviews and reader feedback to help our authors reach more people, improve our books, and grow our business. We would really appreciate it if you took the time to help us out by providing feedback on your recent purchase.

It's really easy, it only takes a second, and it's a tremendous help!

—— NOT SURE WHAT TO SHARE? ——

Here are some ideas to get your review started...

- *What did you learn?*
- *Have you been able to put anything you learned into action?*
- *Would you recommend the book to other readers?*
- *Is the author clear and easy to understand?*

TWO WAYS TO LEAVE AN AMAZON REVIEW

Use the camera app on your mobile phone to scan the QR code or visit the link below to record your testimonial and get your free book.

or

www.quickstartguides.review/finance

SCAN ME   VISIT URL

GET YOUR NEXT
QuickStart Guide®
FOR FREE

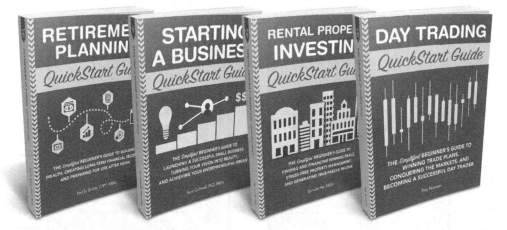

Leave us a quick video testimonial on our website and we will give you a **FREE *QuickStart Guide*** of your choice!

RECORD TESTIMONIAL   **SUBMIT TO OUR WEBSITE**   **GET A FREE BOOK**

SAVE 10% ON YOUR NEXT
QuickStart Guide®

USE CODE: QSG10

RETIREMENT PLANNING QuickStart Guide™

THE *Simplified* BEGINNER'S GUIDE TO BUILDING WEALTH, CREATING LONG-TERM FINANCIAL SECURITY, AND PREPARING FOR LIFE AFTER WORK

Ted D. Snow, CFP®, MBA

SCAN ME

www.quickstartguides.shop/retirement

ACCOUNTING QuickStart Guide™

THIRD EDITION

THE *Simplified* BEGINNER'S GUIDE TO REAL-WORLD FINANCIAL AND MANAGERIAL ACCOUNTING FOR STUDENTS, BUSINESS OWNERS, AND FINANCE PROFESSIONALS

Josh Bauerle, CPA

SCAN ME

www.quickstartguides.shop/accounting

INVESTING QuickStart Guide®

SECOND EDITION

THE *Simplified* BEGINNER'S GUIDE TO SUCCESSFULLY NAVIGATING THE STOCK MARKET, GROWING YOUR WEALTH, AND CREATING A SECURE FINANCIAL FUTURE

Ted D. Snow, CFP®, MBA

SCAN ME

www.quickstartguides.shop/investing

REAL ESTATE INVESTING QuickStart Guide®

THE *Simplified* BEGINNER'S GUIDE TO SUCCESSFULLY SECURING FINANCING, CLOSING YOUR FIRST DEAL, AND BUILDING WEALTH THROUGH REAL ESTATE

Symon He, MBA

SCAN ME

www.quickstartguides.shop/real-esate

Use the camera app on your mobile phone to scan the QR code or visit the link below the cover to shop. Get 10% off your entire order when you use code 'QSG10' at checkout at www.quickstartguides.com

CLYDEBANK MEDIA

QuickStart Guides®

PROUDLY SUPPORT ONE TREE PLANTED

One Tree Planted is a 501(c)(3) nonprofit organization focused on global reforestation, with millions of trees planted every year. ClydeBank Media is proud to support One Tree Planted as a reforestation partner.

Every dollar donated plants one tree and every tree makes a difference!

Made in the USA
Las Vegas, NV
28 August 2023

76681280R00188